THE TRAGEDY OF

MACBETH

William Shakespeare

Katherine Rowe, Editor
Bryn Mawr

J. J. M. Tobin, General Editor
University of Massachusetts-Boston

WADSWORTH
CENGAGE Learning™

Australia • Brazil • Japan • Korea • Mexico • Singapore • Spain • United Kingdom • United States

WADSWORTH
CENGAGE Learning™

**Evans Shakespeare Editions:
Macbeth
Katherine Rowe, Editor
J. J. M. Tobin, General Editor**

Senior Publisher: Lyn Uhl

Publisher: Michael Rosenberg

Development Editor:
Michell Phifer

Assistant Editor: Erin Bosco

Editorial Assistant: Rebecca
Donahue

Media Editor: Janine Tangney

Senior Marketing Manager:
Melissa Holt

Marketing Communications
Manager: Glenn McGibbon

Content Project Manager:
Aimee Chevrette Bear

Art Director: Marissa Falco

Print Buyer: Betsy Donaghey

Rights Acquisition Specialist,
Text: Katie Huha

Rights Acquisition Specialist,
Images: Jennifer Meyer Dare

Production Service: MPS Limited,
a Macmillan Company

Cover Designer: Walter Kopec

Text Designer: Maxine Ressler

Cover Image: Misty Cotton (left)
as a Witch, Henry Woronicz as
Macbeth, and Pat Sibley and
Afton Quast as Witches in the
Utah Shakespeare Festival's
2004 production of *Macbeth*.
(Copyright Utah Shakespeare
Festival. Photo by Karl Hugh.)

Compositor: MPS Limited,
a Macmillan Company

For product information and
technology assistance, contact us at **Cengage Learning
Customer & Sales Support, 1-800-354-9706**

For permission to use material from this text
or product, submit all requests online at
www.cengage.com/permissions
Further permissions questions can be emailed to
permissionrequest@cengage.com

Library of Congress Control Number: 2010942857

ISBN-13: 978-0-495-91120-3

ISBN-10: 0-495-91120-8

Wadsworth
20 Channel Center Street
Boston, MA 02210
USA

Cengage Learning is a leading provider of customized
learning solutions with office locations around the globe,
including Singapore, the United Kingdom, Australia,
Mexico, Brazil, and Japan. Locate your local office at:
international.cengage.com/region

Cengage Learning products are represented in Canada by
Nelson Education, Ltd.

For your course and learning solutions, visit
www.cengage.com

Purchase any of our products at your local college store
or at our preferred online store **www.cengagebrain.com**

Printed in the United States of America
1 2 3 4 5 6 7 14 13 12 11

Other titles in the *Evans Shakespeare Editions*
from Cengage Learning

As You Like It
Heather Dubrow, Volume Editor

Hamlet
J. J. M. Tobin, Volume Editor

King Lear
Vincent F. Petronella, Volume Editor

Measure for Measure
John Klause, Volume Editor

A Midsummer Night's Dream
Douglas Bruster, Volume Editor

Richard III
Nina Levine, Volume Editor

The Tempest
Grace Tiffany, Volume Editor

The Winter's Tale
Lawrence F. Rhu, Volume Editor

TABLE OF CONTENTS

LIST OF ILLUSTRATIONS

ABOUT THIS SERIES

J. J. M. Tobin

THE EVANS Shakespeare Editions are individual editions of essential plays by William Shakespeare, edited by leading scholars to provide college and university students, advanced high school students, and interested independent readers with a comprehensive guide to the plays and their historical and modern contexts. The volume editor of each play has written an introduction to the play and a history of the play in performance on both stage and screen. Central sources and contexts for the play are included, and each editor also has surveyed the critical commentary on the play and selected representative influential essays to illuminate the text further. A guide to additional reading, viewing, and listening concludes the volume and will continue the reader's relationship with the play.

Each volume includes an overview of Shakespeare's life and the world of London theater that he inhabited. Our goal for these editions is that they provide the reader a window into Shakespeare and his work that reminds us all of his enduring global influence.

The text for these plays comes from *The Riverside Shakespeare*, edited with notes and textual commentary by the late Gywnne Blakemore Evans. Evans was known for his unrivaled scholarly precision, and his *Riverside* text is an essential and much-admired modern edition of Shakespeare. The Evans Shakespeare Editions preserve the *Riverside* line numbering, which is the numbering used in the invaluable *Harvard Concordance to Shakespeare* by Marvin Spevack.

Beyond his scholarly work, Evans was a generous mentor to many of the editors in this series and a tremendous influence on all of us. His kind-hearted nature made it impossible for him truly to dislike anyone. However, despite an identification with the most traditional and canonical of cultural texts, he reserved a raised eyebrow and stern words for those whose politics lacked empathy and understanding for the full diversity of human experience. In this attitude too, as in all his writing and teaching, it was evident that he was a scholar who understood Shakespeare. This series is dedicated to his memory.

Shakespeare's Life

J. J. M. Tobin

S HAKESPEARE WAS a genius, but he was no unreachable ivory-tower poet. Instead, Shakespeare was a young man from the provinces who made good in the big city of London. Just when and how he came from the provinces remains a mystery. He was born in 1564, the eldest son of an initially quite successful father whose position as alderman and then bailiff (mayor) of the town of Stratford allowed his son to attend the local Latin Grammar School. There, Shakespeare received an education that, contrary to some critics' belief, provided him with the historical perspective and verbal flexibility that helped define his writing.

The schoolboy grew into a young man who married an older woman, Anne Hathaway, and became the father of a daughter and a set of twins, a boy and a girl, by the age of twenty-one. The boy, Hamnet, would die before his twelfth birthday. When the playwright's father, John Shakespeare, only recently recovered from two decades of legal and financial difficulties, died in 1601, having earlier secured the coat of arms of a gentleman (Duncan-Jones 90–102), Shakespeare was left in Stratford with a family of four women: his wife, his two daughters, and his mother, Mary, *née* Arden. Shakespeare's own familial experiences, from the fluctuations of his father's fortunes, to the strong influence of several female relatives, to the tragic loss of a beloved son, doubtless added heart and depth to the incisive portrayals of characters that he created in his plays and poems.

Accordingly, given the fact that all description is necessarily selective, Shakespeare often had in mind his own experiences when he chose narrative and dramatic sources for the foundation of his comedies, histories, and tragedies. The few facts of his life that survive are open to all sorts of interpretations, some of which reveal more about the interpreter than about the facts themselves, while others carry with them a greater degree of likelihood. A few critics have noted that Shakespeare was the eldest boy in a patriarchal world, the first surviving child born in a time of plague after the infant deaths of two siblings. As a child, he doubtless saw and remembered his father dressed in the furred scarlet gown of a bailiff in 1568, going about his appointed supervisory tasks, a figure both familiar as a person and strangely exalted as an official, and as Stephen Greenblatt has noted, all by means of a costume (Greenblatt 30–31). He was likely to have been the indisputable favorite of his mother, acquiring a self-confidence that often leads young men with even a modicum of talent on to success.

Richard Wheeler has pointed out that Shakespeare's choice of source material in which a female is disguised as a boy, best illustrated in *Twelfth Night*, has psychological roots in the playwright's wish to have repaired the loss of his son, Hamnet, whose twin sister, Judith, remained a constant reminder of the absent boy (Wheeler 147–53). Finally, although his marriage and fatherhood indicate some clear grounds for heterosexuality, Shakespeare also wrote beautiful poems about a young man, and his plays often feature male bonding and pathetic male isolation when the bond is broken by marriage, as in the instances of Antonio and Bassanio in *The Merchant of Venice* and a second Antonio and Sebastian in *Twelfth Night*. These scenarios offer putative evidence of at least homosociability.

Of course, over-reliance on causal links between the playwright and the experiences of his creations would logically have Shakespeare a conscience-stricken killer like Claudius or Macbeth, a disoriented octogenarian like Lear, and a suicidal queen like Cleopatra—interpretative leaps that even the most imaginative critic is unwilling to make.

Between the birth of the twins in February 1585 and the writer Robert Greene's allusion to Shakespeare as an actor-turned-playwright in September 1592, there is no hard evidence of his whereabouts, although many theories abound. Perhaps he was a schoolmaster in the country; perhaps he was attached to the household of a Catholic landowner in Lancashire. Certainly one of the most plausible theories is that Shakespeare joined the traveling theatrical troupe called the Queen's Men in 1587 as it passed through Stratford and then came to London as a member of their company. If so, he joined an exciting theatrical world with competition for the entertainment dollar among several companies with plays written by both authors who were university graduates and a minority who were not. It was a world that on its stages carefully reflected the political issues and events of the moment, but did so indirectly because of restrictions created by governmental censorship and by the potential dangers posed by a personal response to criticism by the powerful men of the time.

These dramas were composed for a public audience of mixed class and gender, from work-cutting apprentices to lords of the realm and every possible class gradation in between. They were also performed occasionally for a private audience of higher status in smaller indoor venues.

The London of these plays was a fast-growing city, even in a time of plague, full of energy, color, commerce, varieties of goods, animals, and people of all social degrees. The population numbered perhaps 200,000 by the end of the sixteenth century. It was governed by a Lord Mayor and a municipal council quite concerned about issues of crowd control, the spread of disease, crime, and the fallout of all three in neighborhoods either just at the edge of their partial jurisdiction, Shoreditch in the north and Southwark, Bankside, in the south, or fully within it, like the Blackfriars. Playhouses, three-tiered amphitheaters, and the earlier open-plan inn-yards with galleries above, brought together all three of these problems and more, and they were threatened constantly with restriction by the authorities, who also had the subtle financial desire of taxing players whose performances were not protected by aristocratic patronage.

By the time he joined the newly formed Lord Chamberlain's Men in 1594, Shakespeare had already written his first four history plays (*1, 2, & 3 Henry VI* and *Richard III*), the farcical comedies *The Taming of the Shrew* and *The Comedy of Errors*, and the grotesquely interesting tragedy *Titus Andronicus*. Many, but certainly not all, of his 154 sonnets were also written in the mid-1590s. When the Lord Chamberlain's Men moved into the newly constructed Globe theater in late 1599, having had five good years at the Theatre and the nearby Curtain in Shoreditch, Shakespeare had scripted four more history plays, *King John*, *Richard II*, and *1 & 2 Henry IV* (and part of a fifth play, *Edward III*), six comedies, including *The Two Gentlemen of Verona*, *Love's Labour's Lost*, three of the five so-called "golden comedies" (*A Midsummer Night's Dream*, *The Merchant of Venice,* and *Much Ado About Nothing*), and *Romeo and Juliet,* the tragic companion to *A Midsummer Night's Dream.*

The opening season at the Globe doubtless included the last of the English history plays written solely by Shakespeare, *Henry V*, the pastoral comedy both debunking and idealistic, *As You Like It*, and the most frequently taught of the plays focused on Roman history, *Julius Caesar*. Before the death of Queen Elizabeth in late March of 1603, Shakespeare had certainly written his most famous play, *Hamlet*, his most intensely claustrophobic tragedy, *Othello*, the bourgeois domestic comedy *The Merry Wives of Windsor*, the last of the "golden comedies," which we find alloyed with both satire and melancholy, *Twelfth Night*, and the uniquely powerful satirical comedy *Troilus and Cressida*, as well as the enigmatic poem about martyrdom, *The Phoenix and Turtle*.

Outbreaks of the plague affected Shakespeare both as a dramatist and as a poet, for the virulence of the disease, when deaths reached more than fifty a week in London, forced the authorities to close the theaters in order to restrict contagion. Shakespeare was thus left with added time free from the incessant pressure to produce dramatic scripts, and he then composed his two Ovidian narrative poems, *Venus and Adonis* (1593) and *The Rape of Lucrece* (1594). The most extended theater closings were from June 1592 to May 1594 and from March 1603 to April 1604, but there were other, briefer closings. The plague was an abiding and overpowering presence in the lives and imaginations of the poet and his audiences.

After the accession in 1603 of James VI of Scotland as James I of England, when the Lord Chamberlain's Men became the King's Men, and before the company activated for themselves the lease in 1608 of the Blackfriars, a smaller, indoor theater that was to draw a higher and more homogeneous class of spectator, Shakespeare created his other great tragedies, *King Lear, Macbeth, Antony and Cleopatra,* and *Coriolanus,* as well as the bitter *Timon of Athens* (although there is no record of its ever having been performed), and the two "bed-trick" plays, *All's Well That Ends Well* and *Measure for Measure,* comedies in which a lecherous man is fooled by the substitution of one woman for another in the darkness of the night. For that indoor spectacle-friendly Blackfriars Theater, Shakespeare wrote the romances *Pericles, Cymbeline, The Winter's Tale,* and *The Tempest,* with their wondrous atmospheres and radiant daughters. By 1611, Shakespeare was moving into partial retirement, co-authoring with John Fletcher, his younger colleague and successor as principal playwright of the King's Men, *Henry VIII, The Two Noble Kinsmen,* and, probably, the lost *Cardenio.*

The division of his plays into these categories—comedies, histories, tragedies, and romances—reminds us that the first step taken by the playwright (indeed any playwright) was to determine the basic genre or kind of play that he wished to write, however much he might expand its boundaries. Genre creates expectations in the mind of the audience, expectations that no dramatist of the time was willing to frustrate. Regarding kind, Polonius tells us with unconscious humor of the versatility of the players who come to Elsinore: "The best actors in the world, either for tragedy, comedy, history, pastoral, pastoral-comical, historical-pastoral, tragical-historical, tragical-comical-historical-pastoral" (2.2.396–399). In that boundary-blurring, increasingly capacious definition of genre, he also informs us of Shakespeare's own gift in all kinds of writing and the fact of his often combining many of these genres in a single work. When, at the end of Plato's *Symposium,* Socrates argues that logically, the greatest tragic writer should also be the greatest comic writer, he was prophetic of Shakespeare, even if he doesn't go on to argue that these principles of tragedy and comedy could and should be connected in the same play. And Shakespeare indirectly repays Socrates for his prophecy by alluding to the philosopher's death in Mistress Quickly's description of the dying Falstaff in *Henry V,* 2.3.

Shakespeare is Shakespeare because of a combination of philosophical tolerance, psychological profundity, and metaphoric genius; that is, he is generous-minded, aware of what makes people tick, and is able to express himself more vividly and memorably than anyone else in the language. And it is his language that truly sets him apart, while simultaneously creating some occasional static in the mind of the modern reader.

There are six areas of this problematic language worth special attention: word choice, false friends, allusions, puns, iambic rhythm, and personification. Shakespeare's vocabulary has words that are no longer part of today's language, chiefly because they refer to things and concepts no longer in use, such as "three-farthings," coins of small value, in the Bastard's metaphoric "Look where three-farthings goes" (*King John*, 1.1.143). Such terms are easily understood by looking at the footnotes, or by checking *The Oxford English Dictionary* or a Shakespearean lexicon, like that of Schmidt; C. T. Onions's *A Shakespeare Glossary;* or *Shakespeare's Words,* by David and Ben Crystal. More difficult are false friends, words spelled the same as words we use today but that have different meanings. One example of this issue is "brave," which as an adjective in the sixteenth and early seventeenth centuries meant primarily "splendid" or "glorious," as in Miranda's expression of awe and excitement in *The Tempest*: "O *brave* new world/That has such people in't" (5.1.183–84), or "virtue," which in Shakespeare's language usually means "strength or power," as in Iago's argument for personal responsibility to Roderigo and the latter's lament that "it is not in my *virtue* to amend it [being in love with Desdemona]": "*Virtue*? A fig! 'tis in ourselves that we are thus or thus" (*Othello*, 1.3.318–20).

Equally problematic, but just as easily understood by reference to footnotes, are instances of classical and biblical allusion, where Shakespeare assumes a recognition by all or some of the audience of glancing references to Greek and Roman deities, frequently to elements in that most abiding narrative in Western literature, the Trojan War, as well as historical and legendary figures, as in Hamlet's "My father's brother, but no more like my father/Than I to *Hercules*" (1.2.152–53) or his subconscious reminder in the graveyard of the fact that his father was the victim of fratricide, "How the knave jowls it to the ground, as if 'twere *Cain's* jaw-bone" (5.1.76–77).

More difficult at times are Shakespeare's puns—plays on words, sometimes comedic and sometimes intentionally non-comedic, but in each case designed to bring more than one meaning in a single word to the attention of the audience and the reader. Shakespeare's puns are almost always thematically significant, revelatory of character, or both, and attention to the possibilities of the presence of punning can only increase our understanding and pleasure in the lines. There are such simple etymological puns as "lieutenant," the military title of Cassio in *Othello*, where the word is defined as one who holds the place of the captain in the latter's absence—exactly the fear Othello has about the relationship that he imagines exists between his wife, Desdemona, and Lieutenant Cassio. There are also puns that fuse the physical and the moral, as in Falstaff's comment that his highway robbery is condoned by the goddess of the moon, "under whose *countenance* we steal" (*1 Henry IV*, 1.2.29), where the word "countenance" means both "face" and "approval." Falstaff's pun is in prose, a good example of how Shakespeare, commonly regarded as the greatest of English poets and dramatists, wrote often in prose, which itself is full of the linguistic devices of poetry.

When Shakespeare was writing in verse, he used iambic pentameter lines, ten syllable lines with five feet, or units, of two syllables each, in the sequence of short-long or unstressed-stressed. Consider, for example, Romeo's "But soft,/what light/through yond/er win/

Fig. 1. Joseph Fiennes as William Shakespeare fighting through writer's block in the film *Shakespeare in Love*: a handsome dramatist without the receding hairline of contemporary portraits and busts.

dow breaks?" (*Romeo and Juliet*, 2.2.1), or Antony's "If you/have tears/ prepare/to shed/them now" (*Julius Caesar*, 3.2.169).

Scanning the rhythm of these lines is made easier by our knowledge that Shakespeare and the English language are both naturally iambic and that proof of the correct rhythm begins with marking the stress on the final syllable of the line and moving right to left. The rhythm with the emphasized syllables will lead the actor delivering the lines to stress certain words more than others, as we imagine Shakespeare to have intended, even as we know that stage delivery of lines with an unexpected stress can create fruitful tension in the ear of the audience. For example, Barnardo's "It was about to speak when the cock crew" (*Hamlet*, 1.1.147) is a pentameter line, but the expected iambic rhythm is broken in the last two feet, especially in the sequentially stressed final two syllables, which by their alliteration and double stress combine in form to underscore the moment of interruption in the play's narrative. Such playing off the expected is part of Shakespeare's arsenal of verse techniques.

In addition to these issues of unknown terms, false friends, allusions chiefly classical and biblical, meaningful puns, and verse rhythm itself, there is the metaphoric language that is the glory of Shakespeare, but each instance of this feature demands careful unpacking. Consider the early example of Romeo's personifying Death as an erotic figure keeping Juliet as his mistress, linking the commonly joined notions of love and death: "Shall I believe/That unsubstantial Death is amorous,/ And that the lean abhorred monster keeps/Thee here in dark to be his paramour?" (5.3.102–05). This link already had been anticipated by the Chorus in the prologue to the play, which speaks of "The fearful passage of their death-marked love" (l.6).

More compactly, later in his career, Shakespeare will have Hamlet, in prose, combine Renaissance and medieval views in similes and metaphors, comparisons with and without "like" or "as," in order to describe the multifaceted nature of man: "…how like an angel in apprehension, how like a god! The beauty of the world; the paragon of animals; and yet to me what is this quintessence of dust?" (*Hamlet*, 2.2.306–08). Macbeth in his play will argue against his wife's view that a little water will cleanse his guilty hands: "No; this my hand will rather/The multitudinous seas incarnadine,/Making the green one red" (2.2.58–60). Here Shakespeare has been careful to combine the mouth-filling hyperbole and its Latinate terms "multitudinous" and "incarnadine" (an illustration of the technique that he had learned from Christopher Marlowe) with a crystal-clear synonymous expression, "Making the green one red," for the benefit of all in the theater, even as everyone hears the hypnotically mellifluous line that comes before it.

Sometimes Shakespeare scorned the opportunity to use high-flown language, even when one might expect it most, as in the Roman play *Antony and Cleopatra*, when the queen uses a noun as a verb in her bitter image of herself live on the Roman stage played by a child actor, "And I shall see/Some squeaking Cleopatra *boy* my greatness/I' th' posture of a whore" (*Antony and Cleopatra*, 5.2.219–221). Shakespeare gives to Cleopatra's handmaiden Charmian the least hyperbolic expression in a context linking the erotic and funereal (analogous to that situation described by Romeo), "Now boast thee, death, in thy possession lies/A *lass* unparallel'd" (5.2.315–16), where the simple pastoral monosyllable charms the audience, which all along had sensed the antithesis of the playful girl within the cunningly imperious and imperial queen.

While nothing can fully explain the development of this language, its raw material comes largely from Shakespeare's reading, as do the basic elements of plot and character. The same man who was to save and increase his money and property in London and Stratford was, as a craftsman, equally economical, preferring to alter and expand upon material given to him in the literary sources that lie behind all his compositions rather than to create from experience alone. He is the chief counter-example to Polonius's admonition "Neither a borrower nor a lender be" (*Hamlet* 1.3.75)—Shakespeare is a world-class borrower, but one who reshapes and transforms the borrowed materials.

Certainly he had a most retentive memory and could and did recall, at times subconsciously, both single expressions and rather lengthy passages from his reading. "It is often as if, at some deep level of his mind, Shakespeare thought and felt in quotation," as Emrys Jones has noted (Jones 21). Dryden's comment that Shakespeare "needed not the spectacles of books to read Nature; he looked inwards and found her there" ignores Shakespeare's conscious manipulations of his reading as a chief source for his achievement. Nevertheless, Dryden gives us the basic image useful for picturing Shakespeare's genius. The playwright's metaphorical spectacles had two lenses, one of which was focused on life as he knew it and one on the writings of his predecessors and contemporaries: historians both classical and English, proto-novelists, poets, pamphleteers, and essayists, and playwrights who had in their own ways dealt with themes that interested him.

It is by looking at what Shakespeare himself perused that we see his manipulative genius at work, omitting, adding, preserving, and qualifying those plots, motifs, and images viewed through one lens of his binoculars. An important question is just how much of the original theme and significance is brought over in the creative borrowing, a question made more difficult to answer by the fact that in the composition of his plays, Shakespeare often modified and sometimes even inverted the gender and number of the persons in the original material. See, for example, the model in the story of Cupid and Psyche from Apuleius' *The Golden Asse* (1566), where Psyche almost murders Cupid, for the description of the deaths of the little princes in *Richard III*, as well as for the presentation of the murder of Desdemona in *Othello*. The closer one looks at this source and the affected passage, the more one sees that the young man from Stratford, despite being accused by his London-educated colleague and rival Ben Jonson of having "small Latin and less Greek," was a sufficiently good Latinist to check the translation of Apuleius that he was using against the original, even as he would later check Golding's translation of the *Metamorphoses* against Ovid's Latin for use in *The Tempest*.

We don't know the workplace of Shakespeare, the desk or table where he kept his books, nor do we know for certain who provided him with these volumes, some of which were quite expensive, such as Holinshed's *Chronicles*, North's *Plutarch*, and bibles, both Bishops' and Geneva. But, if we imagine a bookshelf above his desk and envision the titles that he might have ordered there chronologically, we would first see the classics, most importantly Ovid and Virgil; then the Bible, especially Genesis, the Gospel of St. Matthew, and the Book of Revelation; medieval and Renaissance writers, including Chaucer and Erasmus; and then his own immediate predecessors and colleagues, especially Thomas Kyd, Christopher Marlowe, Robert Greene, and Thomas Nashe. Sometimes the most unlikely source can provide a motif or a character, but for more important ideas, we may note what he would have learned from four exemplary volumes on this imagined shelf.

From Seneca, the Roman philosopher, tutor to the emperor Nero and playwright of closet tragedies (that is, of plays meant to be read in the study rather than performed on stage), Shakespeare learned to balance a sensational theme—fratricide and incest—with a plot structured with care and characters subtly developed with an attitude quite fatalistic. From Plutarch, the Greek historian who wrote parallel lives of Greek and Roman leaders, he learned the importance of the nature of the private man when serving in public office and how that nature is revealed in small gestures with large significance—what James Joyce, the "spiritual son" of Shakespeare, would later refer to as "epiphanies." From Machiavelli, the notorious early-sixteenth-century political theorist, or from the image of Machiavelli, he saw what he had already known about the role of deception and amorality in political life. From Michel de Montaigne, the sixteenth-century father of the essay, he added to his already operative skepticism, a capacity to question received notions about the consistency of the "self" and the hierarchical place of human beings in creation.

Fig. 2. Later, on other writers' bookshelves, would be Shakespeare's own First
Folio (1623), containing thirty-six plays, half of them appearing in print for the
first time. It does not, however, include any of the longer poems or sonnets.

To enjoy Shakespeare, it is not at all necessary to understand the sources that he mined, but to study Shakespeare, the better to appreciate the depth and complexity of the work, it is extremely useful to examine the foundations upon which he has built his characters and plots. We can trace, for example, the many constituent elements that have gone into the creation of Falstaff, who, together with Hamlet, is the most discussed of Shakespeare's creations. The elements include, among still others, the Vice of the morality plays; the rogue from Nashe's *The Unfortunate Traveller;* the *miles gloriosus* or cowardly braggart warrior from the Roman comic playwright (and school text) Plautus; the cheerful toper from the Bacchus of Nashe's *Summer's Last Will and Testament;* parodically, the Protestant martyr Sir John Oldcastle from Foxe's *Book of Martyrs;* and even the dying Socrates of Plato's *Phaedo.* Not that Falstaff is at all times all these figures, but in the course of his career in four plays, alive in *1 & 2 Henry IV*, dying offstage in *Henry V*, and radically transformed in *The Merry Wives of Windsor,* he is each of them by turn and counterturn, and still so much more than the mere sum of all these literary, dramatic, and historical parts.

In terms of giving voice to multiple perspectives, to characters of different ages, genders, colors, ethnicities, religions, and social ranks, Shakespeare is unrivaled. No other playwright, then or since, makes other selves live while simultaneously concealing his own self or selves, a talent described by Keats as "negative capability." Shakespeare was also an actor; that is, a person interested in imitating imaginary persons. He was thus doubly a quite creative mimic. Some of the selves mimicked are versions of the "Other," those foreigners or aliens from around the world, including Africans (Aaron, Morocco, Othello), Jews (Shylock, Tubal, Jessica), Frenchmen and Frenchwomen (the Dauphin, Joan of Arc, Margaret of Anjou), non-English Britons (Irish: Macmorris; Scots: Jamy; Welsh: Fluellen), as well as such other continental Europeans as Spaniards (Don Armado) and Italians (including several Antonios), to say nothing of the indefinable Caliban.

Some of his topics, his subjects for dramatic treatment, came often from already set pieces at school, as Emrys Jones, among others, has shown. For example, a set question to be answered, pro and con, was, should Brutus have joined the conspiracy to assassinate Caesar, the answer to which helps create the tensions in *Julius Caesar* (Jones 16). Such an on-the-one-hand and on-the-other school exercise became part of Shakespeare's dramatic strategy, where plays provide the tension created by opposites and the consequent rich ground for multiple interpretations by readers and audiences. There were also sources in earlier stage productions, including plays about Romeo and Juliet, King John, King Lear, and Hamlet. Marlowe especially provided structures to imitate and diverge from in his plays of a weak king (*Edward II*) and of several extraordinary ambitious characters, among whom are a villainous Jew (*The Jew of Malta*), and a rhetorical conqueror (*Tamburlaine*), brilliant efforts which become in Shakespeare's hands the still more dramatic *Richard II*, *The Merchant of Venice*, and *Henry V*.

Shakespeare's borrowing was frequent and pervasive, but his creative adaptations of those raw materials have made him ultimately not just a borrower but in fact the world's greatest lender, giving us four hundred years of pleasure and providing countless artists, whether painters, novelists, film directors, or even comic book writers, with allusive material. Of course, we would happily surrender our knowledge of a number of these borrowings if only we could have some sense of the quality of the voice of the leading man Richard Burbage, of the facial expressions of the comic actor Will Kemp, the sounds of the groundlings' responses to both the jokes and the set soliloquies, and the reactions of both Queen Elizabeth, who allegedly after watching *1 & 2 Henry IV* wanted to see Falstaff in love, and King James, who doubtless loved the image of his ancestor Banquo in *Macbeth*.

Shakespeare's last years before his death in April 1616 were spent back in Stratford. Although little is known of that time, we are left with the enigmatic coda to his life: his will, in which he famously left to his wife, Anne Hathaway Shakespeare, "the second-best bed"—it is unclear whether it was a cruel slight or a fondly personal bequest. Care of his estate went to his elder daughter, Susannah, while a lesser inheritance went to his wayward younger daughter, Judith, and any children she might have. He died a landowner, a family man, and a once well-known playwright. His will did not cite what has become his greatest legacy—the plays and poems that we read today—but the clues that these works leave about his life, and certainly the testament to his talent that they represent, are more valuable than even the most detailed autobiography. To be sure, however, the local boy who made good, worked hard, had flaws, and lived a complicated family life has more in common with many of his readers, then and now, than does the iconic Shakespeare, who has been mistakenly portrayed as a distant genius paring his fingernails while creating many of the greatest works in world literature.

ELIZABETHAN THEATER

J. J. M. Tobin

MASS ENTERTAINMENT today has become ever more frac-
tured as technology provides myriad ways to take in a film
(and myriad ways for Hollywood to try to make money).
Movie theaters now have to compete with home theaters and couches
in a way they never had to before in order to put people in the seats.
The attractions of high-definition screens and stereo surround-sound
are not the draw they once were now that individuals can access such
technology in their own homes, and stadium seating and chair-side
concessions don't make up the difference. The appeal of first-run films
is fading too, now that movies go to DVD in a matter of weeks and are
also available for immediate streaming through a Netflix subscription.
All of these technologies, however, whether enjoyed in the cinema or
at home, contribute to the moviegoer's sensation of being transported
to another time and place (a journey, moreover, that lasts not much
longer than an hour and a half). Hard to imagine, then, that a little
over four hundred years ago, when the battle for the entertainment
dollar took place on the stage rather than the screen, most members
of the Elizabethan audience gladly stood for more than two hours
without benefit of a padded seat, buttered popcorn, or Junior Mints
(although they did have dried fruit and nuts), or the pause button
in order to watch the plays of Shakespeare and his fellow dramatists
performed. The legendary plays we read today on these pages were
once the sixteenth- and early-seventeenth-century equivalents of the
Harry Potter series or *Avatar*—artistic creations to be sure, but first and
foremost moneymakers for their producers.

Theatrical performances in Elizabethan England took place all over
the country in a wide variety of venues. As we know from the work of
A. Gurr and others, if we put aside the sites used by touring companies
like the Queen's Men of the 1580s (to which Shakespeare himself may
have been attached), the guildhalls and marketplaces in cities and towns
like Norwich, Bristol, and Stratford, or the halls of the universities of
Oxford and Cambridge, and instead concentrate on London itself, we
see that there were five basic performance locales (Gurr, esp. 115 ff.).
There were, of course, the inns and inn-yards, in large part roofed
against the weather and useful especially during the winter months.

The most celebrated of these inns in the history of London theater were the Bel Savage, the Bull, and the Cross Keys, these latter two on the same London street. These were the locations most frequently of concern to the mayor and other municipal authorities anxious about unruly crowds and increased chances of plague contagion, until 1594, when it was declared by the Lord Chamberlain of the Queen's court that there would be only two adult companies—his own, the Lord Chamberlain's Men (Shakespeare's group), and his father-in-law's, the Lord Admiral's Men, troupes that would upon the succession of King James be called the King's Men and Prince Henry's Men—and they would not perform anymore in city inns.

Second, there were two indoor halls, one in a building abutting St. Paul's Cathedral, not too far from the Bel Savage Inn, and the other in the refectory of the old Blackfriars monastery, each used by the children's companies of boys who put on plays with adult political and moral themes. Shakespeare and his company in 1596 had hoped to use the Blackfriars because Blackfriars was a liberty—that is, a district that, for reasons of its religious history, was independent of the secular control of the sheriff—but were refused by a powerful NIMBY (not in my backyard) movement of influential residents. They then leased the building to a second generation of a children's company and had to wait until 1608 to take possession of what would turn out to be both a "tonier" and quite lucrative theatrical space.

Third were the dining halls of the Inns of Court, the London law schools or, perhaps, more accurately, legal societies, where noteworthy performances of *The Comedy of Errors* (Gray's Inn) and *Twelfth Night* (the Middle Temple) took place. There, special audiences with their appetite for contemporary satire allowed for the lampooning of particular individuals whose traits and foibles would be represented by grimace, gesture, voice imitation, and even clothing, as in the case of Dr. Pinch in *The Comedy of Errors*, Malvolio in *Twelfth Night*, and Ajax in *Troilus and Cressida*. When these plays were moved to the larger public stage, the personalized elements could be withdrawn and the characters could continue as general, non-specifically humorous figures.

Fourth was the Queen's court itself (after the death of Elizabeth in 1603, it became the King's court), where at Christmastide, the major companies would be invited to perform for the pleasure of the monarch. Indeed, throughout the long period of tension between the city authorities and the court, the justification for allowing the players to perform their craft in public was that they needed to practice in order to be ready at year's end to entertain the monarch. This argument assumed a quite disproportionate ratio of practice to performance, but it was a convenient semi-fiction that seemed to satisfy all concerned. These court performances were rewarded financially by the Master of the Revels and were less expensive than other kinds of royal entertainment, including masques with elaborate scenery and complicated production devices, the high costs of which later contributed to the downfall of Charles I, James's son and successor. Legend has it that Queen Elizabeth so enjoyed some of the performances featuring the character of Falstaff that she wished to see him in love, a comment which was allegedly the stimulus for *The Merry Wives of Windsor*, which was said to have been written in two weeks, the better to satisfy the queen's request. A close look at the multiple sources used in the creation of this middle-class comedy suggests that the legend may be well founded.

Last, there are the purpose-built amphitheaters, beginning with James Burbage's the Theatre (1576) in Shoreditch, just to the north of the city limits; and the Curtain (1578) nearby. To the south, across the Thames, were the Rose (1587), the site of the Lord Admiral's company and most notably the performances of Christopher Marlowe's plays; the Swan (1596); the Globe (1599), built with the very timbers of the Theatre transported across the river in the winter of 1598 after the twenty-one-year lease on the old property had expired and several subsequent months of renting; and, back to Shoreditch in the north, the Fortune (1600), explicitly built in imitation of the triple-tiered Globe.

There was competition for the same audience in the form of bull-baiting, bear-baiting and cockfighting, and also simple competition for attention from such activities as royal processions, municipal pageants, outdoor sermons, and public executions with hangings, eviscerations, castrations, and quarterings, not to mention the nearby temptation of the houses ("nunneries") of prostitution. Nonetheless, these theatrical structures proved that, if you build it, they will come.

And come they did, with hundreds of performances each year of thirty or more plays in repertory for each company, plays of chronicle history, romance, tragedy (especially revenge tragedy), satire, and comedy (slapstick, farcical, situational, verbal, and, from 1597, "humorous"; that is, comedy dependent upon characters moved by one dominant personality trait into behavior mechanical and predictable, almost monomaniacally focused). The two major companies could and did perform familiar plays for a week or more before adding a new play to the repertory. A successful new play would be performed at least eight times, according to Knutson, within four months to half a year (Knutson 33–34). New plays were house-fillers, and entrance fees could be doubled for openings. When sequels created a two-part play, performances were only sometimes staged in proper sequence, even as moviegoers will still watch on cable *Godfather II* or *The Empire Strikes Back* without worrying that they have not just seen *The Godfather* or *Star Wars*.

Fig. 3. Part of J. C. Visscher's view of London (c. 1616 or slightly earlier) looking north from the Bankside and showing the Beargarden theater and, to the right, the Globe theater (or possibly the Swan).

The players seemed willing to play throughout the week and throughout the year, but municipal officials repeatedly insisted that there be no performances on Sundays and holy days and holidays, nor during Lent. These demands had some effect, although their repetition by the authorities clearly suggests that there were violations, with performances on occasional Sundays, even at court, on some holidays, and on some days in Lent.

Of course, even though almost half of Shakespeare's plays had already been performed at the Theater and elsewhere, we think of the Globe, open for business probably in the late summer of 1599, as the principal venue for Shakespeare's work, perhaps with *As You Like It* the first production. The current New Globe on the Bankside in Southwark, erected in careful imitation of what we know to have been the methods and materials of the sixteenth century, allows for a twenty-first-century experience analogous to that of the Elizabethan theatergoer. It may be that the diameter of the current theater, of one hundred feet, is a bit too wide, and that seventy-two feet is rather closer to the exact diameter of not only the Globe but several of these late-sixteenth-century London theaters. If so, the judgment that such Elizabethan theaters could hold between 2,000 and 3,000 people suggests that spectators, particularly the groundlings—those who had paid a penny to stand throughout the two-to-three hour performance—were packed in cheek by jowl.

The geometry of the Globe itself is that of a polygon, but it appears circular. From a distance, one would know that a play was to be performed that day by the presence of a flag flying high above the tiring house, the dressing area for the actors. Once inside the building, the theatergoer would note the covered stage projecting from an arc of the circle almost to the center of the uncovered audience space, such that the groundlings would be on three sides of the stage, with those in the front almost able to rest their chins on the platform which was raised about five feet from the floor. This stage was not raked—that is, inclined or tilted towards the audience—as it often is in modern theaters today. Raking both creates better sightlines and potentially affects stage business, as in the case of a fallen Shylock in productions of *The Merchant of Venice*, who at one point struggled in vain to stand on a pile of slippery ducats (gold coins). This move is made even more difficult by the slight incline. However, instead of raking the stage, the Rose, and perhaps the Globe and the Fortune, had the ground on which the audience stood slightly raked (Thomson 78–79), to the great advantage of those in the back of the theater.

Behind the stage, protected by a backdrop on the first level, was the tiring house where the actors dressed and from which they came and went through two openings to the left and right. There were few surprise entrances in the Elizabethan theater, as the audience could always see before them the places of entry. Covering the upper stage and a large part of the outer stage would be the "heavens," supported by two columns or pillars behind which characters could hide in order to eavesdrop and which could serve metaphorically as trees or bushes. The underside of the "heavens" was adorned with signs of the zodiac, the better to remind the audience that all the world is a stage. At the back of the stage in the center, between the two openings of exit and entrance, was a discovery space within which, when a curtain was drawn, an additional mini-set of a study, a bed, or a cave could be revealed.

From below the stage, figures, especially ghosts, could ascend through a trapdoor, and mythological deities could be lowered from above. From the second tier of the galleries, still part of the tiring house, characters could appear as on battlements or a balcony. Music was a very great part of Elizabethan theater, and musicians would be positioned sometimes on that second level of the tiring house. Less musical but still necessary sound effects, say one indicating a storm and thunder, were achieved by such actions as the offstage rolling of a cannonball down a metal trestle or repeated drumming.

Although the groundlings were the closest to the talented actors, for those members of the audience who wished to sit in the galleries (Stern, esp. 212–13) and were willing to pay more money for the privilege, there would have been the comfort of the familiar, as V. F. Petronella has pointed out, inasmuch as these galleries included rooms not unlike those in the domestic buildings near the Globe. However, the familiar was balanced with the rare via the figures on the stage who represented kings, nymphs, fairies, and ghosts, personages not usually found in the Southwark area (Petronella, esp. 111–25). These audiences themselves came from a great range of Elizabethan society, male and female, from aristocrats to lowly apprentices, with all gradations of the social spectrum in between. The late Elizabethan and early Jacobean period is so special in theatrical history in part because of the work of a number of gifted playwrights, Shakespeare preeminent among them, but also in part because of the inclusive nature of the audiences, which were representative of the society as a whole.

When the King's Men in 1609 began to perform in the smaller, indoor Blackfriars theater while still continuing at the Globe in the summer months, they were able to charge at Blackfriars five or six times the entry fee at the Globe for productions that pleased a grander and wealthier group, but at the cost of having a more socially homogeneous audience. Although the Blackfriars was a more lucrative venue,

Shakespeare's company still profited from productions at the Globe, to the degree that when the Globe burned down during a performance of *Henry VIII* on June 29 1613, the company immediately set about rebuilding the structure so that it could reopen the very next year. One wonders whether Shakespeare came down from semi-retirement in Stratford for the new opening or was already in London working yet again in collaboration with John Fletcher, his successor as principal playwright of the King's Men.

In the more heterogeneous atmosphere at the Globe, whether the first or second version, audiences watched action taking place on a platform of about twelve hundred square feet, a stage which could be the Roman forum at one moment, the senate house at another, and a battlefield at still another. Yet the audience was never at a loss in recognizing what was what, for the dramatist provided place references in the dialogue between and among characters (and some plays may also have featured signs indicating place). The action was sometimes interrupted by informative soliloquies, speeches directed to the audience as if the character speaking on the stage were totally alone, whether or not he or she actually was. By convention, what was said in a soliloquy was understood to be the truthful indication of the character's thoughts and feelings. These soliloquies must have been in their day somewhat analogous to operatic arias—plot-useful devices, but also stand-alone bravura exercises in rhetorical display. Othello's "flaming minister" speech (5.2.1–22) is a good example of the show-stopping effect of the soliloquy, and Edmund's defense of bastardy in *King Lear* (1605; 1.2.1–22), in a passage of identical length, seldom fails to elicit applause at the last line even from today's audiences, who otherwise are accustomed not to interrupt the flow of a performance.

The actors and the audience were proximate and visible to each other during these daylight performances, putting them on more intimate terms than is the case in theaters today. Performers were dressed onstage in contemporary Elizabethan clothing, with the kings and dukes wearing specially purchased, costly garments whose fate as they grew worn and tattered was to outfit the clowns with social pretensions. There were also attempts to provide historical atmosphere when needed with helmets, shields, greaves and togas appropriate to the ancient world. Perhaps as few as ten men and four boys, who would play the women's roles in this all-male theatrical world, could perform all sixteenth-century plays. The boys would remain with the company until their voices cracked, and some then became adult members of the company when places became available. They were apprentices in a profession where the turnover was not great—a bonus to the dramatist who could visualize the actor who would be playing the character he was creating but not so advantageous for a young actor looking for a permanent place within a stable group. Because plays were very seldom performed in an uninterrupted run, actors needed powerful memories. It was a time when the aural rather than the visual understanding was much greater than in our own time, but even so, the capacity of actors to hold in their heads a large number of roles from many different plays was extraordinary, and new plays were constantly being added to the repertory.

Even as one man in his time plays many parts, so did Shakespeare's company of actors. The skills and particular strengths of these actors must have given Shakespeare a great deal of confidence about the complexity of the roles that he could ask them to create. Such an element of the familiar increased the pleasure of the audience when it could recognize the same actor behind two different characters whose similarity might now be perceived. Celebrated instances of doubling include, in *A Midsummer Night's Dream*, Theseus/Oberon and Hippolyta/Titania; and, in *Hamlet*, Polonius/First Gravedigger and, most strikingly, the Ghost/Claudius. The audience would likewise be affected by their experience with an actor in a current play having performed in a previous play that they had also seen. One example of this link between roles that allows the audience to anticipate the plot comes in *Hamlet,* when Polonius tells us of his having played Caesar. Caesar, of course, was killed by Brutus in Shakespeare's *Julius Caesar.* The actor now playing Polonius had played Caesar previously in *Julius Caesar,* and in that production, he was killed by Brutus, played by Richard Burbage (son of James). In this performance of *Hamlet*, Burbage was playing Hamlet, and he would shortly kill Polonius, in a repeat of history.

The theater is the most collaborative of enterprises. We should think of Shakespeare as a script-writer under considerable pressure to provide material for his colleagues, all of whom viewed the play to come as a fundamentally money-making project. Shakespeare had multiple advantages beyond his inherent verbal and intuitive gifts. Not only did he write for a group of actors whose individual talents he could anticipate in the composition of his characters, but the script that he was creating was often a response to recent successes by rival companies with their own revengers, weak and strong English kings, and disguised lovers.

The performances themselves relied greatly on the power of the audience's imagination to fill in what was missing because of the limitations of the Elizabethan stage, as the self-conscious Prologue in *Henry V* (1599) makes clear by appealing to the audience to imagine whole armies being transported across the sea. Other Elizabethan dramatists did attempt to be "realistic" in ways that are laughable even beyond the well-intended efforts of Quince, Bottom, and the other Mechanicals in *A Midsummer Night's Dream* (1596). Consider, as noted by G. B. Evans, Yarrington's *Two Tragedies in One* (1594–c. 1598), 2.1: "When the boy goeth in to the shop, Merry striketh six blows on his head and, with the seventh, leaves the hammer sticking in his head; the boy groaning must be heard by a maid, who must cry to her master." Three scenes later, a character "Brings him forth in a chair with a hammer sticking in his head" (Evans 71). Such grossly imperfect efforts increasingly gave way to conventional signals expressive of the limitations of the stage. Four or five men with spears and a flag could represent an army, and a single coffin could represent a whole graveyard. While the Globe stage lacked scenery as we know it, it was not lacking in props. Not only were there a trapdoor grave and a bank of flowers, but also a good number of handheld props like swords, torches, chalices, crowns, and skulls, each a real object and potentially a symbol.

Sometimes convention and symbolism gave way to nature in the case of live animals. Men in animal skins are safer, of course, but some animals, like dogs and bears, are trainable. It is certain that Crab, the dog in the *Two Gentlemen of Verona* (1595–96), was "played" by a true canine, and it is quite likely that the bear that pursues Antigonus in *The Winter's Tale* was only sometimes a disguised human being; but at other times, it was a bear, managed but real, possibly even a polar bear reared from the time of its capture as a cub. Further reflection on the known dangers associated with working with bears and our knowledge of the props listed in *Henslowe's Diary* of 'j beares skyne' (Henslowe 319) suggest that Elizabethan actors were more comfortable with artificial bears, thereby avoiding any sudden ursine aggression, revenge for all the suffering their colleagues had endured at the bear-baiting stake.

The authorities whose powers of censorship were real and forceful did not worry much about whether animals were live onstage or not, but they did care about theological issues being discussed explicitly and about urban insurrection, as we know from the strictures applied to *The Book of Sir Thomas More*, a manuscript play in which Shakespeare most probably had a hand. For all their apparent sensitivity to political issues, the government seems not to have interfered with plays that show the removal—or even the murder—of kings, although the scene of the deposing of Richard in *Richard II* (1596) was thought too delicate to be printed during the lifetime of Queen Elizabeth, who recognized Richard as a parallel figure and pointedly said: "I am Richard the Second, know ye not that?" Scholars debate whether some of these potent themes regarding right versus might, illegitimate succession, and successful usurpation were recognized imperfectly by the government and so escaped into performance if not always into print. Another theory is that the authorities allowed the audiences to be excited and then pacified by these entertaining productions, a release of energies that returned the audience at the play's end to an unchanged social and political reality.

While it is now customary to refer to this reality as part of the Early Modern Period, it is still important to remember that the two main cultural forces of the time, the Renaissance and the Reformation, came together in a perfect storm of new ideas about values. The Renaissance brought us the rebirth of classical culture and an emphasis on the dignity of human beings, and the Reformation stripped levels of interpretative authority in favor of the individual's more direct reliance on Scripture. These new ideas, sometimes in concert and sometimes in tension, have led increasingly over four hundred years to our current distant but clearly related theories of skepticism and pragmatism.

It is just as important to remember that when James Burbage built his theater in 1576, he was not so much interested in the idea of the dignity of human beings or in the proper interpretation of Scripture as in the making of money. When his son, Richard, and his son's friend and partner, William Shakespeare, and their fellow shareholders were creating and performing their scripts, they were counting the house above all else. Theater was an essential part of the entertainment industry, and for some, it was especially lucrative. If a man was an actor, he made a little bit of money; if a playwright, a little more; if a shareholder in the company that put on the play, a very great deal more; and if a householder in the building in which the plays were performed, even more still. Shakespeare was all four, and as we read his scripts, we should remember that the artist was also a businessman, interested in the box office as much as or more than any hard-to-imagine immortality. The Elizabethan theater was the forerunner of the multiplex, a collaborative, secular church in which the congregation/audience focused on the service before them, and Shakespeare and his fellows focused on both the service and the collection plate.

And yet with all the primary focus on material gain, Shakespeare and his competitors and collaborators were aware of the cultural importance and historical traditions of drama itself. Their own work continued myths and rituals that had begun in Athens and elsewhere more than two thousand years ago. It may well be true, as Dr. Samuel Johnson famously said, that no man but a blockhead ever wrote for anything but money, and Mozart might have been partially correct when he said that good health and money were the two most important elements in life. Yet we also know that just because a work has been commissioned doesn't rule out the presence of beauty and truth, as indeed Mozart's own works reveal. Michelangelo was paid by Pope Julius II to paint the Sistine Chapel, but nobody thinks of the fee the artist earned when she or he looks at the creation of Adam or the expulsion of Adam and Eve from the Garden of Eden. Shakespeare's career in the Elizabethan theatrical world turned out to be quite lucrative, but given the many profound reasons for which we read and study *A Midsummer Night's Dream*, *King Lear*, and *The Tempest* today (among so many other plays and poems), we see that the dramatist who created these works and gained so much material success was nevertheless grossly underpaid.

INTRODUCTION

Katherine Rowe

S HORT, SPOOKY, intensely psychological, violently political, William Shakespeare's *Macbeth* has been popular throughout its history. The tragedy begins with a description of its hero slicing his enemy "from the nave to th' chops" and ends in a battle with trees walking. Yet it also offers the most disturbingly intimate of Shakespeare's portraits of a husband and wife. *Macbeth* has been adapted frequently: burlesqued in early minstrel shows; reimagined for opera, radio, television, film, and the Internet; and retold in historical novels. It has been a staple of political satire and commentary from the seventeenth century to the present. Lady Macbeth in particular is fixed in the Western popular imagination. She may appear as an ambitious warrior-queen, as in John Singer Sargent's beautiful painting (see Color Plate 1), or more negatively, as a masculine woman, ambitious wife, or over-reaching First Lady. The iconic threesome of the witches, captured in Henry Fuseli's illustration (see Color Plate 2), has become a visual shorthand for occult meddling. And the play's nine soliloquies have been a fertile source of quotations. Writers have regularly used them at times of revolution—in England, the United States, Europe, and South Africa—to meditate on the psychology of terror. Welcome Msomi's Zulu adaptation of the play, *uMabatha* (1972), offers a recent example of this long tradition of political adaptation (see Color Plate 3).

Reread and rehearsed in all these ways, a surprising amount of the play's pithy, memorable language has been absorbed into modern English usage. Expressions such as "what's done, is done" now sound like old proverbs. We rarely recall their connection to the play's haunting depiction of individuals and governments irrecoverably committed to violence.

Despite its supernatural thrills and military exploits, the tragedy also works on its audience in quieter ways, demanding different kinds of attention. Its language is compact, evocative, and ambiguous. The imagery is so richly interwoven that some critics have read the play more as a dramatic poem than a work for the stage. Its plot accelerates unevenly, leaving us unsure of the exact order of events. The story of Macbeth's encounter with the witches and his decision to take the throne of Scotland draws on literary traditions with which we may be only partly familiar, including Senecan revenge plots, the fall of tyrants, and medieval Scottish history. The play adapts these sources in surprising ways—inventing a tyrant, for example, whose isolation makes him very different from the fiery rulers who stormed about the Renaissance stage. Less obvious still may be the contemporary concerns that the play takes up, such as the nature of the supernatural, the proper role of a monarch, or the relations between the Scots and the English.

Together with the critical essays and contextual materials reprinted here, this introduction aims to fill in some of these less familiar contexts for *Macbeth*, to explore the surprises that it offers modern readers, and to sketch the wide range of interpretations that it invites. Feelings of strangeness evoked by the play should not in themselves be obstacles to understanding or pleasure. As the nineteenth-century writer Thomas De Quincey observed, the ambiguous language and furious action in *Macbeth* elicit those feelings (see his discussion in the "Critical Essays" section in this volume).

The play disorients us by design. Thus, a reader's or audience member's capacity to sense something strange in a scene or passage of text may be a valuable tool for interpretation. One early scene, at Macbeth's banquet, is a good example of this dynamic. Macbeth has just ordered the murder of his fellow general, Banquo. In this scene, Banquo's ghost appears, silently accusing him. The ghost looks extremely bloody, Macbeth observes, with "gory locks." It is solid enough to take up space at the table. Yet only Macbeth can see it, and because of this, his horror and fury seem bizarre to the company of thanes in the banquet hall.

How should a production stage this apparition, at once solidly material and phantasmal? From undergraduates to professionals, many performances founder at this difficult moment. If the actor playing Banquo sits on the stool covered in stage blood, the apparition can appear as clunky as a zombie in a horror film, making the audience laugh. Yet if there is no actor onstage, audience members will be limited to the confused perspective of Macbeth's court—no longer granted their privileged view of his mental experience, they may find his horror unmotivated, over the top, or outright crazy.

As Neil Forsyth observes, modern stage and film revivals typically handle this and other supernatural events in *Macbeth* by dividing them into two categories (see the "Critical Essays" section of this volume). We understand them either as "real" supernatural events, external to character, or "imaginary" psychological ones, emanating from Macbeth's subconscious, guilty conscience or disturbed emotions. Even when we interpret these apparitions as psychological, however, the question of exactly how material they are remains open to debate. We may see them as immaterial symbols of a Freudian unconscious, or biological effects of neural pathology, like the voices heard by schizophrenics. In performance, the cues that Banquo's physical body is onstage in this scene, although only Macbeth sees him, sustain a sense of dissonance and even crisis in our modern sensibilities. This ghost appears at once external and psychological, physical and imaginary.

Early English science understood the mind as embodied (as modern current cognitive science does) and the soul as well. Thus, Renaissance audiences would have accepted the paradox of a material spirit, assuming no absolute divide between bodily things and spiritual or psychological ones. Yet, the dissonance that Banquo's ghost generates in performance—the problem of who perceives it—remains critical. Where we may puzzle over the question of how "real" psychological phenomena are, Renaissance Europe puzzled over the nature of the afterlife and the possibility—even the obligation—for continued contact between the living and the dead. Great transformations of theology and belief, brought by the Reformation and by Henry VIII's establishment of an independent Church of England in 1534, made for radical divergence between official state religions and individual practices. England's state religion changed repeatedly (along with the monarchs) in the sixty years following Henry's death in 1547.

The degree to which the dead affected the living was thus a matter of theological debate and popular concern for several generations, as Reformation views of the afterlife replaced, revised, and recombined with earlier Catholic ones. Macbeth himself is explicit about this concern: Banquo's ghost raises questions about the afterlife that Macbeth thought were settled. Guilty and fearful, insisting with fury that the corpse should stay dead ("thy bones are marrowless"), Macbeth feels deeply unnerved that it did not (3.4.93). Indeed, he names the apparition as a new and alien thing:

> . . . The [time] has been,
> That when the brains were out, the man would die,
> And there an end; but now they rise again
> With twenty mortal murthers on their crowns,
> And push us from our stools. This is more strange
> Than such a murther is.
>
> (3.4.77–82)

Presenting the walking ghost as strange and newfangled, the scene links its appearance (which is otherwise utterly conventional in a revenge tragedy) to a transition in beliefs about death. Indeed, the very condition of mortality seems to be in flux in Macbeth's account, along with our uncertain knowledge of it.

This example presses home a larger point about how to read in a way that is alert to historical differences. Knowledge of particular cultural contexts will enrich but not resolve the ambiguities of *Macbeth*, for the concerns at the heart of this play were themselves unresolved in the years it was first performed. Instead of clearly asserting a single position in these debates, *Macbeth* dramatizes the uncertainties within them. In the matter of beliefs about the supernatural, for example, the play poses the question of influence in Macbeth's first encounter with the witches and wrestles with it as the plot develops. "The earth hath bubbles, as the water has,/And these are of them," Banquo decides, after the witches disappear (1.3.79–80). His analysis is solidly materialist. It agrees with early geological theory, in which the basic elements of earth, water, fire, and air were assumed to behave in analogous ways. Macbeth seems less certain of this logic, linking the witches with the thinnest of these elements, air: "what seem'd corporal melted,/As breath into the wind" (1.3.81–82). In an important way, he suggests, the question of whether the weird sisters are material fails to address the more urgent question of what their prophecies mean and what kind of power they have.

At this point in the play, the witches certainly have "more than mortal knowledge," as Macbeth believes. Later, it becomes less clear how much force their "supernatural soliciting" may have. Do they sway Macbeth's imagination in a new direction or spur what he had already planned? Contemporary witch trials in Europe debated such questions, along with the nature of the evidence required to resolve them. In Macbeth's crimes, the links between his actions and evil intentions—his own, Lady Macbeth's, and the witches'—may seem clear at first. Yet by the time Macbeth encounters the phantasmal dagger on his way to murder Duncan, it is hard to separate supernatural causes from psychological ones in his "fatal vision." And by the time he draws his actual weapon to hand, the relation between causes and their effects has become wholly confused. "Thou marshal'st me the way that I was going," he muses, as if in some occult way, the instrument leads or realizes his desires before he knows them. Hands in this play, as in others of the period, are often figures for "agency": the relationship between intentions, actions, instruments, and effects. Yet at this moment in *Macbeth*, the normal links between these different components of human action seem radically unstable and unclear. What agency moves that dagger?

The play regularly challenges its audience with conundrums of sequence and causation like these. Historical context does not resolve these puzzles, but it can gain us a deeper understanding of the historical differences that shape our experience of them. Above all, as the example of Banquo's ghost suggests, *Macbeth* defamiliarizes conventional systems of belief, calling our attention to paradoxes at the heart of our ideas about the supernatural and moral action. The play accomplishes this by dramatizing competing perspectives on such concerns. It offers us a kind of double vision of the illusory and invented qualities of things that seemed certain, such as the boundary between life and death. First performed at the Globe Theatre in daylight, *Macbeth* represents a *tour de force* of theatrical illusion, successfully conjuring two-thirds of its scenes in darkness (Brooke, 1). It is equally successful in conjuring—and exposing—the stories that a culture uses to establish political and social facts: Duncan is filled with kingly virtues; Macbeth is a tyrant; it is unnatural for the dead to walk. Indeed, so successful is this conjuring that we feel the force and persuasion of these stories even as we are pressed to recognize them *as* fictions, scripted along conventional lines that may not match the evidence at hand: Duncan is a less than effectual ruler; Malcolm decries a kind of tyranny that does not quite match Macbeth's behavior; and a living woman walks like a ghost. Among the most powerful of these double visions is the extraordinary degree to which the play gets us attached to Macbeth—on his side and wanting his success even when he seems most vividly monstrous.

This double vision does not involve simple binary oppositions (tyrant vs. good king, hero vs. monster). Instead, *Macbeth* injects uncertainty into the very categories that organize our interpretation of the action. In the case of the play's political plot, for example, it is not that Macbeth is *not* a tyrant. His bloody, illegitimate rule certainly makes him one, as does his susceptibility to external influences—especially the witches and Lady Macbeth. A king's will and actions should be his own. Yet neither is Macbeth the source of all things evil in Scotland. The way his tyranny is misnamed by other characters should make us wonder: How reliable are the speakers making this charge? What interests does the charge serve? How stable a category is tyranny in the first place? As the chant, "double, double" suggests, the play offers multiple perspectives on any given problem—whether it be the nature of good government or relations between the living and the dead.

This dramatic double vision invites broader questions: How can we believe stories about good government if they are the ones that all leaders tell about themselves, whether they are bad or good? How should we act on the basis of conflicting beliefs? How autonomous are our actions and the desires from which they spring? These were pressing questions for Shakespeare's audience and they are ones we repeat for ourselves, in our own contexts, when we watch or read *Macbeth*.

TYRANNY, RENAISSANCE PSYCHOLOGY, AND LITERARY SOURCES

Macbeth was composed and, it is believed, first staged in 1606, roughly three years after Elizabeth I died and James I took the throne of England. The play is often called the last of Shakespeare's "great tragedies" (Bradley, 331). In the most likely order of composition, it follows *Hamlet, Othello*, and *King Lear*. By expanding our time frame slightly, we might observe that *Macbeth* comes towards the end of a twelve-year period (roughly 1596–1608) during which Shakespeare was experimenting with a variety of tragic modes, from the romantic *Romeo and Juliet* to the harshly cerebral *Coriolanus*. Yet Shakespeare was not the only playwright experimenting in the first decade of the seventeenth century. These were boom years in the London theater. In both public and private playhouses, late medieval revivals played alongside classically influenced tragedies and the latest city comedies. Theatrical performances punctuated public life as well. On noble estates and in city streets, elaborately staged events such as royal progresses and Lord Mayor's pageants celebrated the new king, much as parades in U.S. cities celebrated the return of astronauts in the Apollo missions. James Stuart was the central subject of (and sometimes participant in) these public entertainments. The relatively cheap print versions commemorating them spread news of the court and its intrigues and opinions widely. This hospitable climate fostered cross-pollination between various dramatic genres, played in public, private, and courtly venues. It also fostered creative exchanges between the theater and popular print forms such as prose history, news, and religious pamphlets.

Macbeth is altogether typical of this period in the wide range of resources the play text draws on, imitates, and adapts. These include classical tragedy and rhetoric, early histories of Scotland and England, contemporary writings on witchcraft and political theory (including those by James I himself), early psychological theory, medieval English drama, popular murder pamphlets, dances and songs from other plays, court entertainments, and civic pageants. Yet despite this variety of source material, *Macbeth* does not convey an overall sense of collage. Consider, for example, Lady Macbeth's celebrated invocation to the spirits, a passage that seamlessly fuses a wide range of sources in a few lines:

... Come, you spirits
That tend on mortal thoughts, unsex me here,
And fill me from the crown to the toe topful
Of direst cruelty! Make thick my blood,
Stop up th' access and passage to remorse,
That no compunctious visitings of nature
Shake my fell purpose, nor keep peace between
Th' effect and [it]! Come to my woman's breasts,
And take my milk for gall, you murth'ring ministers ...

(1.5.40–48)

This terrifying vision of female aggression evokes the story of Seneca's Medea, a vengeful witch-mother who murdered her children. This story circulated widely in the Renaissance. It also recalls Thomas Nashe's cannibal mother Miriam, from *Christ's Tears over Jerusalem* (1593). The imagery of diabolical lactation in the soliloquy derives in part from European witch lore (witches were supposed to suckle their familiars). The figures of bodily transformation and moving fluids draw on the classical theory of the four "humors," the basis of Renaissance ideas about physiology and psychology. With all these, the speech invokes early ethnic stereotypes about Scottish warrior women, sketched by early historians such as John Bellenden (1540) and William Harrison (see Mary Floyd-Wilson's discussion in the "Critical Essays" section of this volume).

Lady Macbeth's character recombines these resources in surprising and strategic ways. Comparisons to vengeful Medea spin what might otherwise be a figure of valiant femininity in negative terms. What this passage frames most negatively is Lady Macbeth's paradoxical effort to open herself to supernatural influences and at the same time make herself impervious to natural feelings and to conscience. Harrison's bold Scots are naturally open, as Floyd-Wilson observes: integrated with and conditioned by their rugged environment, raised by hardy and fierce warrior women whose temperate habits suit the landscape and climate (see Floyd-Wilson, "English Epicures," in the "Critical Essays" section, for quotations from Harrison). In Lady Macbeth's attempt to make herself bold, bloody, and resolute, we can see a degenerate version of these hardy Scottish women.

The transformations that Lady Macbeth envisions may be read both metaphorically and literally. In a metaphorical sense, taking "milk for gall" can mean turning kindness to bitter and caustic feelings, or forsaking the role of a nurturer for that of a destroyer. "Unsex me" implies a radical transgression of the categories of sex, gender, and sexuality themselves, connecting to the motifs of vulnerable masculinity and monstrous femininity that Janet Adelman traces through the play (see the "Critical Essays" section of this volume). Paired with "come to my women's breasts," the entreaty "unsex me here" can even sound like an erotic invitation. (It has been played this way in a number of film productions.) Yet these commands also have specific, literal meanings that have to do with Renaissance ideas about the workings of an embodied mind. These ideas are so resonant in the play and yet so strange to most modern readers that some explanation is required.

Renaissance science understood the human body and mind as porous and permeable. As in the case of the supernatural, what modern audiences might classify as distinct parts of our inner lives—mental, emotional, spiritual, and physical—were fully integrated with each other. Moreover, they were understood to be malleable, altered by what we think of as external conditions: social behaviors, nutrition, and the weather (see Floyd-Wilson's discussion of "passibility" in "English Epicures," in the "Critical Essays" section). Thus, Lady Macbeth's "compunctious visitings" denote external forces that might affect her resolve: the sensory perceptions that press on feelings and on conscience, or heaven crying out against the crime. Yet they also denote internal forces: the feelings themselves, specifically the tragic passion of "remorse." Consciousness was understood as a direct product of such influences and the physical body that they altered, with its dynamic balance of fluids ("humors") and its internal communication systems ("animal spirits," coursing through "passages," carrying messages between body, mind, and soul) (Paster, 113).

In early-seventeenth-century Europe, still deeply influenced by classical theory, a key hallmark of civility and temperate character was the ability to discipline this malleable system by controlling the environmental factors that affect bodily fluids, such factors as diet, climate, travel, education, and even fashions in clothes (see Floyd-Wilson, 2003, and Schoenfeldt). Different kinds of persons were thought to have different—and more or less changeable—balances of humors: the young more vulnerable to impressions than the old, northerners more than southerners, women more than men. Renaissance psycho-physiology may sound farfetched when sketched out this way, but in certain respects, its logic is still with us. It is still a Western cliche that women and children are more temperamentally impulsive, impressionable, and changeable than men. Commercial culture assures us that we can improve ourselves and our moods using the same strategies used by Renaissance gentlemen: traveling, shopping for a new outfit, or changing our diet. Such deliberate alteration of character and emotions raised fundamental questions for Renaissance writers: How much control do we actually have in this process, if we depend on external inputs to manage our internal lives? Are the changes that result authentic and natural, or do they involve an artificial transformation that somehow estranges us from ourselves?

Such parallels offer familiar points of contact in a deeply unsettling passage. And they get us some way toward understanding how Lady Macbeth's language, at once metaphorical and literal, invokes contemporary physiological theory. What may be less obvious to us, precisely because we share similar questions, is exactly how much at odds her diabolical self-discipline is with cultural traditions that regularly described self-discipline as a good thing (see Schoenfeldt). The way that Lady Macbeth attempts to control her emotions matters as much here as the emotions themselves. In the logic of humoral psychology, Lady Macbeth attempts an especially severe self-discipline—so severe that she imagines one internal fluid transformed to another, milk for gall. If she could achieve it, such unbending sternness would be exceptional in several respects. First, it would contradict a humoral hierarchy that held women to be more impressionable than men. (Nashe's Miriam decides to kill her son because she is so vulnerable to maternal pity that she wants to save him from starvation.) Second, Lady Macbeth's "unsexing" involves so radical a departure from gender norms that it makes self-discipline itself look unnatural. Finally, the forces that she invites in to effect these transformations profoundly undermine her apparent autonomy.

The soliloquy closes in a way that suggests how interested the play is in this unnatural mastery of emotions and its converse state, the radical openness to external forces such as malevolent spirits. Lady Macbeth concludes with a command:

> Come, thick night,
> And pall thee in the dunnest smoke of hell,
> That my keen knife see not the wound it makes,
> Nor heaven peep through the blanket of the dark
> To cry, "Hold, hold!"
>
> (1.5.50–54)

Even in imagination, she cannot allow herself to visualize the crime that she contemplates. So she displaces the faculties of sight to the knife and to heaven, here personified as blinded witnesses who "see not" and "peep" not in her place. The rhetorical device of *preteritio* used here—telling us what she is not going to acknowledge, letting us see what she will not let herself witness—gives us a double vision of the emotions and perceptions that would move her if she did not short-circuit them. Ironically, the effect of this deliberate effort at repression is to break the crucial connections between will and action that would constitute true self-control. Importantly, the self-deception imagined here is enabled by night and smoke—reminding us of the "filthy air" of the opening scenes that was associated with the witches. Is Lady Macbeth in control of her own mental discipline here, or is she giving herself over to demonic forces? Her final appearance on stage in Act 5, scene 1, sleepwalking and "infected" of mind, suggests the latter.

We might assume that this destructive mental discipline belongs only to Lady Macbeth (a "fiend-like queen" who overturns proper gender hierarchies), except that Macbeth takes the throne through parallel efforts at self-mastery and with parallel losses of autonomy. Just as Lady Macbeth's transformation is illuminated by its literary contexts, so his behavior invites comparison with stage tyrants of the period. As suspicions of Macbeth grow, they harden into a public description of him as a butcher whose misrule makes widows and orphans of the nation. Tyrannical rulers of this kind were a staple of English Renaissance tragedy, from Thomas Preston's *Cambyses* (c. 1569) to John Webster's *The Duchess of Malfi* (c. 1614). Antitypes of the good ruler, they typically gained or held power illegally and ruled capriciously, unable to govern their emotions with the discipline valued by classical writers such as Seneca, whose treatises on governance were required reading in Renaissance political theory. A ruler who cannot govern his own desires cannot govern others, these Stoic philosophers held. Therefore, the hallmark of a good leader is self-mastery, and that of a tyrant is inordinate desire. This is the tradition to which Malcolm alludes when he tests Macduff, describing himself as even more abusive than Macbeth:

> I grant him bloody,
> Luxurious, avaricious, false, deceitful,
> Sudden, malicious, smacking of every sin
> That has a name; but there's no bottom, none,
> In my voluptuousness . . .
> . . . and my desire
> All continent impediments would o'erbear
> That did oppose my will.
>
> (4.3.57–65)

Given proclivities like these, tyrants will always make for sensational theater. But the spectacle of an abusive, impulsive ("sudden") leader also offers an opportunity for serious theorizing about the nature of good government—and for taking public positions on this question. Jacobean tragedy modeled itself on its classical roots in seeing theater as a critical vehicle for education: a venue for shaping as well as reflecting contemporary political and social debates. George

Puttenham observed in his 1589 treatise on rhetoric that the ancient role of theater was reform. The particular business of tragedy is to illustrate and reproach the bad behavior of "great Princes," "to th' intent that such exemplifying (as it were) of their blames and adversities . . . might worke for a secret reprehension to others that were alive, living in the same or like abuses" (Puttenham, 50).

Is Macbeth a tyrant? It may seem odd to ask this question, given the number of characters who assert this as fact. However, the precise definition of a tyrant was as much a matter of debate in Renaissance Europe as it was in the classical period. The play clearly takes pains to establish that its protagonist rules illegally, as a result of regicide; one lord points out "the tyrant" withholds "the due of birth" from Malcolm (3.6.24–25). Yet Macbeth is not technically a usurper because he is properly invested at Scone. Interestingly, the historical Macbeth took the throne through a form of limited election (the medieval Scottish mode of succession) rather than inheritance. The play contains oblique references to this practice in 2.4.29–41, and when Macduff calls for the thanes to hail Malcolm, 5.9.22–24. (Henry Paul explores these issues in *The Royal Play*.) To finesse this matter, the text plays down elements of its historical sources that describe Macbeth's reign as legitimate and sound. Beyond the question of legitimacy, the nature of Macbeth's tyranny is also in question. Most peculiarly, the tyrannical abuse that matters in this play appears not to be aggressive passions that dominate those of others but passions that are too easily swayed or perversely contained. As Janet Adelman famously observed, the play dramatizes these conditions in gendered terms. Unfolding "the fantasy of a virtually absolute and destructive maternal power" represented by the witches and Lady Macbeth, it then devolves to an "equally destructive fantasy of absolute escape from this power" (see the first paragraph of Adelman's discussion in the "Critical Essays" section). Fittingly, Macbeth reflects on his growing dispassion precisely at the moment when he learns of his wife's death:

> I have almost forgot the taste of fears.
> The time has been, my senses would have cool'd
> To hear a night-shriek, and my fell of hair
> Would at a dismal treatise rouse and stir
> As life were in't. I have supp'd full with horrors;
> Direness, familiar to my slaughterous thoughts,
> Cannot once start me.

$$(5.5.9-15)$$

The reactions Macbeth has lost—rising hair, a sudden start—epitomize the capacity to respond emotionally to the evidence of the senses. We see him in that mode earlier in the play, responding fearfully to external signs. Here, however, his dispassion divides him so radically from the rest of the world that he walks continually apart and awake, cut off from the human community of sleepers. This physical and social isolation is an important index of his failure to lead. Successful leaders in *Macbeth* turn out neither to be excessively vulnerable to external influences nor invulnerable to them. Instead, they respond in kind and in community, moving others and being moved by them in effectual ways. As the lengthy exchanges in Act 4, scene 3 testify, both Malcolm and Edward I seem particularly skilled at this governance of emotion.

THE SCOTTISH PLAY

The characters in *Macbeth* may seem a homogenous lot from a modern perspective: all of them white Europeans, all of them from a region we now call "the United Kingdom," most of them courtiers. At the turn of the seventeenth century, however, England and its northern neighbor Scotland were different nations: historical enemies a long century away from the formal union of their separate governments, churches, and legal systems. Ethnic distinctions between and within the nations were the subject of much contemporary debate. In ways that are sometimes hard to see from a modern perspective, the behaviors and emotions of different characters in *Macbeth* dramatize those differences.

Theater professionals traditionally call this tragedy "the Scottish play," heedful of a curse said to haunt revivals throughout its history (see Braunmuller and Garber). Customarily, people who work in the theater ward off bad luck by taking care not to utter Macbeth's name backstage or offstage—only doing so when the script requires it onstage. Yet Scottishness matters to *Macbeth* in other ways as well. The action develops careful distinctions between different kinds of Scots: barbaric Highlanders such as Macdonwald, so rebellious that one can only do battle with them and hope to destroy them; and more civil and civilizable midlanders, such as Macduff, who eventually join forces with a third group, the prospering English court of Edward I. To understand what is at stake in these distinctions, we need some sense of the context in which Renaissance cultures explored questions of ethnicity. Then, as now, ethnic differences implied physical as well as cultural variations. In the Renaissance, these variations were associated—on the basis of classical tradition—with differences in native climate and geography. Skin color was not a primary sign of ethnicity or race, as it is so often in modern societies. Instead, ethnicity was understood as a predisposition for certain temperaments, qualities of mind, and behaviors. Mary Floyd-Wilson's essay in this volume explores these concepts of ethnicity in detail.

Two early portraits of an Englishman and a Scotsman provide a good example of the stereotypes English writers inherited and wrestled with. These appear in one of the first travel guides in English, written by the physician Andrew Boorde: *The Fyrst Boke of the Introduction of Knowledge* (1555). The monologues that accompany these portraits (Figs. 5 and 6 in the "Sources and Contexts" section of this volume) suggest both the differences and the connections between contemporary stereotypes of the two nations.

In his portrait of an Englishman (Fig. 5), Boorde mocks a goofy, effeminate, but vigorous and even likable figure. The Englishman's pretensions to culture and education (described in his monologue and evoked in the woodcut by his hat) suit him oddly—as oddly as Henry VIII's head suits a half-naked body. His belly and chest look round, feminine, soft; the knot on his loincloth seems embarrassingly small. The fabric and shears that he brandishes symbolize a constitutional giddiness that the monologue explains: he is so vulnerable to changes of fashion and so consumed by the desire to improve himself that he "cannot tell what" to wear. These props also suggest a different kind of weakness: the economic vulnerability associated with the English passion for Continental fashions, in turn associated with an imbalance of trade in raw materials and finished clothing.

By contrast, the woodcut of the Scot shows a man elegantly dressed (Fig. 6). He poses with one elbow akimbo, an "in-your-face" stance used in Renaissance portraits of noblemen to indicate their status and authority. The Scot reinforces this hostile disposition, referring to his natural dislike of the English and his country's long alliance with France (see the first and last lines of his monologue in the "Sources and Contexts" section of this volume), a source of both political and cultural anxiety in England. Although Scotland lies even farther north than England, geographically more distant from cities like Paris, it had closer ties to the cultural centers of early Renaissance Europe.

Stereotypes usually slant toward particular interests, and Boorde's are no exception. His negative portrait of Scottish duplicity reflects the long hostilities between the two nations. By contrast, Boorde's lumpy Englishman has surprising appeal, although he is clearly also a figure of satire. His monologue suggests native vigor, candid confidence, and loyalty to God and king. He frisks in a thriving natural landscape. It may be a stretch to call this scene Edenic, but the Englishman (his lower half, at least) appears integrally connected to his environment in a way that the Scotsman, posed indoors in his woodcut, does not. According to type, the Englishman's monologue makes it clear that he lacks suaveness and self-control, qualities about which Boorde's Scot boasts. Boorde's Scot tells us, for example, that while he is "true" to France, he remains invulnerable to French fashions, refusing to update his look, "Although the frenchmen go never so gay" (l. 16 of his monologue, in the "Sources and Contexts" section of this volume). *Macbeth* reworks such stereotypes, as it reworks its other source materials, in strategic ways. In this play, what Scots can apparently learn from the English is a productive kind of civil openness: it is only after traveling to Edward's court that both Macduff and Malcolm show us that they can govern their feelings (and in Malcolm's case, those of others) in politic ways. The importance of this quality and its association with Englishness in the play are brought home by the brief eyewitness account that Malcolm gives of Edward in Act 4, scene 3, the scene that takes place in England. Filled with generous pity, as Malcolm describes him, Edward performs the ceremony of the King's Touch, laying hands on petitioners so scrofulous they seem repulsive even at secondhand.

Despite Edward's saintliness, negative stereotypes are hard to erase. Anxiety about the English vulnerability to impressions lingers in the play, displaced northwards in the motif of ill-fitting clothes. Caithness observes Macbeth's unfitness to govern in these terms; he "cannot buckle his distemper'd cause/Within the belt of rule" (5.2.15–16). Angus answers in kind: "Now does he feel his title/Hang loose about him, like a giant's robe/Upon a dwarfish thief" (5.2.20–22). That motif echoes the more dramatic moments in which the radical openness of the Macbeths to external influences leads to a loss of autonomy and agency, as discussed above.

Effectively, this English play offers multiple, even contradictory visions of Scottishness. Scottish characters show themselves by turns as violent, cautious, open to influence, sternly repressed, deeply loyal, turncoats, implacable enemies, successful allies, too credulous, and canny. These contradictions expose deep fractures within contemporary ethnic and national identities, which the play dramatizes. Thus, the Scots in *Macbeth* can seem as terrifyingly barbarous as those described by William Harrison, and yet they can also dissemble artfully. That ability cannot be ill (Malcolm uses it to great effect in Act 4, scene 3). Yet it cannot be good (Lady Macbeth espouses it to cover a regicide). Nor can these contradictions be resolved by sorting the *dramatis personae* into good and bad Scots or civil and barbarous Scots. From a certain angle, even apparently good, southern Scots such as Macduff appear duplicitous. Lady Macduff presses this point in uncomfortable terms that the play never fully answers. Indeed, we cannot even be sure that we know what the Scottish landscape is like in *Macbeth*, for all the vivid descriptions we hear. Is the air at Inverness sweet and gentle, as Banquo and Duncan find it, or is it the smoky pall that Lady Macbeth evokes a few lines earlier? As with much in Macbeth's Scotland, the question is unresolvable. This surreal setting captures deep uncertainties about ethnic identities that—like questions about the afterlife—were far from settled.

THE NEW COURT, POLITICS, AND POLITICAL THEATER

Uneasiness about ethnic differences may well have been highlighted by the succession to the English throne, in 1603, of a Scottish ruler. Before and after he took the English throne, James I was also James VI of Scotland. After the defeat of the Spanish Armada in 1588, Elizabeth I had solidified a sense of English nationalism; yet she never married nor produced an heir. The animosity between England and Scotland had been so heated in the later decades of her reign that in 1587, Elizabeth ordered the execution of her cousin and political rival, Mary Stuart (James I's mother), who styled herself "Queen of England and Scotland" but who is best known to history as "Mary, Queen of Scots." James Stuart's accession brought Scotsmen into key positions at court and for the first time broached seriously the possibility of unifying these historical enemies into one nation.

The presence of the king of another country on the throne of England required of the nation its own kind of double vision. James I himself was ambitious for union and the imperial possibilities that it promised. His speeches to Parliament in the first decades of his reign reassured the English that they could continue to think of themselves as English, their national sovereignty intact; yet he also repeatedly asked them to include Scotland in that sovereign nation for the first time. The metaphors governing the relationship between monarch and commonwealth changed significantly as well. Elizabeth Tudor had presented herself as a virgin queen and described the nation as her spouse. Welcoming James I meant welcoming a family to the throne in the persons of a new royal lineage, the Stuarts. It may be hard for us to grasp quite how vertiginous the process of succession could be in this transitional period: at once tenuous—up for grabs until someone assumed the throne—and then absolute once the monarch was installed.

With its other double visions, *Macbeth*'s story of transfers of power among three kings gives us a vivid picture of the anxieties of succession. Scholars have long discussed the play's investment in contemporary political theory and concerns of the court. *Macbeth* has been understood to praise the new Stuart monarchy, to warn against dangers and potential errors, or both. Scenes of conspiracy evoke actual plots against James I: the Gowrie plot in 1600 and the Gunpowder Plot in November 1605. Duncan's court dramatizes the vulnerability of any regime to deception, self-interest, and disloyalty. The spectacle of the witches touches on concerns that James I himself wrote about in his *Daemonologie* (1597). This treatise on witchcraft engaged contemporary debates about its dangers, representing occult practices as the systematic inversion of natural hierarchies in the family, in the state, and in spiritual life (see Clark, 69–72). In a wave of popular witch plays, English theater explored these inversions. For contemporary legal theorists, witches posed challenges to the legal process, particularly in matters of evidence, which also deeply concern the play. The evil actions of a witch were by definition occulted: beyond the range of ordinary knowledge, not perceptible to the senses. How could a court prove or disprove agency when the causal links between evil intentions and effects were essentially untraceable in this way? Although the witches in *Macbeth* are palpable presences for much of the play, the degree of their evil influence remains an open question, as we have seen. Again, rather than settling the urgent questions that English writers on witchcraft wrestled with, *Macbeth* builds them into its dramatic action.

Macbeth addresses the question of Anglo-Scottish union more obliquely, offering a national backstory for the project that James I pursued unsuccessfully but passionately. The Show of Kings, some carrying "twofold balls and treble sceptres" (emblems of the two nations) dramatizes an unbroken line from Banquo (James Stuart's legendary ancestor) to James I (4.1.121). This procession of eight kings corresponds to a mythical lineage that circulated in the period, illustrated by the broadside in Figure 4. The family tree shows the pedigree of Prince James (not yet crowned as James VI) descending from "a mythical Banquo's mythical son Fleance, whose son Walter, we are told, was the first of the line to bear the name Stuart" (Evans, 1306).

Similarly, Malcolm's England-sponsored return to the throne and his replacement of Scottish titles ("thane") with English titles ("earl"... "the first that ever Scotland/In such an honor nam'd") projects the strong and virtuous arm of English rule deep into Scotland's past, making James I's accession seem an inevitable return, as triumphal as Malcolm's (5.9.29–30). Dancing witches who compliment the monarch seem clearly designed for court performance (4.1.120–132). James I had a strong and well-known preference for entertainments that involved more dancing than moralizing or exposition. (See the "Note on the Text" section for speculations on dating).

In all these respects, Shakespeare's company, relicensed as the King's Men in 1603, seem to be earning their court patronage with this play.

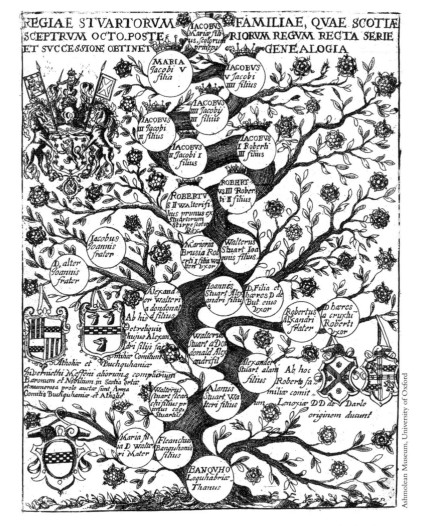

Fig. 4. Banquo's royal line and James I. From a broadside in the Sutherland Collection, Ashmolean Museum, Oxford.

However, *Macbeth* would be much less compelling and unsettling if such glorifying gestures were all it offered. The narrative that Malcolm closes with—the triumph of a virtuous Anglo-Scottish force over the evils wrought by the "dead butcher and his fiend-like queen"—may seem an apt summation of the moral action as a whole. Yet the play reflects on the uses of such narratives in a way that undercuts the political mythology that they present. Duncan's capacity for organizing trustworthy supporters seems tenuous. Images of "dysfunctional solidarity" run through the military language of Act 1, scene 2, undercutting the early triumph of Duncan's forces against the northern rebels (Berger, 7). The sergeant who reports on the battle begins with a telling simile. He describes the battle as a self-defeating action, like that of two swimmers who drown each other in their attempts to stay afloat: "Doubtful it stood,/As two spent swimmers that do cling together/And choke their art" (1.2.7–9). The word "doubtful" will echo through the opening scenes, not only describing the battle and its outcome but extending to other joint endeavors in the play, prone to undercut their own ends. Both clinging and choking, the two swimmers may be friends or enemies. Moreover, the metaphor suggests, friendship all too easily converts to its opposite as both swimmers risk drowning because of their mutual striving. The uncertainty about motive and outcome evoked by these twinned figures resonates with the "doubly redoubled strokes" that Macbeth and Banquo furiously lay on in battle. Graphic reports of their fury only partly hide the fact that this is a similar pair of strivers: allies now, perhaps, but for how long? Their violence may seem to guarantee the nation's safety, but ultimately it will be self-defeating. The verbal signs of this political and moral dysfunction are repetition and antithesis, echoing later in the witches' "double, double" and "fair is foul, and foul is fair."

The political situation at the close of the play vividly conveys this paradoxical vision. Scotland's fortunes turn almost full circle, from Duncan's precarious reign, through the dark period of Macbeth's bloodthirsty rule, to the restoration of Malcolm. For many decades, critics understood that restoration in wholly positive terms. Malcolm certainly seems to promise more able leadership than his immediate predecessors, and yet the play suggests unsettlingly that every change of regime comes with a significant cost. These costs are imagined sweepingly: the hardening of human minds, the corrosion of intimacy between spouses, the cancellation of loyalties, the dependence of a nation on its neighbor, even demonic threats to the order of nature as horses turn cannibal, day turns to night, and forests walk. Indeed, even though the tragedy revolves mostly around a single character— Macbeth is onstage for a remarkably high percentage of scenes—it is equally interested in the social consequences of regicide. The steady attrition of Macbeth's court dramatizes what it takes to turn the loyalties of a courtier, servant, or spouse. The final act finds him in terrible isolation, a leader without counselors to moderate his "slaughterous thoughts." And it finds the nation, as Rosse puts it, floating upon "a wild and violent sea," unable to generate leadership without the support of its southern neighbor (4.2.21). To be sure, the closing battle unifies Edward's England with the good southern Scots. Yet that union has a distinctly partisan flavor that leaves Scotland's autonomy in question.

Although Malcolm seems to have learned from his father's example, he repeats Duncan's error in his closing speech. He invests his nobles with new titles (as James I did, on his succession to the English throne, doling out more than a thousand new knighthoods, largely to the Scots he had brought with him to London). It is true that the natural world symbolically returns with Birnam Wood, reborn in a kind of spring Maying ritual (Holloway, 73–74). Yet such seasonal returns of ceremony, health, and fruitfulness have an incomplete corollary in the political world of the play. A ritual procession of green branches might appear to restore the "sere, the yellow leaf" of Macbeth's court, reprising the apocalyptic apparition of a "Child crowned, with a tree in his hand" (4.1.86sd). This masque-like procession and the salutation of Malcolm as the new king serve to restore the ceremony that was disrupted at Macbeth's feast. Yet, the promise of fruitful succession remains uncertain at the play's close, still tied to equivocal, supernatural prophecies that Banquo's heirs will one day inherit Scotland's throne. Moreover, as Janet Adelman makes clear, the new regime offers an equally dysfunctional alternative to the old. Scotland exchanges the demonically infused, upside-down world of Lady Macbeth and the witches for a world that is only apparently more benign: a hyper-masculine, military world in which the king is "unknown to woman" and all children are dead or fled (see the "Critical Essays" section of this volume).

The "secret reprehension" that Puttenham describes as the function of tragedy—private self-knowledge gained by a playgoer—seems directed at a courtly audience. Yet it is also directed more widely, at lawmakers, merchants, and others in commercial and public theaters (Kinney, 21). The mirror held up in the Show of Kings may reflect any playgoer, flatteringly or critically, as a given production determines. If the audience for such self-reflection is varied, so are the political concerns addressed. As many scholars have observed, *Macbeth* reworks early histories of Scotland (such as accounts of Macbeth's reign, 1034–57) into an argument about the dangers of absolutist monarchy. At the same time, the play explores a more general problem in political discourse: the self-promoting narratives that every regime spins to solidify its power. Macduff begins his encounter with Malcolm, late in the play, with a familiar motive for military action: a patriotic call to protect a nation personified by its most vulnerable subjects, "widows and orphans." The terrible irony of this rhetoric is brought home when Macduff learns of his own immediate loss, the death of the family that he abandoned. Yet as the scene closes, Malcolm helps convert

Macduff's guilt and grief into a second motive for war—the manly "tune" of just retribution. A few moments later, Siward confronts the loss of his son with similar military logic, what might now be called the logic of "acceptable costs." Both emotional reactions have troubled modern audiences. While a discourse of honor and stoic reticence inform their restrained grief, the play refuses to allow that rhetoric to fully obscure the political expedience that it also serves.

Macbeth signals its interest in such political packaging early on, in official descriptions of the rebellions against Duncan. Within a few scenes, we hear such contradictory public accounts of the Thane of Cawdor that the reversal in stories seems as pressing as what happens to Cawdor. First censured as a traitor, Cawdor dies an exemplary death on the scaffold, begging forgiveness for his treason. In Malcolm's description, he frankly confesses, repents, and yet still displays a proper aristocratic *sprezzatura* (unstudied grace) in the face of death. This scaffold story recalls that of Thomas More, who famously went to his own execution with a graceful gesture. More was innocent of many of the charges against him, while Cawdor is not. Yet the manner of death serves the same political function in both cases, confirming the power of the Crown to contain rebellion and dissent. Macbeth's entrance on the heels of this tidy wrap-up presses several ironic points—most obviously Duncan's failure to "find the mind's construction in the face" (1.4.12). The timing of this entrance also calls into question the degree to which packaged political narratives such as Cawdor's confession can produce the order that they self-servingly describe. Macbeth ultimately rejects Cawdor's graceful death, and typically his defiance invites competing interpretations. On the one hand, it might imply the immoral state of reprobation. Grounded in a false certainty that his sin will never be forgiven, Macbeth is too proud to repent. On the other hand, his doomed resistance also appears heroic as he defies the tidy wrap-up Malcolm's party hopes for. The tension between these two possibilities, reprobation and heroic resistance, derives in part from the way the play interweaves its classical and Christian frameworks.

MURDER, DESPAIR, POPULAR THEOLOGY

The small but dramatically telling moment of the decision to repent or not marks a critical turning point, not only for these exemplary favorites-turned-pariahs, but also in contemporary religious narratives. The Christian plot of sin and providential redemption provided a deep structure for literary genres as diverse as medieval cycle plays and the newest entertainments in cheap print. Like many hybrid texts of the period, *Macbeth* grafts this Christian plot onto its classical one.

From the beginning, therefore, the murder of Duncan appears as a kind of primal sin, a sacrilegious violation of natural and divine laws of kinship, obedience, and hospitality. Duncan's "virtues" Macbeth tells himself, "Will plead like angels, trumpet-tongue'd, against/The deep damnation of his taking-off" (1.7.18–20). Interestingly, repentance seems an option for Macbeth only once—when he expresses regret at the murder of Macduff's family (5.8.5–6). Instead, the play explores both the temptation to sin and the anguish and horror of reprobation. It does so in graphic, even sensational terms: from the gruesome witches' Sabbath to Macbeth's terrible imaginings, anxiety, and despair. He realizes "I am in blood/Stepp'd in so far that, should I wade no more,/Returning were as tedious as go oe'r" (3.4.135–7).

The tragedy's most magnificent, nihilistic passages capture this state of fixed sin as a cognitive condition. Reprobation emerges as the way that the mind—imagination, will, and memory—operates. Once one has "jumped" "the life to come," risked, and also passed over the promise of eternal life, one's capacity to imagine any future progressively deteriorates. "To-morrow" shrinks to a repetitive, empty utterance, its promise of futurity diminished to agonizing slowness as it "Creeps in this petty pace from day to day,/To the last syllable of recorded time." Reaching to imagine that last moment, Macbeth's fancy can only loop obsessively back, in despair, to an equally empty yesterday as "full of sound and fury" as the Apocalypse, but bereft of salvational meaning and "signifying nothing" (5.5.19–28). The prophecy that Macbeth will beget no kings translates this loss into dynastic terms, making Banquo's heirs—and by extension the Stuart line that culminates in James I—the promised ending that Macbeth's reign will never fulfill.

For a period in which the most urgent questions of identity involved spiritual as well as political issues, such vivid portraits of reprobation were understandably popular. They became the staple of a new genre—the murder pamphlet, which flourished in the growing market for inexpensive print. Macbeth's plot line follows the pattern of these short religious pamphlets closely: a criminal solicited by demonic forces commits a mortal sin, only to be discovered in his or her crime and punished (Lake and Questier, 380–92). Tales of notorious murders served a mixed set of needs, joining Protestant concerns about spiritual reform to the economic interests of a new entertainment market. Accordingly, the pamphlets indulge in sensational reports of violent disorder (wives killing husbands, children killing parents). Yet they also control such subversive material by concluding with order restored. Scaffold speeches of the kind Cawdor gives, in which the sinner confesses and repents, reassure readers of the inevitability of providential and political control. In *Macbeth*, Cawdor's death offers an early taste of such conservative closure. But by reporting it secondhand, in ways that foreground the interests of the reporter, the play frustrates generic expectations, sapping the moral plot of dramatic and political closure. Indeed, the play quickly leaves such neat packaging behind, to conclude in terms almost opposite to the narrative satisfactions offered by the pamphlets, with Macbeth's final, determined refusal to "be the show and gaze o' th' time" (5.8.24). Similarly self-conscious gestures characterize the play's borrowings from medieval drama. The English tradition of cycle dramas, last performed a generation earlier than *Macbeth* (in 1575), included daylong sequences of short plays retelling the entire Christian story, from Creation to the end of time. As scholars have long observed, the Porter scene in *Macbeth* adapts material from a specific play, the *Harrowing of Hell*, which served as a theatrical and theological climax to these biblical dramas. That tradition partly explains the mixed dramatic moods that sometimes trouble modern audiences at this point in *Macbeth*. *Harrowing* plays describe Christ's descent from heaven to free the saints for eternal life and shunt sinners down the hellmouth forever. They are at once triumphal, horrifying, and wickedly funny. (In the Towneley version of the *Harrowing* play, one talkative Rybald, whose name means "vulgar and lewd", is the demonic gatekeeper to hell.) Borrowing from the cycle tradition, *Macbeth* does not straightforwardly incorporate these symbolic roles as much as it cites them *as* roles, in all their theatricality. When the Porter briefly treats us to his hung-over version of a "devil-porter," miming the entrance of sinners at hell's gate, he makes playful allusion to a familiar dramatic scene, giving us a kind of generic double vision of an earlier form behind his miming. By implication, such playacting casts Macduff in the part of Christ descending. Macduff's nativity legend and the double action of defeating the tyrant and crowning Malcolm confirm him in this role (Harcourt, 402).

Still, the larger patterns of apocalyptic resolution rarely stabilize in *Macbeth*. Time remains thematically "out of joint"—compressed, accelerating or suspended, rather than progressive—so that Macbeth may "feel the future in an instant," only to find himself locked in the backward look of the "tomorrow" speech. In this way, eschatological time, dynastic cycles, and the characters' experience of time passing never quite line up with each other. Neither do symbolic roles seem settled. For example, we cannot read Macduff straightforwardly, as a force of divine retribution. Janet Adelman's analysis of Macduff's own nativity legend traces a strain of misogyny in the theme of a man "not of woman born," making it clear how far he is from that of Christ, whose humanity (in the Renaissance) is symbolized by his human birth. The Porter himself explicitly rejects any simple mapping of the allegorical landscape of medieval drama onto the Scottish north: "this place is too cold for hell. I'll devil-porter it no further" (2.3.16–17).

STUTTERING, REPETITIONS, AND ECHOES

The aesthetic dissonance that the Porter scene often generates— when bawdy banter interrupts the tense lead-in to murder—derives in part from its generic sources. Yet these contradictory moods are also part of rhetorical patterns that dominate the play, shaping a sense of unease. Thomas DeQuincey's eloquent reading of this scene captures the uncertainty that such oppositions generate for an audience (see his discussion in the "Critical Essays" section of this volume). L. C. Knights ascribed similar effects to the poetic work of antithesis and paradox and to iambic lines full of metrical substitutions (trochees and triple feet) and abrupt pauses (caesuras). These formal effects contribute to the "sickening see-saw rhythm" that Knights finds in Macbeth's guilty thoughts as they swerve from one idea to its opposite, never settling for a middle ground of description: "This supernatural soliciting/Cannot be ill; cannot be good" (1.3.130–31) (Knights, 38). Queasy antitheses like these belong to most of the characters, not just Macbeth. The witches use them, as does Lady Macbeth: "What thou wouldst highly,/That wouldst thou holily; wouldst not play false,/And yet wouldst wrongly win" (1.5.20–22). Banquo solicits the witches with a marvelous pair of parallel antitheses, swerving verbally in a way that seems to cancel the request even as he makes it. "Speak then to me, who neither beg nor fear/Your favors nor your hate," he commands (1.3.60–61). The more we unpack these paired phrases, the more disorienting they are. Is Banquo boasting that he does not beg favors nor fear hate, or is it that he does not beg nor fear favors? (Certainly, a witch's favors may be as dangerous as her hate.) Several more permutations are possible here and all of them may be relevant. Each gives a slightly different spin on this request-that-is-not-a-request.

The verbal contagion that pervades the play is even more disorienting than riddling speeches such as Banquo's. Characters echo and reprise each other as if unwittingly catching each other's thoughts, often to deeply ironic effect. Macbeth's first line offers the most famous instance of this contagion. He enters, observing the weather, in words that echo the witches' incantation, "So foul and fair a day I have not seen" (1.3.38). This effect includes all the characters. Rosse picks up Lady Macduff's anxieties about treason. Lady Macbeth and Macbeth echo and complete each others' lines ("If we should fail," "We fail?"). Malcolm sharpens Macduff's feelings: "Be this the whetstone of your sword, let grief/Convert to anger; blunt not the heart, enrage it," the prince urges. In response, Macduff imagines himself and Macbeth face to face, within a sword's length of each other (4.3.228–234). His posture ironically echoes that of Macbeth himself, in the opening combat against Macdonwald (1.2.15ff) and Norway (1.2.55ff).

At critical moments, the language of the play becomes so compact that it seems as cryptic and equivocal as the witches' prophecies. Restoration adapters of the play, such as William Davenant, revised this quality away. Later, critics found such compactness magnificently ambiguous, a deliberate verbal parallel of the epistemological fog that grows as the play proceeds. Syntax often suspends definite meaning, as when Macbeth confesses, "My thought, whose murther yet is but fantastical,/Shakes so my single state of man that function/Is smother'd in surmise . . ." (1.3.139–41). The gloss reminds us to watch out for the typically flexible Renaissance grammar. The pronoun "whose" should be read as if it were a prepositional phrase, "in which." Thus: "My thought—in which the idea of murder is just an inkling—is still enough to horrify me into inaction . . ." This kind of paraphrasing helps to make sense of a cryptic line; yet to reduce such evocative phrases to single ideas is to oversimplify and miss the other, more troubling suggestions lurking there. Is Macbeth in the process of destroying his own cognitive faculties—as the voice he hears later tells him he has, by murdering sleep? Such thematic connections (murdered Sleep/murdered thought) have a secondary effect, suggesting the overdetermined consequences of action—particularly violent action—in the play. Lady Macbeth's helpless refrain, "what's done, is done," resonates through her later speeches up to the final "what's done cannot be undone."

Knights argues that Renaissance playgoers listened for such complex effects of verbal repetition and compression, trained to a high level of aural "athleticism" by a culture whose popular and elite art forms emphasized rich verbal patterning (Knights, 10). Similar claims might be made for the visual perceptions of modern audiences, trained to parse the juxtapositions of modern video and film editing. Literary and visual arts do train perceptions in profound and interesting ways. However, we should be careful not to generalize too far about this because familiarity with a medium does not guarantee sophistication (as film teachers regularly complain). Moreover, we ought to ask whether early playgoers would have drawn the same sense of troubling uncertainty—the almost existential *nausée*—that Knights and De Quincey find in Shakespeare's ambiguous antitheses.

Scholars, directors, and actors have long described *Macbeth* as a psychological study: of ambition, of evil, of moral reprobation, of will, and more recently of national disposition. Yet, as the foregoing discussions of early English psychological theory, spiritual debates, and political concerns suggest, the concerns of the play are ones we can share only partly and not always intuitively. Even when we find uneasiness clearly represented as an onstage reaction (as in the case of Banquo's ghost), we should be cautious about assuming that that uneasiness means the same thing as our own. Such caution reminds us to interpret comparatively, exploring the imperfect but stimulating match between earlier ideas and experiences and our own.

Literary texts invite us to practice anachronism in this particular, fruitful way. In the process of reading, past forms and present expectations converge, our understanding of the one shaped by the other and vice versa. *Macbeth* deals in exactly these kinds of anachronistic exchanges, exploring how past forms survive into and make demands on the present. *Macbeth's* anachronisms are not ours. But the problems that it explores—of influence and autonomous action, of political ambition and loyalty, of national, ethnic, and sexual identity—are integral to our engagement with the play. Its formal structures of double vision dramatize Renaissance puzzles of belief. Yet the play also teaches us to read them *as* puzzles: not problems to be resolved, but cues to seek the contradictions in our own ways of knowing.

PERFORMANCE HISTORY

THIS DISCUSSION focuses on Anglo-American performances of *Macbeth*. The global history of non-Anglophone Shakespeare onstage is far more robust than a brief introduction can trace (though admittedly, what counts as "Anglo-American" is itself in question when modern productions such as *uMabatha*, Welcome Msomi's Zulu adaptation, travel so widely). Suggestions in the "Further Reading, Viewing, and Listening" section provide more resources for those interested in this broader performance context.

Stage performances are themselves only one part of the multifaceted experiences that audiences may have of *Macbeth*, including reading the text, viewing it in the cinema or at home, exploring video and online adaptations, and even enjoying parodies in fiction and in politics. All these adaptations borrow freely from one another, linking versions of the play across time and media. For a discussion of *Macbeth* on film, see Neil Forsyth's excellent treatment in the "Secondary Essays" section of this volume.

Macbeth is the only play in the canon that has a negative reputation among actors themselves. There is a belief that the play is unlucky, and that one of the ways to avoid the bad luck is never to refer to the play by its proper title. Better to call it "the Scottish play," and its protagonist "Harry Lauder," after the hugely popular Scottish singer of the early twentieth century. It is understandable that a drama with swordplay and considerable action conducted onstage in the dark should have its share of accidents. It is also true to note that there are recorded incidents of deadly fights among armed individuals in the audiences of the play, as well as the fact that the 1849 Astor Place riots in New York City, which resulted in the death of more than thirty people, began at a performance of *Macbeth*. Modern actors and directors, either skeptical of the truth of this negative aura surrounding the play or confident in the power of magical thinking, concern themselves with different issues: How noble is Macbeth? How dominant is his wife? What is the nature of their relationship? How should the witches and the ghost of Banquo be presented? How much violence is acceptable? How much of the Porter's combination of vulgarity and seventeenth-century political allusion should be preserved? Where should the interval come? Has the net always been down so that any amount of cutting, adding, and rearranging of this already cut play is permissible?

Ideas about heroism, gender relationships, the place of comedy in tragedy, and the role of the imagination drive the directorial decisions behind the performances in *Macbeth*. Throughout the history of Western stage productions, these decisions have been complicated by both such modest immediate needs as finding employment for comedians in the company, protecting the self-image of the leading actors, and avoiding misplaced laughter from the audience, as well as the deeper need to adjust to the shifts in audience expectation about issues like violence, the supernatural, and the nature of masculinity. The story of these performances in the Anglo-American theater begins in the lifetime of Shakespeare himself and comes through to the present day in a Dante's *Inferno* version of the play at the New Globe Theatre in London in 2010.

EARLY STAGE HISTORY, THE SEVENTEENTH CENTURY

Macbeth appears to be an occasional play—that is, a drama composed for a particular occasion and subsequently moved to a public theater. Shakespeare seldom practiced this tactic, but there is a persuasive argument that *Macbeth*, which among other things celebrates the triumph of King James in surviving the Gunpowder Plot of November 5, 1605, was composed for the entertainment of King James and his brother-in-law, King Christian IV of Denmark, at Hampton Court in early August 1606. Presumably, James was pleased by the presence of the witches (creatures about which he had written somewhat skeptically), the allusion to the Gunpowder Plot, and, especially, the virtue displayed by Banquo, an ancestor of James, in not succumbing to temptation as his colleague Macbeth does.

There is no description of that royal performance, but we do have the comments of the astrologer and quack doctor Simon Forman in the manuscript *Book of Plays* (see the "Sources and Contexts" section of this volume). A version of Forman can be seen in the film *Shakespeare in Love* (1998), where he is the Early Modern psychiatrist helping young Will Shakespeare to overcome his writer's block and related issues. The historical Forman, who is recalling both the play he had seen at the Globe (a public theater) on April 20, 1611, and his reading of the source of the play in Holinshed's *Chronicles*, describes Macbeth (and Banquo) as entering upon horseback. Dogs and bears were used on the Elizabethan-Jacobean stage, and it is not impossible that a horse or a pair of horses could have been used at the Globe (Bartholomeusz, 4). The reappearance of the horses would have to wait until the arrival of twentieth-century film, when they could be seen, for example, in the headlong tracking shots of galloping horses that dominate the opening scenes of Akira Kurosawa's *Komonosu-jō* (*Throne of Blood;* 1957). Forman does describe an elegant bit of stage business whereby the ghost of Banquo sits in Macbeth's chair while the tyrant toasts the apparently absent Banquo. The principle of discrepant awareness, whereby the audience always knows more than the protagonist and other characters, must have allowed that 1611 Globe Theatre audience a particular pleasure in anticipating the shock that Macbeth is about to receive when he turns around to see the bloody specter.

The first performance of the play came after the Restoration of the monarchy and more than twenty years after the Puritans closed the London theaters in 1642. William Davenant produced a cut-down and added-to version of the play, and his version was used by others as well for about eighty years afterward. Davenant, a playwright who specialized in elaborate entertainments, had been one of the producers of the masques that so delighted Charles I. These highly artificial, mythological, dance-filled compliments to king and court required cranes and pulleys for "flying" machines, the better to move about fairies and deities. In his version of *Macbeth*, Davenant had the witches flying, singing, and dancing, thereby turning the play in the direction of opera. These witches did not inspire dread and were in fact humorous; Davenant wanted to give employment to the comedians in his company, and that was how he did it. More importantly, Davenant wrote scenes for Lady Macduff. In one scene, she visits with Lady Macbeth while their husbands are fighting for King Duncan; in another, which serves as a kind of mirror-image of the exchanges between Lady Macbeth and Macbeth, Lady Macduff offers her husband good counsel.

The effect of these revisions is to turn the drama into a clear-cut morality play, with the enhanced Macduffs a counterweight to the reduced Macbeths (Williams, 57). Such cuts and additions were thought to be quite legitimate; after all, Davenant was doing no more to Shakespeare's script (which shows signs not only of having been cut, but added to by Thomas Middleton in the witches' scenes) than Shakespeare had done with his own sources. Davenant's increase in spectacle and moral didacticism held the stage until the London actor David Garrick restored much of Shakespeare's text in 1744.

EIGHTEENTH AND NINETEENTH CENTURIES

Garrick (1717–79), the dominant actor-manager of his time, was a short man with a great power of mimicry. His facial expression and body language more than compensated for his small stature. His style of relatively naturalistic acting worked well for him, although later, stages and auditoriums became larger and his subtlety got lost in these cavernous venues. This naturalistic style replaced the older declamatory style of the previous successful Macbeth, James Quin (1693–1766), even as Garrick's text replaced Davenant's script.

Yet that new text, while closer to Shakespeare's play as it appears in the Folio of 1623, nonetheless had not only its own cuts but also one extraordinary rearrangement and accompanying addition. Garrick removed Lady Macbeth from the scene of the discovery of Duncan's murder, where in Shakespeare's script she faints, in order to avoid the unseemly laughter that this gesture had produced in mid-eighteenth-century audiences (Williams, 60). Further, not only did he delete the lines about his title "hang[ing] loose about him, like a giant's robe/Upon a dwarfish thief" (5.2.20–2) in order to avoid drawing attention to his own lack of commanding stature, and excise the killing of Lady Macduff and her children, the better not to detract further from Macbeth's dignity (Prescott, 84–5), but he also had Macbeth killed onstage and gave him a dying aria in which he expresses remorse and contrition for his crimes. Of course, in this version, these crimes probably would never have been committed but for the irresistible influence of Lady Macbeth. Garrick's Lady Macbeth was played by Hannah Pritchard, the first in a long line of powerful and sometimes subtle Lady Macbeths, including Sarah Siddons, Charlotte Cushman, Helen Faucit, and Ellen Terry. (This group later expanded to include more recent actresses, the most critically successful of whom was Judi Dench in 1976.) When Pritchard retired, Garrick did not continue performing the role of Macbeth.

Sarah Siddons (1755–1831) was partnered in the play with her brother, John Philip Kemble (1757–1823). She is almost always labeled the greatest tragic actress of her time, made even more famous by the portrait of her painted by Sir Joshua Reynolds. Adjusting to the large stages that he and she performed on, Kemble returned to a more formal declamatory style, an example of how the physical environment of a theater can affect the performances therein. A declaiming thane and his lady who hold precise poses are inevitably quite different from a more naturalistic couple who seem to respond dynamically, in the moment. Sarah Siddons's Lady Macbeth was dominant, truly ambitious, contemptuous of her hesitant spouse, but not without her own weakness: "Since she did appreciate her character's vulnerability, Siddons might have managed the faint in the discovery scene (2.3.118), but the Garrick-Pritchard promptbook she used cut Lady Macbeth from the scene. . . ." (Kliman, 36). Over the years, Siddons adjusted her performance: "Siddons went through three ways of saying 'we fail?': first, a question, then an emphasis on *we* and finally the simple declarative. . . . Her way was different from Pritchard's scornful exclamation" (Kliman, 35).

Kemble's younger rival was Edmund Kean (1787–1833), an actor praised by the most influential of critics, the poet Samuel Taylor Coleridge. He was slight of stature and less formal in delivery than Kemble. Kean actually might have unwittingly contributed to the tradition of *Macbeth* as an unlucky play when, as a boy playing a goblin in Kemble's *Macbeth*, he stumbled and sent a row of other actors falling like dominoes. Critics have found in this episode an emblem of the rivalry between Kemble and Kean as they played *Macbeth*, a tragedy about political rivalry.

Following Kean, who had made himself the center of early productions partly by means of reducing secondary characters, thus beginning a tradition that continued into the twentieth century, the next great Macbeth was William Macready (1793–1873), an actor-manager who was an enthusiast of spectacular settings, and perhaps almost as well known for his partnering with the American actress Charlotte Cushman (1816–76). Charlotte Cushman was a woman of mannish face and large stature, who used her "trangressive masculinity" (Rowe, 126) to create a fearsome Lady Macbeth. Some sense of her dominance is seen in the anecdote that Edwin Booth, playing Macbeth during the extended run of the play and tired of being hectored by Lady Macbeth, was once tempted (or succumbed to the temptation) to say, "Why don't you kill him? You're a great deal bigger than I am" (Rowe, 127).

Two other elements in the life and career of Macready deserve mention. It was he who, in rivalry with the American Edwin Forrest (1806–72), whose own Macbeth had been hissed on a London visit, ran afoul of the violent behavior of New Yorkers in 1849, the notorious Astor Place riots. He also had in his company Helen Faucit (1817–98), ultimately a less physically dominating but more feminine queen than Pritchard, Cushman, or even Siddons. The nineteenth-century critic Henry Morley analyzed her performance and focused on a particular bit of stage business that suggested something of the genius of both the actress and the playwright: "We have seen Miss Faucit praised for representation of smooth treachery in the tender playing of her fingers about the head of the child Fleance while Macbeth is sending father and child into the toils set for them. Miss Faucit knows her Shakespeare better than that. The fingers of the woman who has been a woman, and has murder on her soul, wander sadly and tenderly over the type of her lost innocence" (Salgado, 310–11).

Henry Irving (1838–1905), the first actor ever to be knighted, was like Charles Kean (1811–68), an enthusiast of spectacle to the point where he resuscitated Davenant's flying and singing witches. This is a good illustration of "what goes around comes around," and of the parallel between the repeated devices and strategies of the theater and the frequent scenarios in Shakespeare of the overthrow of kings who are themselves overthrown. The historian in Irving led him back to Holinshed, where Macbeth lives long enough to become an old man, justification for the actor's portrayal of Macbeth as elderly in Act 5.

Irving's Lady Macbeth was the celebrated Ellen Terry (see the famous portrait of whom by John Singer Sargent in Color Plate 1), whose understanding of Macbeth is clear in her notebook comment: "A man of great *physical* courage frightened at a *mouse*. A man who talks and talks and works himself up rather than have had a neglectful mother—who never taught him the importance of self control—He has none!" While Faucit's "Lady Macbeth was domestic and gentle...Ellen Terry's Lady Macbeth was domestic and practical" (Bartholomeusz, 200). Terry also invested her with considerable ambition, as her marginal annotations for her first entrance (reading Macbeth's letter) make clear: "'Steady. Breathe hard. Excited. Not too quick'" (Wilders, 97).

By the end of the nineteenth century, *Macbeth* had proven its theatrical success, but not without some difficulties, for the play is not an easy one to stage and the audience's expectations are high. Braunmuller notes that "The Porter's speeches were omitted by Davenant, Garrick, Kemble, and others" (Braunmuller, 164), chiefly because of their vulgarity and elusive references to political events. What is needed is some subtlety in creating the moment of "crossing," the point in the play where dominant Lady Macbeth and dominated Macbeth reverse their positions. Even with that moment achieved, there remains the problem described by Orson Welles: "[N]o actor in the history of theater has ever been a great Macbeth. Why? Because there has never been an actor who could perform the first and second part of the play. For this play has a great defect . . . the Macbeth who is the victim of Lady Macbeth is not the one who then becomes king. . . . The actor must be brutally simple and completely natural to play the first part, and extremely cerebral to play the second part. In other words, Laurence Olivier would have to play in the first part, and John Gielgud in the second" (Kliman, 62). Welles's assessment came from a deep knowledge of the play, acting and directing for radio, the stage (including his "Voodoo Macbeth," for the Federal Theater Project, 1936), and film (*Macbeth*, 1948).

TWENTIETH TO TWENTY-FIRST CENTURIES

Five stage productions in the twentieth to twenty-first centuries deserve special mention for the ways in which they address these staging challenges. These are the 1955 Glen Byam Shaw effort, starring

Laurence Olivier and Vivien Leigh; the 1976 Trevor Nunn work with Ian McKellen and Judi Dench; the 2007 Rupert Good achievement with Patrick Stewart and Kate Fleetwood; the 2009 interactive American Repertory Theater/Punchdrunk staging; and the 2010 Lucy Bailey–directed production with Elliot Cowan and Laura Rogers at the New Globe Theatre.

The athletic Olivier, dressed in Highland attire, according to Kenneth Tynan in the *Observer*, "gave the impression of 'having already killed Duncan time and time again in his mind'" (Bartholomeusz, 255). In keeping with Welles's division of the play with Olivier as the ideal Macbeth of the first half, Olivier was "this sinuous tigerish Macbeth," according to the critic of the *Financial Times* (Bartholomeusz, 257). The banquet scene was particularly well presented, with the thrones of the king and queen raised on a platform above a semicircular table, with the guest thanes seated to either side of a vacant chair reserved for Macbeth. The king descends to join the thanes, only to see Banquo's ghost in the chair reserved for him. When the ghost exits by passing between Macbeth and Lady Macbeth, the king recovers, toasts the absent Banquo, and then sees Banquo again, this time standing, quite appropriately, between the two thrones. Olivier dropped the wine cup, retreated, and then, recovering as the ghost walked towards the table, jumped onto the table in a challenge to the ghost, which then descended through a trapdoor (Bartholomeusz, 262–64). Such athleticism and recovered courage restored the audience's grudging admiration for the protagonist. Even at the end, even after the barbaric slaying of Lady Macduff and her children, Olivier elicits the sympathy of the audience, "pity for the latent nobility of the man and at the same time [the audience] could recognize the evil that flowed from him" (Bartholomeusz, 265). Frequently, Olivier has been likened to Garrick, however much the two differed: "Both men were able to reconcile the discordant elements of Macbeth's character—along with his evil, they could integrate the man of sensibility, whose suffering engenders pity, and the man of courage, whose intrepidity earns admiration" (Kliman, 64).

The chief difference in the two performances, one in the eighteenth century and one in the twentieth, derived in large part from the actress playing opposite Macbeth, a difference "between their two ladies, the impressively obdurate, physically dominant Mrs. Pritchard, so unlike the visually frail, delicately beautiful, snake-like Vivien Leigh. Garrick's Macbeth was the more noble, more uxorious, Olivier's the stronger, more self-motivated" (Kliman, 64–5).

Trevor Nunn's 1976 production with Ian McKellen and Judi Dench, and featuring John Woodvine as a richly ambiguous Banquo, was performed with a simple set of crates surrounding a magical circle into which actors entered while others whose characters were not yet involved in the action watched as if at a rehearsal. Macbeth himself always moved about the circle counterclockwise, as if already of the Devil's party. The forces of good and evil were juxtaposed early on, as Duncan chants the Agnus Dei as the witches mutter their doggerel lines as a version of the Dies Irae. A rarely achieved balance was kept between the clear moral responsibility of the Macbeths and the otherworldly force represented by the witches. The critics found Judi Dench's Lady Macbeth especially successful, chiefly because of her skill in smoothing over the awkwardness created by the shift of her role from dominant partner to excluded wife without any transitional phase. Dench showed a woman devastated by her loss of Macbeth's need for her counsel and support, a feeling exacerbated by being replaced in those roles by his servant Seyton.

The freedom to move passages, and even scenes, from their order in the Folio text—which, as we have noted, began at least as early as Davenant—continues in the twenty-first century. One sterling example is the 2007 production by Rupert Good, starring Kate Fleetwood as Lady Macbeth and Patrick Stewart as Macbeth. (Stewart, better known as Captain Jean-Luc Picard of *Star Trek: The Next Generation*, was also the finest Claudius in *Hamlet* of our time—Claudius's being, among many other things, an earlier version of Macbeth). This production involved with true shock the blood, gore, and horror of modern action films. It used a "set . . . unchanged throughout, a large gloomy white-tiled utility room, equipped with a large sink downstage left and a big old-fashioned refrigerator with a television set perched on it upstage right, with a centre-stage rear entrance in the form of a grille-doored industrial lift [elevator]" (Dobson, 347). Combining Act 1, scene 1, and Act 1, scene 3, the production has nurses giving the bleeding sergeant what turns out to be a deliberately lethal injection—after which the nurses take off their masks and become the self-satisfied witches waiting for the arrival of Macbeth and Banquo. This production was marked with a number of clever bits of stage business, including Duncan's visiting the kitchen where Lady Macbeth has to wipe her hands of the blood from the meat that she is cutting up for the guests' dinner, and the use of the sink as a urinal by the drunken Porter in Act 2, scene 3.

In this 2007 production, Banquo's ghost appeared to the audience and to Macbeth walking across the banquet table toward Macbeth at the head of it, when the lights suddenly went out. Then the lights went up for the interval, and upon its return, the audience realized that "the production having told us exactly what Macbeth was about to see, the scene re-started from the beginning, this time with the murderers inaudible, and this time with the ghost appearing solely to Macbeth" (Dobson, 349).

Stewart played Macbeth as a tyrant, but a particular tyrant—Stalin. Another figure who serves as a shared referent for Shakespeare productions, Stalin had a withered arm that made him a fine model for some of Ian McKellen's Richard III, an early version of Macbeth "cultivating a sort of self-congratulatory peasant wiliness for his dealings with his underlings, and employing a security apparatus visibly modeled on the KGB . . ." (Dobson, 349).

The twenty-first century continues the stage evolution of *Macbeth* in ways that Davenant could not have imagined, but which, if he were alive today, he would understand as still related to the script that he had once manipulated so successfully. In 2009, an old schoolhouse in Massachusetts hosted an interactive *Macbeth*, and in 2010, London's New Globe Theatre hosted a medieval version of the tragedy that Dante might have recognized.

Perhaps none of the stage productions is so unusual as *Sleep No More*, an "installation theater piece" by the Punchdrunk Theater Company in collaboration with the American Repertory Theater of Cambridge, Massachusetts, in the fall of 2009 (Rizzo). In *Sleep No More*, based on the 2003 version of this play produced in England, the audience moves in small groups and however they like through forty-four rooms of an old schoolhouse. All the scenes in the play are operative, each with accompanying sounds, sights, and smells (of food, perfume, sweat, and so on). The audience is totally immersed in the world of the play, the production of which is "part installation art, part dance-theater, part Uncle Will's Haunted House Tour" (Rizzo).

Indeed, there is a strong flavor of Halloween about the entire performance, where one expects to put one's hand in a bowl of peeled grapes representing eyeballs left over from a witches' brew as one listens to menacing background music. There are no peeled grapes here, but there are foodstuffs left over from the banquet scene, while in the distance and partial darkness, some amorous partying with flashes of nudity can be made out. One room conjures Birnam Wood, with fragrant fir trees. The entire experience involves the audience, following its unplanned sequence of scenes, where actors mime episodes from the play and episodes that are not in the play but connected to its action. The whole enterprise is the working through of a mobile mosaic, where the mobility occurs in each room and in the freedom of the audience to turn to other rooms, left or right, up or down. That audience of about three hundred enters "at staggered times, and outfitted with masks, [is] set loose in small groups of as few as five — or, for a lucky handful, one" (Anderman). Codirector/choreographer Maxine Dagle described the nature of the production, which was clearly visual, aural, olfactory, and tactile, but not verbal, as "We've lifted the quintessential images and created an alternative physical and visual text of the play" (Anderman). While the audience members have the freedom to create their own experience of *Macbeth*, the actors are as choreographed in their moves as ballet dancers. The experience lasted about three hours—three times the hour needed to show the plot if followed directly but enough time to go back to see what one had missed by too long an involvement in one or another of the fascinating scenes.

Somewhat more traditional—insofar as Shakespeare's words are used and insofar as only some members of the audience are employed as participants—was the *Macbeth* performed in May and June 2010 at Shakespeare's Globe, directed by Lucy Bailey. The distinctive element in this production was the idea that the seemingly circular Globe galleries evoke the circles of Dante's *Inferno*. This effect was achieved in part through the spectacular use of a tarpaulin covering the groundlings (the standing members of the audience) so that their heads appear through and above the black sheeting, rather as the heads of the damned poke through the ice of the ninth circle in Gustave Doré's illustration of the bottom of hell.

This production casts the Macbeths as a relatively young couple. Their relationship is not only that of two halves of one personality, as Freud suggested, but that of two erotically charged lovers eager to embrace one another at the first opportunity. Some human touches amid all the violence appealed to some reviewers: "There is also a lethal jocularity to the way Macbeth pops a crown on the head of Banquo's son [Fleance], only to snatch it back when the boy threatens to abscond with it" (Billington), and "no one will forget Frank Scanlon's grotesque porter, who brings a new meaning to the phrase 'comic relief'" (Hemming) with his impressive micturition.

CONCLUSION

Actors continue to enjoy treating "the Scottish play" as if it were unlucky, but they have shown what splendid good luck audiences have in seeing this special play, and even sometimes participating in it, whether as visitors in Macbeth's castle or as damned souls with heads above an infernal tarpaulin. That actors continue to perform the play despite its allegedly unlucky history reinforces the central role that *Macbeth* has played in the dramatic tradition. Superstition is just another part of the theater's magic.

WORKS CITED IN THE INTRODUCTION
AND PERFORMANCE HISTORY

Adam, Eve, ed. *Mrs. J. Comyns Carr's Reminiscences.* London: Hutchinson & Co., 1926.

Adelman, Janet. "'Born of Woman': Fantasies of Maternal Power in *Macbeth.*" In *Cannibals, Witches, and Divorce: Estranging the Renaissance.* Selected papers from the English Institute, 1985. Ed. Marjorie Garber. Baltimore: Johns Hopkins UP, 1985. 90–121.

Anderman, Joan. "Mystery Theater." *Boston Globe*, October 4, 2009, Living Arts 1.

Bartholomeusz, Dennis. *Macbeth and the Players.* Cambridge, UK: Cambridge UP, 1969.

Berger, Harry. "The Early Scenes of *Macbeth*: Preface to a New Interpretation." *ELH* 47 (1980): 1–31.

Billington, Michael. "*Macbeth*, Shakespeare's Globe, London," *The Guardian*, 30 April 2010.

Boorde, Andrew. "An English man," and "A Scottish man," *The Fyrst Book of the Introduction of Knowledge.* (1547; ed. F. J. Furnivall.) Early English Text Society. 10. London: Trübner, 1870.

Bradley, A. C. *Shakespearean Tragedy: Lectures on Hamlet, Othello, King Lear, Macbeth.* 2d ed. London: Macmillan, 1905.

Braunmuller, A.R., ed. *Macbeth.* 2d ed. Cambridge, UK: Cambridge UP, 2008.

Brooke, Nicholas, ed. *Macbeth.* Oxford: Clarendon Press, 1990.

Clark, Stuart. *Thinking with Demons: the Idea of Witchcraft in Early Modern Europe.* Oxford: Clarendon, 1997.

Davenant, William. *Macbeth, a Tragedy: With All the Alterations, Amendments, Additions, and New Songs, As It's Now Acted at the Duke's Theatre.* London, 1674.

De Quincey, Thomas. "On Knocking at the Gate." *The London Magazine*, 1823.

Dobson, Michael. "Shakespeare Performance in England." *Shakespeare Survey* 61 (2008): 346–59.

Evans, G. Blakemore, Gen. Ed. *The Riverside Shakespeare.* Cambridge, MA: Houghton Mifflin Company, 1974.

Floyd-Wilson, Mary. "English Epicures and Scottish Witches." *Shakespeare Quarterly* 57:2 (Summer) 2006, 131–161.

———. *English Ethnicity and Race in Early Modern Drama.* Cambridge, UK: Cambridge UP, 2003.

Forsyth, Neil. "Shakespeare the Illusionist: Filming the Supernatural." *The Cambridge Companion to Shakespeare on Film.* Ed. Russell Jackson. Cambridge, UK: Cambridge UP, 2000. 274-284.

Garber, Marjorie. "Macbeth, The Male Medusa." *Shakespeare's Ghostwriters: Literature as Uncanny Causality*. New York: Methuen, 1987. 87–123.

Harcourt, John B. "I Pray You, Remember the Porter." *Shakespeare Quarterly* 12 (1961): 393–402.

Harrison, William. "The description of Scotland." In Raphael Holinshed, *The Second volume of Chronicles*. London, 1587. Sig. B5v.

Harrowing of Hell: A Miracle Play. Introduction by J. O. Halliwell. London: Halliwell, 1840.

Hemming, Sarah. "*Macbeth*, Shakespeare's Globe, London," *The Financial Times*, May 3, 2010.

Holloway, John. *The Story of the Night: Studies in Shakespeare's Major Tragedies*. London: Routledge & K. Paul, 1961.

King James I. *Daemonology, In Form of a Dialogue*. Edinburgh, 1597.

Kinney, Arthur. "Scottish History, the Union of the Crowns, and the Issue of Right Rule: The Case of Shakespeare's *Macbeth*." In *Renaissance Culture in Context: Theory and Practice*. Ed. Jean R. Brink and William F. Gentrup. Brookfield, VT: Scolar, 1993. 18–53.

Kliman, Bernice W. *Macbeth (Shakespeare in Performance)*. 2d ed. Manchester, UK: Manchester UP, 2004.

Knights, L.C. *How Many Children Had Lady Macbeth? An Essay in the Theory and Practice of Shakespeare Criticism*. Cambridge, UK: The Minority Press, 1933.

Lake, Peter, with Michael Questier. *The Antichrist's Lewd Hat: Protestants, Papists, and Players in Post-Reformation England*. New Haven: Yale UP, 2002.

Paster, Gail Kern. "The Unbearable Coldness of Female Being: Women's Imperfection and the Humoral Economy." *English Literary Renaissance* 28 (1998): 416–40.

Paul, H.N. *The Royal Play of Macbeth*. New York: Macmillan, 1950.

Prescott, Paul. "Doing All That Becomes a Man: The Reception and Afterlife of the *Macbeth* Actor, 1774–1889." *Shakespeare Survey* 57 (2004), 81–95.

Puttenham, George. *The Arte of English Poesie*. Kent, OH: The Kent State UP, 1970.

Rizzo, Frank. "Sleep No More." *Variety*, October 19, 2009.

Rowe, Katherine. "The Politics of Sleepwalking: American Lady Macbeths." *Shakespeare Survey 57, Macbeth and Its Afterlife*, ed. Peter D. Holland, 2004: 126–36.

Salgado, Gamini. *Eyewitnesses of Shakespeare: Firsthand Accounts of Performances 1590–1890*. London: Sussex UP, 1975.

Schoenfeldt, Michael C. *Bodies and Selves in Early Modern England: Physiology and Inwardness in Spenser, Shakespeare, Herbert, and Milton*. Cambridge, UK: Cambridge UP, 1999.

Wilders, John, ed. *Shakespeare in Production: Macbeth*. Cambridge, UK: Cambridge UP, 2004.

Williams, Simon. "Taking Macbeth out of Himself: Davenant, Garrick, Schiller, and Verdi," *Shakespeare Survey* 57 (2004): 54–68.

ABBREVIATIONS

F1, F2, etc. First Folio, Second Folio, etc.
O1, O2, etc. First Octavo, Second Octavo, etc.
Q1, Q2, etc. First Quarto, Second Quarto, etc.
(c) corrected state
(u) uncorrected state
cf. compare
conj. conjecture
ed(s). editor(s); edition(s)
fol(s). folio(s)
(JM) updates by the General Editor
l(l). line(s)
MS manuscript
n.s. new series
om. omit(s), omitted
o.s.d. opening stage direction
(KR) updates by the Editor
s.d(d). stage direction(s)
ser. series
sig(s). signature(s)
s.p(p). speech-prefix(es)
subs. substantially
v verso

KEY TO WORKS CITED IN EXPLANATORY
AND TEXTUAL NOTES

Reference in explanatory and textual notes is in general by last name of editor or author. Not included in the following list of works so cited are editions of *Macbeth* or special studies referred to in the introduction, performance history, further reading lists, and selected bibliographies appended to the Note on the Text.

BULLOUGH, Geoffrey, *Narrative and Dramatic Sources of Shakespeare*, 1957–75 (7 vols.)

CAPELL, Edward, ed., *Works*, [1768] (10 vols.)

COLLIER, John P., ed., *Works*, 1842–44 (8 vols.); 1853; 1858 (6 vols.)

DAVENANT, William, *Macbeth*, 1674

DOUAI MS (*Macbeth*), Douai MS. 7.87, in the Douai Public Library (see G.B. Evans, *PQ*, XLI [1962], 158–72)

DYCE, Alexander, ed., *Works*, 1857 (6 vols.); 1864–67 (9 vols.); 1875–76 (9 vols.) *Works of Beaumont and Fletcher*, 1843–46 (11 vols.)

GLOBE, ed. William G. Clark and W.A. Wright, *Works*, 1864

HANMER, Thomas, ed., *Works*, 1743–44 (6 vols.); 1745; 1770–71 (6 vols.)

HOLINSHED, Raphael. See BULLOUGH

HUNTER, John, ed., *Macbeth*, 1870

JENNENS, Charles, ed., *Hamlet* (1773), *Julius Caesar* (1773, 1774), *King Lear* (1770), *Macbeth* (1773), *Othello* (1773)

JOHNSON, Samuel, ed., *Works*, 1765 (2 eds., 8 vols.); 1768 (8 vols.)

KITTREDGE, George L., ed., *Works*, 1936

MALONE, Edmond, ed., *Works*, 1790 (10 vols.)

MUIR, Kenneth, ed., *Macbeth*, 1951

NEILSON, William A., ed., *Works*, 1906

PELICAN, *Works*, general ed. Alfred Harbage (rev. 1-vol. ed.), 1969

POPE, Alexander, ed., *Works*, 1723–25 (6 vols.); 1728 (8 vols.)

RIDLEY, M.R., ed., *Works* (New Temple), 1935–36 (40 vols.)

ROWE, Nicholas, ed., *Works*, 1709 (2 eds., 6 vol.); 1714 (8 vols.)

SEWARD, Thomas (see THEOBALD, *Works of Beaumont and Fletcher*, 1750)

SINGER, S.W., ed., *Works*, 1826 (10 vols.); 1855–56 (10 vols.)

STAUNTON, Howard, ed., *Works*, 1858–60 (3 vols.)

STEEVENS, George, ed., *Works*, 1773 (with Samuel Johnson, 10 vols.); 1778 (10 vols.); 1793 (15 vols.)

THEOBALD, Lewis, ed., *Works*, 1733 (7 vols.); 1740 (8 vols.); 1757 (8 vols.) (with Thomas Seward and J. Sympson), *Works of Beaumont and Fletcher*, 1750 (vol. X: *The Two Noble Kinsmen*)

WHITE, Richard Grant, ed., *Works*, 1857–66 (12 vols.); 1883 (6 vols.)

WILSON, John Dover (with A. Quiller-Couch et al.), ed., *Works* (New Cambridge Shakespeare), 1921–66 (39 vols.)

THE TRAGEDY OF

MACBETH

[DRAMATIS PERSONAE

DUNCAN, *King of Scotland*
MALCOLM ⎫
DONALBAIN ⎭ *his sons*
MACBETH ⎫
BANQUO ⎭ *generals of the King's army*
MACDUFF ⎫
LENNOX ⎪
ROSSE ⎪
MENTETH ⎬ *noblemen of Scotland*
ANGUS ⎪
CATHNESS ⎭
FLEANCE, *son to Banquo*
SIWARD, *Earl of Northumberland, general of the
    English forces*
YOUNG SIWARD, *his son*
SEYTON, *an officer attending on Macbeth*
BOY, *son to Macduff*
ENGLISH DOCTOR
SCOTS DOCTOR
SERGEANT
PORTER
OLD MAN
Three MURDERERS
LADY MACBETH
LADY MACDUFF
GENTLEWOMAN *attending on Lady Macbeth*
Three WITCHES, *the Weïrd Sisters*
Three other WITCHES
HECAT
APPARITIONS
LORDS, GENTLEMEN, OFFICERS, SOLDIERS, ATTENDANTS,
    and MESSENGERS

SCENE: SCOTLAND; ENGLAND]

Act I

SCENE I

Thunder and lightning. Enter three WITCHES.

1. WITCH When shall we three meet again?
In thunder, lightning, or in rain?
2. WITCH When the hurly-burly's done,
When the battle's lost and won.
3. WITCH That will be ere the set of sun.   5
1. WITCH Where the place?
2. WITCH   Upon the heath.
3. WITCH There to meet with Macbeth.
1. WITCH I come, Graymalkin.
[2. WITCH] Paddock calls.
[3. WITCH] Anon.   10
ALL Fair is foul, and foul is fair,
Hover through the fog and filthy air.   *Exeunt.*

SCENE 2

Alarum within. Enter KING [DUNCAN], MALCOLM,
DONALBAIN, LENNOX, *with* ATTENDANTS, *meeting a bleeding*
[SERGEANT].

DUNCAN What bloody man is that? He can report,
As seemeth by his plight, of the revolt
The newest state.

Words and passages enclosed in square brackets in the text above are either emendations of the copy-text or additions to it. The Textual Notes immediately following the play cite the earliest authority for every such change or insertion and supply the reading of the copy-text wherever it is emended in this edition. The glosses have been lightly updated for the Evans Shakespeare Edition.

1.1. Location: An open place.   **3. hurly-burly:** commotion, uproar, i.e. the battle that is described in the following scene.   **6. heath:** heather, wild open space. **8, 9. Graymalkin, Paddock:** i.e. grey cat, toad; the names of the familiars or spirits who serve the witches. In 4.1.3 we learn that the familiar of the Third Witch is called Harpier, apparently meaning "harpy." **10. Anon:** right away, coming (spoken to her familiar).

MALCOLM This is the sergeant,
Who like a good and hardy soldier fought
'Gainst my captivity. Hail, brave friend!   5
Say to the King the knowledge of the broil
As thou didst leave it.
[SERGEANT]   Doubtful it stood,
As two spent swimmers that do cling together
And choke their art. The merciless Macdonwald
(Worthy to be a rebel, for to that   10
The multiplying villainies of nature
Do swarm upon him) from the Western Isles
Of kerns and [gallowglasses] is supplied,
And Fortune, on his damned [quarrel] smiling,
Show'd like a rebel's whore. But all's too weak;   15
For brave Macbeth (well he deserves that name),
Disdaining Fortune, with his brandish'd steel,
Which smok'd with bloody execution,
(Like Valor's minion) carv'd out his passage
Till he fac'd the slave;   20
Which nev'r shook hands, nor bade farewell to him,
Till he unseam'd him from the nave to th' chops,
And fix'd his head upon our battlements.
DUNCAN O valiant cousin, worthy gentleman!
[SERGEANT] As whence the sun gins his reflection   25
Shipwracking storms and direful thunders [break],
So from that spring whence comfort seem'd to come
Discomfort swells. Mark, King of Scotland, mark!
No sooner justice had, with valor arm'd,
Compell'd these skipping kerns to trust their heels,   30
But the Norweyan lord, surveying vantage,

---

12. Filthy air: fireworks were used to generate the "Thunder and light-ning" indicated in the s. d., fouling the theater air with smoke and the smell of gunpowder. **1.2.** Location: Scotland. A camp. **o.s.d. Alarum:** trumpet call to arms. **6. broil:** battle. **9. art:** skill (in swimming). **10. that:** i.e. that end. **12. Western Isles:** islands west of Scotland. **13. Of:** with. **kerns:** light-armed foot soldiers, usually the poorer class of "wild Irish," sometimes mercenaries. **gallowglasses:** heavy-armed Irish foot soldiers. **14. quarrel:** cause. **15. Show'd:** appeared. **16. name:** i.e. designation "brave." **19. minion:** male favorite, darling. Also a follower, underling, servant (cf Boorde, pp. 152, l. 11, in the Sources and Contexts section). **21. shook hands:** i.e. took leave. **22. nave:** navel. **chops:** jaws. **24. cousin:** kinsman (used familiarly of any collateral relative except a brother or sister). Duncan and Macbeth were grandsons of King Malcolm. **25. gins his reflection:** begins its turning back (at the vernal equinox). **27. spring:** (1) spring season; (2) source. **28. swells:** wells up. **Mark:** listen. **30. skipping:** highly mobile (because light-armed, but with implication that they are quick to retreat).

With furbish'd arms and new supplies of men,
Began a fresh assault.
DUNCAN   Dismay'd not this
Our captains, Macbeth and Banquo?
[SERGEANT]   Yes,
As sparrows eagles; or the hare the lion.   35
If I say sooth, I must report they were
As cannons overcharg'd with double cracks, so they
Doubly redoubled strokes upon the foe.
Except they meant to bathe in reeking wounds,
Or memorize another Golgotha,   40
I cannot tell—
But I am faint, my gashes cry for help.
DUNCAN So well thy words become thee as thy wounds,
They smack of honor both. Go get him surgeons.
                              [*Exit Sergeant, attended.*]
                    Enter ROSSE *and* ANGUS.

Who comes here?
MALCOLM   The worthy Thane of Rosse.   45
LENNOX What a haste looks through his eyes! So should he look
That seems to speak things strange.
ROSSE   God save the King!
DUNCAN Whence cam'st thou, worthy thane?
ROSSE   From Fife, great King,
Where the Norweyan banners flout the sky
And fan our people cold.   50
Norway himself, with terrible numbers,
Assisted by that most disloyal traitor,
The Thane of Cawdor, began a dismal conflict,
Till that Bellona's bridegroom, lapp'd in proof,
Confronted him with self-comparisons,   55

---

31. surveying vantage: seeing his opportunity, taking the advantage. **36. sooth:** truth. **37. cracks:** charges. **so:** in such a way. **39. Except:** unless. **40. memorize another Golgotha:** make the field as memorable for slaughter as Golgotha, i.e. Calvary, "the place of skulls." **45. Thane:** A Scottish clan chief; one who holds the king's lands through military service. **47. seems to:** seems about to. **49–50. flout . . . cold:** mock the sky and fan cold fear into our people. It has been suggested that Rosse begins his account in the so-called historic present tense. **51. Norway:** the King of Norway. **53. dismal:** ill-boding. **54. Till that:** Until. **Bellona's bridegroom:** i.e. Macbeth. Bellona was the goddess of war; she was a virgin, but Shakespeare is making a conceit, not a mistake, since *1 Henry IV,* 4.1.114, proves that he knew the facts. **lapp'd in proof:** clad in tested armor. **55. self-comparisons:** i.e. scoffing remarks about deeds as valorous as his own.

Point against point, rebellious arm 'gainst arm,
Curbing his lavish spirit; and to conclude,
The victory fell on us.

DUNCAN   Great happiness!

ROSSE   That now
Sweno, the Norways' king, craves composition;
Nor would we deign him burial of his men   60
Till he disbursed at Saint Colme's inch
Ten thousand dollars to our general use.

DUNCAN No more that Thane of Cawdor shall deceive
Our bosom interest. Go pronounce his present death,
And with his former title greet Macbeth.   65

ROSSE I'll see it done.

DUNCAN What he hath lost, noble Macbeth hath won.

Exeunt.

SCENE 3

Thunder. Enter the three WITCHES.

1. WITCH Where hast thou been, sister?
2. WITCH Killing swine.
3. WITCH Sister, where thou?
1. WITCH A sailor's wife had chestnuts in her lap,
   And mounch'd, and mounch'd, and mounch'd.
   "Give me!" quoth I.   5
   "Aroint thee, witch!" the rump-fed ronyon cries.
   Her husband's to Aleppo gone, master o' th' *Tiger;*
   But in a sieve I'll thither sail,
   And like a rat without a tail,
   I'll do, I'll do, and I'll do.   10
2. WITCH I'll give thee a wind.
1. WITCH Th' art kind.
3. WITCH And I another.
1. WITCH I myself have all the other,
   And the very ports they blow,   15
   All the quarters that they know

---

57. lavish: unrestrained, wild.   **59. craves composition:** begs terms of peace.
61. Saint Colme's inch: Inchcolm, a small island in the Firth of Forth.
64. bosom interest: dearest concerns. **present:** immediate.   1.3. Location: A
heath.   **6. Aroint:** be gone. **rump-fed:** fed with meat, perhaps fat-rumped(?). **ronyon:** fat woman.   **7. Aleppo:** Syrian city, center of trade.   **9. like:** in the shape of.
11. wind. Northern witches were believed to sell winds and control the weather.
Cf. 4.1.52.   **15. blow:** i.e. blow from; the ships are kept out of port by winds.

I' th' shipman's card.
I'll drain him dry as hay:
Sleep shall neither night nor day
Hang upon his penthouse lid;   20
He shall live a man forbid;
Weary sev'nnights, nine times nine,
Shall he dwindle, peak, and pine;
Though his bark cannot be lost,
Yet it shall be tempest-toss'd.   25
Look what I have.

2. WITCH Show me, show me.

1. WITCH Here I have a pilot's thumb,
Wrack'd as homeward he did come.   *Drum within.*

3. WITCH A drum, a drum!   30
Macbeth doth come.

ALL The weïrd sisters, hand in hand,
Posters of the sea and land,
Thus do go, about, about,
Thrice to thine, and thrice to mine,   35
And thrice again, to make up nine.
Peace, the charm's wound up.

Enter MACBETH *and* BANQUO.

MACBETH So foul and fair a day I have not seen.

BANQUO How far is't call'd to [Forres]? What are these
So wither'd and so wild in their attire,   40
That look not like th' inhabitants o' th' earth,
And yet are on't? Live you? or are you aught
That man may question? You seem to understand me,
By each at once her choppy finger laying
Upon her skinny lips. You should be women,   45
And yet your beards forbid me to interpret
That you are so.

MACBETH   Speak, if you can: what are you?

1. WITCH All hail, Macbeth, hail to thee, Thane of Glamis!

2. WITCH All hail, Macbeth, hail to thee, Thane of Cawdor!

3. WITCH All hail, Macbeth, that shalt be King hereafter!   50

---

17. shipman's card: compass card; or, possibly, chart. **20. penthouse lid:** i.e. eyelid (*penthouse* = lean-to with a sloping roof). **21. forbid:** under a curse. **23. peak:** grow emaciated. **32. weïrd.** Spelled *weyard* or *weyward* in F1. From Old English *wyrd*, "fate." The word comprises our current senses of uncanny, fated, and also wayward or uncontrolled. (KR) **33. Posters of:** swift travelers over. **37. wound up:** i.e. ready for action. **43. question:** converse with. **44. choppy:** chapped.

BANQUO Good sir, why do you start, and seem to fear
    Things that do sound so fair?—I' th' name of truth,
    Are ye fantastical, or that indeed
    Which outwardly ye show? My noble partner
    You greet with present grace, and great prediction   55
    Of noble having and of royal hope,
    That he seems rapt withal; to me you speak not.
    If you can look into the seeds of time,
    And say which grain will grow, and which will not,
    Speak then to me, who neither beg nor fear   60
    Your favors nor your hate.
1. WITCH Hail!
2. WITCH Hail!
3. WITCH Hail!
1. WITCH Lesser than Macbeth, and greater.   65
2. WITCH Not so happy, yet much happier.
3. WITCH Thou shalt get kings, though thou be none.
    So all hail, Macbeth and Banquo!
1. WITCH Banquo and Macbeth, all hail!
MACBETH Stay, you imperfect speakers, tell me more: 70
    By Sinel's death I know I am Thane of Glamis,
    But how of Cawdor? The Thane of Cawdor lives
    A prosperous gentleman; and to be king
    Stands not within the prospect of belief,
    No more than to be Cawdor. Say from whence   75
    You owe this strange intelligence, or why
    Upon this blasted heath you stop our way
    With such prophetic greeting? Speak, I charge you.

                                         Witches vanish.

BANQUO The earth hath bubbles, as the water has,
    And these are of them. Whither are they vanish'd?   80
MACBETH Into the air; and what seem'd corporal melted,
    As breath into the wind. Would they had stay'd!
BANQUO Were such things here as we do speak about?
    Or have we eaten on the insane root

---

53. fantastical: imaginary.   **54. show:** appear to be.   **55. with present grace:** i.e.
by his present title, as Thane of Glamis.   **55–56. prediction . . . noble having:**
i.e. as Thane of Cawdor.   **57. rapt:** carried out of himself. **withal:** with (by) it.
60–61. beg . . . hate: beg your favors nor fear your hate.   **66. happy:** lucky,
fortuitous, blessed.   **67. get:** beget.   **70. imperfect:** giving an incomplete account.
71. Sinel: Macbeth's father, according to Holinshed.   **76. owe:** possess. **intelligence:**
information.   **77. blasted:** blighted, barren.   **84. on:** of. **insane:** causing insanity.
The root has been variously identified.

That takes the reason prisoner?   85
MACBETH Your children shall be kings.
BANQUO   You shall be king.
MACBETH And Thane of Cawdor too; went it not so?
BANQUO To th' self-same tune and words. Who's here?

Enter ROSSE *and* ANGUS.

ROSSE The King hath happily receiv'd, Macbeth,
   The news of thy success; and when he reads   90
   Thy personal venture in the rebels' fight,
   His wonders and his praises do contend
   Which should be thine or his. Silenc'd with that,
   In viewing o'er the rest o' th' self-same day,
   He finds thee in the stout Norweyan ranks,   95
   Nothing afeard of what thyself didst make,
   Strange images of death. As thick as tale
   [Came] post with post, and every one did bear
   Thy praises in his kingdom's great defense,
   And pour'd them down before him.
ANGUS   We are sent   100
   To give thee from our royal master thanks,
   Only to herald thee into his sight,
   Not pay thee.
ROSSE And for an earnest of a greater honor,
   He bade me, from him, call thee Thane of Cawdor;   105
   In which addition, hail, most worthy thane,
   For it is thine.
BANQUO   What, can the devil speak true?
MACBETH The Thane of Cawdor lives; why do you dress me
   In borrowed robes?
ANGUS   Who was the thane lives yet,
   But under heavy judgment bears that life   110
   Which he deserves to lose. Whether he was combin'd
   With those of Norway, or did line the rebel
   With hidden help and vantage, or that with both
   He labor'd in his country's wrack, I know not;

92–93. His . . . his: i.e. Duncan does not know whether to speak of his astonishment or his admiration. **93. that:** i.e. the conflict between his astonishment and his admiration. **96. Nothing:** not at all. **97. images:** figures, forms. **As . . . tale:** as fast as they could be "told" or counted. **98. post with post:** one messenger after another. **104. earnest:** token, pledge. **106. addition:** title. **109. Who . . . thane:** he who once held that title. **111. combin'd:** allied. **112. line:** support. **the rebel:** i.e. Macdonwald.

But treasons capital, confess'd and prov'd,   115
Have overthrown him.
MACBETH   [*Aside.*] Glamis, and Thane of Cawdor!
The greatest is behind. [*To Rosse and Angus.*] Thanks for your pains.
[*Aside to Banquo.*] Do you not hope your children shall be kings,
When those that gave the Thane of Cawdor to me
Promis'd no less to them?
BANQUO   [*Aside to Macbeth.*] That, trusted home, 120
Might yet enkindle you unto the crown,
Besides the Thane of Cawdor. But 'tis strange;
And oftentimes, to win us to our harm,
The instruments of darkness tell us truths,
Win us with honest trifles, to betray 's   125
In deepest consequence.—
Cousins, a word, I pray you.
MACBETH   [*Aside.*] Two truths are told,
As happy prologues to the swelling act
Of the imperial theme.—I thank you, gentlemen.
[*Aside.*] This supernatural soliciting   130
Cannot be ill; cannot be good. If ill,
Why hath it given me earnest of success,
Commencing in a truth? I am Thane of Cawdor.
If good, why do I yield to that suggestion
Whose horrid image doth unfix my hair   135
And make my seated heart knock at my ribs,
Against the use of nature? Present fears
Are less than horrible imaginings:
My thought, whose murther yet is but fantastical,
Shakes so my single state of man that function   140
Is smother'd in surmise, and nothing is
But what is not.
BANQUO   Look how our partner's rapt.
MACBETH [*Aside.*] If chance will have me king, why, chance
        may crown me
Without my stir.

---

117. **behind:** beyond, to come.   120. **home:** completely.   121. **enkindle you
unto:** give you cause to hope for.   126. **deepest consequence:** the very important
events that follow.   127. **Cousins:** i.e. fellow lords.   128. **swelling act:** grand dramatic action.   130. **soliciting:** incitement, temptation (so also *suggestion* in line
134).   137. **use:** custom. **fears:** objects of fear.   139. **whose:** in which. **fantastical:**
imagined.   140. **single . . . man:** weak human constitution. **function:** the normal
operation of its powers.   141. **surmise:** imagined action, guess. 141–42. **nothing . . .
not:** i.e. nothing has reality for me but what is imaginary.

BANQUO　　　　New honors come upon him,
Like our strange garments, cleave not to their mould　　　145
But with the aid of use.
MACBETH　　　　　　[*Aside*.] Come what come may,
Time and the hour runs through the roughest day.
BANQUO Worthy Macbeth, we stay upon your leisure.
MACBETH Give me your favor; my dull brain was wrought
With things forgotten. Kind gentlemen, your pains　　　150
Are regist'red where every day I turn
The leaf to read them. Let us toward the King.
[*Aside to Banquo*.] Think upon what hath chanc'd; and at more time,
The interim having weigh'd it, let us speak
Our free hearts each to other.
BANQUO　　　　　　　　　Very gladly.　　　　　　　155
MACBETH Till then, enough.— Come, friends.　　　　*Exeunt*.

SCENE 4

Flourish. Enter KING [DUNCAN], LENNOX, MALCOLM,
DONALBAIN, *and* ATTENDANTS.

DUNCAN Is execution done on Cawdor? [Are] not
Those in commission yet return'd?
MALCOLM　　　　　　　　　My liege,
They are not yet come back. But I have spoke
With one that saw him die; who did report
That very frankly he confess'd his treasons,　　　　　5
Implor'd your Highness' pardon, and set forth
A deep repentance. Nothing in his life
Became him like the leaving it. He died
As one that had been studied in his death,
To throw away the dearest thing he ow'd,　　　　　10
As 'twere a careless trifle.
DUNCAN　　　　　　　There's no art
To find the mind's construction in the face:

---

144. stir: exertion, initiative.　**145. strange:** new. **their mould:** i.e. the shape
of him who wears them.　**148. stay:** wait.　**149. favor:** pardon. **wrought:**
agitated.　**150. pains:** efforts.　**151–52. regist'red . . . them:** i.e. recorded in my
memory, invoking the metaphor of the book of memory. (KR)　**154. weigh'd:**
considered.　**155. Our free hearts:** i.e. our thoughts freely.　1.4. Location: Forres.
The palace.　**2. in commission:** i.e. delegated to see the execution carried
out. **liege:** sovereign.　**9. been studied:** made it his study.　**10. ow'd:** owned.
11. careless: uncared-for.

He was a gentleman on whom I built
An absolute trust.

Enter MACBETH, BANQUO, ROSSE, *and* ANGUS.

O worthiest cousin!
The sin of my ingratitude even now   15
Was heavy on me. Thou art so far before,
That swiftest wing of recompense is slow
To overtake thee. Would thou hadst less deserv'd,
That the proportion both of thanks and payment
Might have been mine! Only I have left to say,   20
More is thy due than more than all can pay.
MACBETH   The service and the loyalty I owe,
In doing it, pays itself. Your Highness' part
Is to receive our duties; and our duties
Are to your throne and state children and servants;   25
Which do but what they should, by doing every thing
Safe toward your love and honor.
DUNCAN   Welcome hither!
I have begun to plant thee, and will labor
To make thee full of growing. Noble Banquo,
That hast no less deserv'd, nor must be known   30
No less to have done so, let me infold thee
And hold thee to my heart.
BANQUO   There if I grow,
The harvest is your own.
DUNCAN   My plenteous joys,
Wanton in fullness, seek to hide themselves
In drops of sorrow. Sons, kinsmen, thanes,   35
And you whose places are the nearest, know
We will establish our estate upon
Our eldest, Malcolm, whom we name hereafter
The Prince of Cumberland; which honor must
Not unaccompanied invest him only,   40
But signs of nobleness, like stars, shall shine
On all deservers. From hence to Enverness,
And bind us further to you.

---

16. before: ahead.   **19–20. That . . . mine:** so that I could thank you and
reward you as you deserve.   **27. Safe toward:** to secure.   **34. Wanton:** unrestrained.   **37. establish our estate:** settle the succession.   **39. Prince of Cumberland:** title of the Scottish heir apparent.   **42. Enverness:** Inverness, seat of the
Thane of Cawdor.

MACBETH The rest is labor, which is not us'd for you.
I'll be myself the harbinger, and make joyful 45
The hearing of my wife with your approach;
So humbly take my leave.
DUNCAN   My worthy Cawdor!
MACBETH [Aside.] The Prince of Cumberland! that is a step
On which I must fall down, or else o'erleap,
For in my way it lies. Stars, hide your fires, 50
Let not light see my black and deep desires;
The eye wink at the hand; yet let that be
Which the eye fears, when it is done, to see. Exit.
DUNCAN True, worthy Banquo! he is full so valiant,
And in his commendations I am fed; 55
It is a banquet to me. Let's after him,
Whose care is gone before to bid us welcome:
It is a peerless kinsman. Flourish. Exeunt.

SCENE 5

Enter MACBETH'S WIFE alone, with a letter.

LADY MACBETH [Reads.] "They met me in the day of
success; and I have learn'd by the perfect'st report,
they have more in them than mortal knowledge. When
I burnt in desire to question them further, they made
themselves air, into which they vanish'd. Whiles I 5
stood rapt in the wonder of it, came missives from the
King, who all-hail'd me 'Thane of Cawdor,' by which
title, before, these weïrd sisters saluted me, and re-
ferr'd me to the coming on of time with 'Hail, King
that shalt be!' This have I thought good to deliver 10
thee, my dearest partner of greatness, that thou mightst
not lose the dues of rejoicing by being ignorant of what
greatness is promis'd thee. Lay it to thy heart, and
farewell."
Glamis thou art, and Cawdor, and shalt be 15
What thou art promis'd. Yet do I fear thy nature,
It is too full o' th' milk of human kindness

---

44. The rest . . . you: i.e. leisure which is not spent in your service is weari-
some. **45. harbinger:** one sent ahead to arrange for lodging. **52. wink . . .
hand:** be blind to what the hand does. **be:** come to pass. **54. full so valiant:**
i.e. every bit as valiant as you say. **1.5. Location:** Inverness. Macbeth's castle.
2. perfect'st report: most reliable information. **6. missives:** messengers.
10. deliver: inform. **16. fear:** fear for, feel uneasy about.

To catch the nearest way. Thou wouldst be great,
Art not without ambition, but without
The illness should attend it. What thou wouldst highly, 20
That wouldst thou holily; wouldst not play false,
And yet wouldst wrongly win. Thou'ldst have, great Glamis,
That which cries, "Thus thou must do," if thou have it;
And that which rather thou dost fear to do
Than wishest should be undone. Hie thee hither, 25
That I may pour my spirits in thine ear,
And chastise with the valor of my tongue
All that impedes thee from the golden round,
Which fate and metaphysical aid doth seem
To have thee crown'd withal.

Enter MESSENGER.

                What is your tidings? 30
MESSENGER The King comes here to-night.
LADY MACBETH   Thou'rt mad to say it!
Is not thy master with him? who, were't so,
Would have inform'd for preparation.
MESSENGER So please you, it is true; our thane is coming.
One of my fellows had the speed of him, 35
Who, almost dead for breath, had scarcely more
Than would make up his message.
LADY MACBETH   Give him tending,
He brings great news.   *Exit Messenger.*
          The raven himself is hoarse
That croaks the fatal entrance of Duncan
Under my battlements. Come, you spirits 40
That tend on mortal thoughts, unsex me here,
And fill me from the crown to the toe topful
Of direst cruelty! Make thick my blood,
Stop up th' access and passage to remorse,

---

20. illness: wickedness. **24. fear to do:** shrink from doing. **25. Hie:** hasten. **26. spirits:** inspiration; but also "animal spirits", very thin substances understood to carry information between the senses, mind, and soul, as agents of cognition, memory, feeling, and imagination. Cf. 1.5.40. **28. round:** crown. **29. metaphysical:** supernatural. **30. withal:** with. **35. had . . . of:** outdistanced. **40. spirits:** demonic powers; also "animal spirits", cf. 1.5.26. **41. mortal:** deadly, murderous. **unsex:** make me sexless, unfemale, or unhuman. (KR) **44. th'access...remorse:** eyes, that register pitiful sights (cf. *sightless, see, peep*, ll. 49-53), also blood vessels and nerves, the conduits for the movements of spirits and humors that comprise emotions. (KR)

That no compunctious visitings of nature   45
Shake my fell purpose, nor keep peace between
Th' effect and [it]! Come to my woman's breasts,
And take my milk for gall, you murth'ring ministers,
Wherever in your sightless substances
You wait on nature's mischief! Come, thick night,   50
And pall thee in the dunnest smoke of hell,
That my keen knife see not the wound it makes,
Nor heaven peep through the blanket of the dark
To cry, "Hold, hold!"

> *Enter* MACBETH.

Great Glamis! worthy Cawdor!
Greater than both, by the all-hail hereafter!   55
Thy letters have transported me beyond
This ignorant present, and I feel now
The future in the instant.
MACBETH   My dearest love,
Duncan comes here to-night.
LADY MACBETH   And when goes hence?
MACBETH To-morrow, as he purposes.
LADY MACBETH   O, never   60
Shall sun that morrow see!
Your face, my thane, is as a book, where men
May read strange matters. To beguile the time,
Look like the time; bear welcome in your eye,
Your hand, your tongue; look like th' innocent flower,   65
But be the serpent under't. He that's coming
Must be provided for; and you shall put
This night's great business into my dispatch,
Which shall to all our nights and days to come
Give solely sovereign sway and masterdom.   70
MACBETH We will speak further.
LADY MACBETH   Only look up clear:

---

45. compunctious: compassionate. (KR) **nature:** natural feeling. **46. fell:** cruel. **keep peace:** intervene. **47. Th' effect and it:** i.e. my purpose and its accomplishment. **48. for:** in exchange for. **gall:** bile (a humoral fluid); poison; bitterness. (KR) **49. sightless:** invisible. **50. nature's mischief:** evil done to, or within, nature. **51. pall thee:** wrap yourself as with a pall, or coffin cover. (KR) **dunnest:** darkest. **56. letters:** letter (cf. Latin *litterae*). **57. ignorant:** i.e. ignorant of what the future will bring. **63. beguile the time:** deceive the world. **68. dispatch:** management. **71. clear:** serene.

To alter favor ever is to fear.
Leave all the rest to me.   *Exeunt.*

SCENE 6

Hoboys and torches. Enter KING [DUNCAN], MALCOLM,
DONALBAIN, BANQUO, LENNOX, MACDUFF, ROSSE, ANGUS, *and*
ATTENDANTS.

DUNCAN This castle hath a pleasant seat, the air
Nimbly and sweetly recommends itself
Unto our gentle senses.

BANQUO   This guest of summer,
The temple-haunting [marlet], does approve,
By his lov'd [mansionry], that the heaven's breath   5
Smells wooingly here; no jutty, frieze,
Buttress, nor coign of vantage, but this bird
Hath made his pendant bed and procreant cradle.
Where they [most] breed and haunt, I have observ'd
The air is delicate.

                    Enter LADY [MACBETH].

DUNCAN   See, see, our honor'd hostess!   10
The love that follows us sometime is our trouble,
Which still we thank as love. Herein I teach you
How you shall bid God 'ield us for your pains,
And thank us for your trouble.

LADY MACBETH   All our service
In every point twice done, and then done double,   15
Were poor and single business to contend
Against those honors deep and broad wherewith
Your Majesty loads our house. For those of old,
And the late dignities heap'd up to them,
We rest your ermites.

---

72. favor: expression. **to fear:** i.e. to create fear.   1.6. Location: Inverness. Before Macbeth's castle. **o.s.d. Hoboys:** oboes.   **1. seat:** situation.   **3. gentle:** noble.   **4. temple-haunting:** given to building its nest in churches. **marlet:** martin.   **5. mansionry:** i.e. nest-building.   **6. jutty:** projection.   **7. coign of vantage:** convenient corner.   **10. delicate:** soft.   **12. Which:** i.e. the trouble. **thank as love:** are grateful for because it arises from love.   **13. God . . . pains:** God reward *me* for *your* trouble. Duncan is gently facetious.   **16. single:** feeble.   **16–17. contend Against:** i.e. try to match.   **20. We . . . ermites:** we are ever your hermits, i.e. we will always gratefully pray for you.

82

DUNCAN   Where's the Thane of Cawdor?   20
We cours'd him at the heels, and had a purpose
To be his purveyor; but he rides well,
And his great love, sharp as his spur, hath holp him
To his home before us. Fair and noble hostess,
We are your guest to-night.

LADY MACBETH   Your servants ever   25
Have theirs, themselves, and what is theirs, in compt,
To make their audit at your Highness' pleasure,
Still to return your own.

DUNCAN   Give me your hand.
Conduct me to mine host, we love him highly,
And shall continue our graces towards him.   30
By your leave, hostess.   *Exeunt.*

SCENE 7

*Hoboys, torches. Enter a SEWER and divers SERVANTS with dishes
and service over the stage. Then enter MACBETH.*

MACBETH   If it were done, when 'tis done, then 'twere well
It were done quickly. If th' assassination
Could trammel up the consequence, and catch
With his surcease, success; that but this blow
Might be the be-all and the end-all—here,   5
But here, upon this bank and [shoal] of time,
We'ld jump the life to come. But in these cases
We still have judgment here, that we but teach
Bloody instructions, which, being taught, return
To plague th' inventor. This even-handed justice   10
Commends th' ingredience of our poison'd chalice
To our own lips. He's here in double trust:
First, as I am his kinsman and his subject,

---

22. be his purveyor: i.e. get here ahead of him and arrange for his welcome (a purveyor being one who goes ahead to secure food and lodging). **23. holp:** helped. **26. in compt:** in trust; subject to account. **27. audit:** accounting. **28. Still:** always. **1.7.** Location: Inverness. Inner court of Macbeth's castle. **o.s.d. Sewer:** butler. **3. trammel up:** entangle as in a net. **the consequence:** the events arising from it. **4. his surcease:** its (the assassination's) conclusion (?) or Duncan's death (?). **5. here:** in this world. **6. shoal.** This emendation of Theobald's is generally accepted; but some prefer to read *school* after F1, taking *bank* to mean "bench" and citing lines 8–9 in support. **7. jump:** risk. **8. still:** always. **have judgment:** are punished. **that:** in that. **10. even-handed:** impartial. **11. Commends:** presents. **ingredience:** contents, ingredients.

Strong both against the deed; then, as his host,
Who should against his murtherer shut the door,   15
Not bear the knife myself. Besides, this Duncan
Hath borne his faculties so meek, hath been
So clear in his great office, that his virtues
Will plead like angels, trumpet-tongu'd, against
The deep damnation of his taking-off;   20
And pity, like a naked new-born babe,
Striding the blast, or heaven's cherubin, hors'd
Upon the sightless couriers of the air,
Shall blow the horrid deed in every eye,
That tears shall drown the wind. I have no spur   25
To prick the sides of my intent, but only
Vaulting ambition, which o'erleaps itself,
And falls on th' other—

Enter LADY [MACBETH].

                              How now? what news?
LADY MACBETH He has almost supp'd. Why have you left the
    chamber?
MACBETH Hath he ask'd for me?
LADY MACBETH   Know you not he has?   30
MACBETH We will proceed no further in this business:
He hath honor'd me of late, and I have bought
Golden opinions from all sorts of people,
Which would be worn now in their newest gloss,
Not cast aside so soon.
LADY MACBETH   Was the hope drunk   35
Wherein you dress'd yourself? Hath it slept since?
And wakes it now to look so green and pale
At what it did so freely? From this time
Such I account thy love. Art thou afeard
To be the same in thine own act and valor   40
As thou art in desire? Wouldst thou have that
Which thou esteem'st the ornament of life,
And live a coward in thine own esteem,

---

17. **faculties:** royal powers. 18. **clear:** blameless. 22. **Striding:** bestriding. **cherubin.** Construed as singular, with plural *cherubins,* everywhere else in Shakespeare; hence many editors emend to *cherubins* here, in view of *couriers* in line 23. **hors'd:** riding. 23. **sightless couriers:** invisible runners, i.e. winds. 25. **tears . . . wind.** As rain stills the wind. 28. **other:** other side. 32. **bought:** won. 34. **would:** want to. 37. **green:** sickly. 42. **the ornament of life:** i.e. the crown.

Letting "I dare not" wait upon "I would,"
Like the poor cat i' th' adage?
MACBETH   Prithee peace!   45
I dare do all that may become a man;
Who dares [do] more is none.
LADY MACBETH   What beast was't then
That made you break this enterprise to me?
When you durst do it, then you were a man;
And to be more than what you were, you would   50
Be so much more the man. Nor time, nor place,
Did then adhere, and yet you would make both:
They have made themselves, and that their fitness now
Does unmake you. I have given suck, and know
How tender 'tis to love the babe that milks me;   55
I would, while it was smiling in my face,
Have pluck'd my nipple from his boneless gums,
And dash'd the brains out, had I so sworn as you
Have done to this.
MACBETH   If we should fail?
LADY MACBETH   We fail?
But screw your courage to the sticking place,   60
And we'll not fail. When Duncan is asleep
(Whereto the rather shall his day's hard journey
Soundly invite him), his two chamberlains
Will I with wine and wassail so convince,
That memory, the warder of the brain,   65
Shall be a fume, and the receipt of reason
A limbeck only. When in swinish sleep
Their drenched natures lies as in a death,
What cannot you and I perform upon
Th' unguarded Duncan? what not put upon   70
His spungy officers, who shall bear the guilt
Of our great quell?

---

45. th' adage: i.e. "The cat would eat fish, and would not wet her feet."
47. none: not a man, i.e. either more than human or less.   **48. break:** broach.
52. Did then adhere: were then suitable. **would:** wanted to.   **53. that their fit-**
ness: that fitness of theirs.   **60. But:** only. **sticking place:** probably, the mark to
which a soldier screwed up the cord of a crossbow or to which a musician tuned
an instrument.   **63. chamberlains:** personal attendants.   **64. wassail:** carousing.
convince: overpower.   **66. receipt:** receptacle.   **67. limbeck:** alembic, upper
part of a still to which the fumes rise. It was believed that the fumes of wine rose
from the stomach to the brain and intoxicated it.   **71. spungy:** spongy, i.e. soaked
with drink.   **72. quell:** killing, murder.

MACBETH   Bring forth men-children only!
For thy undaunted mettle should compose
Nothing but males. Will it not be receiv'd,
When we have mark'd with blood those sleepy two   75
Of his own chamber, and us'd their very daggers,
That they have done't?
LADY MACBETH   Who dares receive it other,
As we shall make our griefs and clamor roar
Upon his death?
MACBETH   I am settled, and bend up
Each corporal agent to this terrible feat.   80
Away, and mock the time with fairest show:
False face must hide what the false heart doth know.

Exeunt.

73. **mettle:** physical and mental composition, temperament. 74. **receiv'd:** believed. 77. **other:** otherwise. 78. **As:** inasmuch as. 79. **bend up:** make taut, strain. 80. **corporal agent:** active part of the body. 81. **mock the time:** deceive the world.

Act 2

SCENE I

Enter BANQUO, *and* FLEANCE *with a torch before him.*

BANQUO How goes the night, boy?

FLEANCE The moon is down; I have not heard the clock.

BANQUO And she goes down at twelve.

FLEANCE   I take't, 'tis later, sir.

BANQUO Hold, take my sword. There's husbandry in heaven,
Their candles are all out. Take thee that too.   5
    [*Gives him his belt and dagger.*]
A heavy summons lies like lead upon me,
And yet I would not sleep. Merciful powers,
Restrain in me the cursed thoughts that nature
Gives way to in repose!

Enter MACBETH, *and a* SERVANT *with a torch.*

                        Give me my sword.
Who's there?   10
MACBETH A friend.

BANQUO What, sir, not yet at rest? the King's a-bed.
He hath been in unusual pleasure, and
Sent forth great largess to your offices.
This diamond he greets your wife withal,   15
By the name of most kind hostess, and shut up
In measureless content.

MACBETH   Being unprepar'd,
Our will became the servant to defect,
Which else should free have wrought.

BANQUO   All's well.

2.1. Location: Inverness. Inner court of Macbeth's castle. **4. husbandry:** economy. **6. heavy summons:** i.e. sleepiness. **7. would not sleep:** do not want to go to bed and to sleep. **14. largess:** gifts. **offices:** kitchens and other household departments. **16. shut up:** concluded. **17. In:** i.e. with an expression of. **18. defect:** deficiency. **19. free:** fully, without limitation.

I dreamt last night of the three weïrd sisters: 20
To you they have show'd some truth.
MACBETH   I think not of them;
Yet when we can entreat an hour to serve,
We would spend it in some words upon that business,
If you would grant the time.
BANQUO   At your kind'st leisure.
MACBETH If you shall cleave to my consent, when 'tis, 25
It shall make honor for you.
BANQUO   So I lose none
In seeking to augment it, but still keep
My bosom franchis'd and allegiance clear,
I shall be counsell'd.
MACBETH   Good repose the while!
BANQUO Thanks, sir; the like to you!   30
        Exit Banquo [with Fleance].
MACBETH Go bid thy mistress, when my drink is ready,
She strike upon the bell. Get thee to bed.
          Exit [Servant].

Is this a dagger which I see before me,
The handle toward my hand? Come, let me clutch thee:
I have thee not, and yet I see thee still.   35
Art thou not, fatal vision, sensible
To feeling as to sight? or art thou but
A dagger of the mind, a false creation,
Proceeding from the heat-oppressed brain?
I see thee yet, in form as palpable   40
As this which now I draw.
Thou marshal'st me the way that I was going,
And such an instrument I was to use.
Mine eyes are made the fools o' th' other senses,
Or else worth all the rest. I see thee still;   45
And on thy blade and dudgeon gouts of blood,
Which was not so before. There's no such thing:
It is the bloody business which informs
Thus to mine eyes. Now o'er the one half world
Nature seems dead, and wicked dreams abuse 50
The curtain'd sleep; witchcraft celebrates

---

25. clave . . . 'tis: support my cause when the time comes. **28. franchis'd:** free
from guilt. **clear:** unstained. **29. counsell'd:** willing to listen. **36. sensible:**
perceptible. **39. heat-oppressed:** fevered. **46. dudgeon:** handle. **gouts:** drops.
48. informs: creates shapes. **49. half world:** hemisphere. **50. abuse:** deceive.

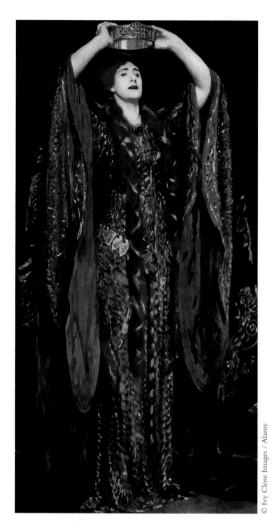

Pl. 1. The English actress Ellen Terry as Lady Macbeth (1889) in a costume designed for Henry Irving's production at the Lyceum Theatre in 1888. Painted by the American artist John Singer Sargent (1856-1925). Sargent captures a striking combination of anguish and ambition in Terry's eyes. He also captures the dramatic impact of the dress designed by Terry, her costume consultant Alice Comyns-Carr and her dressmaker. Their design depicts Lady Macbeth as a diabolical warrior-queen: elaborately-embroidered silk was "sewn all over with real green beetle wings," to "look as much like soft chain armour as [possible], and yet have something that would give the appearance of the scales of a serpent" (Comyns-Carr 211).

Pl. 2. *The Three Witches, or the Weird Sisters* (after 1783). Among the most famous illustrations of Shakespeare's witches, painted by Henry Fuseli (1741–1825), an artist who specialized in the supernatural. With their fierce focus and coordinated gestures, these witches are clearly the powerful prophetic agents of the first acts of *Macbeth*. The indistinct, smoky atmosphere that surrounds them evokes the infected Scottish climate of "fog and filthy air" through which their influence moves.

Pl. 3. The Three Sangomas (Witches), in ritual dance. *uMabatha / The Zulu Macbeth*. Shakespeare's Globe Theatre, April 2001. In this adaptation by Welcome Msomi, first staged in the early 1970s, Msomi reimagines the witches as sangomas, or shamans. Part of a long tradition of political adaptations of the play, *uMabatha* sets the story of *Macbeth* in nineteenth century South Africa, a period of tribal warfare and emerging nation-states.

Pale Hecat's off'rings; and wither'd Murther,
Alarum'd by his sentinel, the wolf,
Whose howl's his watch, thus with his stealthy pace,
With Tarquin's ravishing [strides], towards his design   55
Moves like a ghost. Thou [sure] and firm-set earth,
Hear not my steps, which [way they] walk, for fear
The very stones prate of my whereabout,
And take the present horror from the time,
Which now suits with it. Whiles I threat, he lives: 60
Words to the heat of deeds too cold breath gives.

                                  A bell rings.

I go, and it is done; the bell invites me.
Hear it not, Duncan, for it is a knell,
That summons thee to heaven or to hell.   *Exit.*

SCENE 2

Enter LADY [MACBETH].

LADY MACBETH That which hath made them drunk hath made me
    bold;
What hath quench'd them hath given me fire. Hark! Peace!
It was the owl that shriek'd, the fatal bellman,
Which gives the stern'st good-night. He is about it:
The doors are open; and the surfeited grooms   5
Do mock their charge with snores. I have drugg'd their possets,
That death and nature do contend about them,
Whether they live or die.
MACBETH [*Within.*]   Who's there? What ho?
LADY MACBETH Alack, I am afraid they have awak'd,
And 'tis not done; th' attempt, and not the deed,   10
Confounds us. Hark! I laid their daggers ready,

---

52. Pale Hecat's off'rings: its rites to Hecate (goddess of witchcraft and also of the moon, hence "pale"). **53. Alarum'd:** given the signal for action. **54. watch:** watchword (like the announcement of the hour called out by a watchman). **55. Tarquin:** ravisher of Lucrece. **design:** plan; figuratively, his intended victim. (KR) **58. prate:** tell, blab, scold. (KR) **59. horror:** dread, fear; (KR). 2.2. Location: Scene continues. **3. fatal bellman:** night watchman who rang a bell at midnight outside the cell of prisoners scheduled for execution in the morning. The screech owl is often thought to presage death. **5. surfeited:** filled to excess, overfed. (KR) **grooms:** servants; here the chamberlains of 1.7.63. **6. mock their charge:** make a mockery of their assigned duty. **possets:** drinks made with wine and hot milk. **10. th' attempt … deed:** the deed unsuccessfully attempted. **11. Confounds:** ruins utterly.

He could not miss 'em. Had he not resembled
My father as he slept, I had done't.

Enter MACBETH.

My husband!

MACBETH I have done the deed. Didst thou not hear a noise?

LADY MACBETH I heard the owl scream and the crickets cry.   15
Did not you speak?

MACBETH   When?

LADY MACBETH   Now.

MACBETH   As I descended?

LADY MACBETH Ay.

MACBETH

        Hark! Who lies i' th' second chamber?

LADY MACBETH Donalbain.

MACBETH   This is a sorry sight.

[*Looking on his hands.*]

LADY MACBETH A foolish thought, to say a sorry sight.

MACBETH There's one did laugh in 's sleep, and one cried,
"Murther!"   20
That they did wake each other. I stood and heard them;
But they did say their prayers, and address'd them
Again to sleep.

LADY MACBETH   There are two lodg'd together.

MACBETH One cried, "God bless us!" and "Amen!" the other,
As they had seen me with these hangman's hands.   25
List'ning their fear, I could not say "Amen,"
When they did say "God bless us!"

LADY MACBETH   Consider it not so deeply.

MACBETH But wherefore could not I pronounce "Amen"?
I had most need of blessing, and "Amen"
Stuck in my throat.

LADY MACBETH   These deeds must not be thought   30
After these ways; so, it will make us mad.

MACBETH Methought I heard a voice cry, "Sleep no more!
Macbeth does murther sleep"—the innocent sleep,
Sleep that knits up the ravell'd sleave of care,
The death of each day's life, sore labor's bath,   35
Balm of hurt minds, great nature's second course,
Chief nourisher in life's feast.

---

22. address'd them: i.e. settled down. **25. hangman's.** His hands would
be bloody after quartering his victim. **30. thought After:** thought about.
34. knits . . . sleave: straightens out the tangled skein.

LADY MACBETH   What do you mean?
MACBETH Still it cried, "Sleep no more!" to all the house;
"Glamis hath murther'd sleep, and therefore Cawdor
Shall sleep no more —Macbeth shall sleep no more."   40
LADY MACBETH Who was it that thus cried? Why, worthy thane,
You do unbend your noble strength, to think
So brain-sickly of things. Go get some water,
And wash this filthy witness from your hand.
Why did you bring these daggers from the place?   45
They must lie there. Go carry them, and smear
The sleepy grooms with blood.
MACBETH   I'll go no more.
I am afraid to think what I have done;
Look on't again I dare not.
LADY MACBETH   Infirm of purpose!
Give me the daggers. The sleeping and the dead   50
Are but as pictures; 'tis the eye of childhood
That fears a painted devil. If he do bleed,
I'll gild the faces of the grooms withal,
For it must seem their guilt.   *Exit. Knock within.*
MACBETH   Whence is that knocking?
How is't with me, when every noise appalls me?   55
What hands are here? Hah! they pluck out mine eyes.
Will all great Neptune's ocean wash this blood
Clean from my hand? No; this my hand will rather
The multitudinous seas incarnadine,
Making the green one red.   60

Enter LADY [MACBETH].

LADY MACBETH My hands are of your color; but I shame
To wear a heart so white. (*Knock.*) I hear a knocking
At the south entry. Retire we to our chamber.
A little water clears us of this deed;
How easy is it then! Your constancy   65
Hath left you unattended. (*Knock.*) Hark, more knocking.
Get on your night-gown, lest occasion call us
And show us to be watchers. Be not lost

---

42. unbend: loosen, let go slack. **44. witness:** evidence. **53. gild.** Blood was
often called golden. See 2.3.118. Note the punning resonance with *guilt* in the next
line (KR). **59. multitudinous seas:** multitudes of seas. **incarnadine:** turn blood-
red. **60. one red:** completely red. **65. constancy:** firmness, determination (KR).
66. left you unattended: i.e. deserted you. **67. night-gown:** dressing gown.
68. watchers: people who have stayed up.

So poorly in your thoughts. 69
MACBETH To know my deed, 'twere best not know myself. *Knock.*
Wake Duncan with thy knocking! I would thou couldst! *Exeunt.*

SCENE 3

Enter a PORTER. *Knocking within.*

PORTER Here's a knocking indeed! If a man were
porter of Hell Gate, he should have old turning the
key. (*Knock.*) Knock, knock, knock! Who's there,
i' th' name of Belzebub? Here's a farmer, that hang'd
himself on th' expectation of plenty. Come in time!   5
Have napkins enow about you, here you'll sweat for't.
(*Knock.*) Knock, knock! Who's there, in th' other
devil's name? Faith, here's an equivocator, that could
swear in both the scales against either scale, who committed treason enough for God's sake, yet could   10
not equivocate to heaven. O, come in, equivocator.
(*Knock.*) Knock, knock, knock! Who's there? Faith,
here's an English tailor come hither for stealing
out of a French hose. Come in, tailor, here you may
roast your goose. (*Knock.*) Knock, knock! Never   15
at quiet! What are you? But this place is too
cold for hell. I'll devil-porter it no further. I had
thought to have let in some of all professions that go

70. To . . . myself: if I am to come to terms with what I have done, I shall need
to avoid self-scrutiny (?) or if not being lost in my thoughts means seeing clearly
what I have done, I'd better remain lost in my thoughts (?).   2.3. Location: Scene
continues.   2. old: plenty of.   4–5. Belzebub: a devil. (KR) farmer . . . plenty:
i.e. one who had hoarded grain to sell at high prices and foresaw his ruin when
the prospect of plentiful crops threatened to bring the prices down.   5. Come in
time: opportunely arrived.   6. napkins: handkerchiefs. here you'll sweat: one
expects heat and heavy labor in hell.   7–8. other devil's name. He cannot remember the name of a second devil. Faith: by my faith. (KR)   8. equivocator.
A reference to Jesuits, and particularly to Father Garnet, who claimed the right to
make ambiguous answers when under examination so as not to incriminate himself. The word was current during the investigation that followed the Gunpowder
Plot of 1605, for which Garnet was put on trial in 1606. (KR)   9. both . . . scale:
either scale (of Justice) against the other.   14. French hose: French breeches. There
were two kinds, one loose, the other tight. Presumably the tailor stole cloth from the
supply brought to him by a customer for making the former. Or perhaps, relying
too much on his skill, he tried it on the latter and so was found out. In either case,
the phrase plays on the proverbial English weakness for French fashions (cf Boorde,
pp. 152, Sources and Contexts section. (KR)   15. roast your goose: heat your
iron.   17. I'll devil-porter it: i.e., I'll stop play-acting the Porter at Hell's gate, a
role familiar from medieval drama. (KR)

the primrose way to th' everlasting bonfire.   (*Knock.*)
Anon, anon! [*Opens the gate.*] I pray you remember   20
the porter.

Enter MACDUFF *and* LENNOX.

MACDUFF Was it so late, friend, ere you went to bed,
That you do lie so late?
PORTER Faith, sir, we were carousing till the second
cock; and drink, sir, is a great provoker of three things.   25
MACDUFF What three things does drink especially pro-
voke?
PORTER Marry, sir, nose-painting, sleep, and urine.
Lechery, sir, it provokes, and unprovokes: it provokes
the desire, but it takes away the performance. There-   30
fore much drink may be said to be an equivocator
with lechery: it makes him, and it mars him; it sets him
on, and it takes him off; it persuades him, and dis-
heartens him; makes him stand to, and not stand to; in
conclusion, equivocates him in a sleep, and giving him   35
the lie, leaves him.
MACDUFF I believe drink gave thee the lie last night.
PORTER That it did, sir, i' the very throat on me; but
I requited him for his lie, and (I think) being too strong
for him, though he took up my legs sometime, yet I   40
made a shift to cast him.
MACDUFF Is thy master stirring?

Enter MACBETH.

Our knocking has awak'd him; here he comes.
LENNOX Good morrow, noble sir.
MACBETH   Good morrow, both.
MACDUFF Is the King stirring, worthy thane?
MACBETH   Not yet.   45
MACDUFF He did command me to call timely on him,
I have almost slipp'd the hour.

24–25. the second cock: i.e. 3 a.m.   **28. Marry:** indeed (originally, the name
of the Virgin Mary used as an oath). **Nose-painting:** reddened nose, lechery.
35. equivocates . . . sleep: deceives him in a dream.   **35–36. giving . . . lie.** The
passage puns on at least three senses of *give one the lie:* (1) call one a liar; (2) lay
one out flat (copulating or passed out); (3) cause one to urinate (*lie* = *lye*, slang
for "urine").   **38–41. That . . . him.** These lines describe the effects of too much
drink in terms of a wrestling match.   **41. made a shift:** managed. **cast:** (1) throw
off; (2) vomit.   **46. timely:** early.   **47. slipp'd the hour:** arrived late. (KR)

MACBETH   I'll bring you to him.
MACDUFF I know this is a joyful trouble to you;
  But yet 'tis one.
MACBETH The labor we delight in physics pain.   50
  This is the door.
MACDUFF   I'll make so bold to call,
  For 'tis my limited service.   *Exit Macduff.*
LENNOX Goes the King hence to-day?
MACBETH   He does; he did appoint so.
LENNOX The night has been unruly. Where we lay,
  Our chimneys were blown down, and (as they say)   55
  Lamentings heard i' th' air; strange screams of death,
  And prophesying, with accents terrible,
  Of dire combustion and confus'd events
  New hatch'd to th' woeful time. The obscure bird
  Clamor'd the livelong night. Some say, the earth   60
  Was feverous, and did shake.
MACBETH   'Twas a rough night.
LENNOX My young remembrance cannot parallel
  A fellow to it.

Enter MACDUFF.

MACDUFF O horror, horror, horror! Tongue nor heart
  Cannot conceive nor name thee!
MACBETH *and* LENNOX   What's the matter?   65
MACDUFF Confusion now hath made his masterpiece!
  Most sacrilegious murther hath broke ope
  The Lord's anointed temple, and stole thence
  The life o' th' building!
MACBETH   What is't you say—the life?
LENNOX Mean you his Majesty?   70
MACDUFF Approach the chamber, and destroy your sight
  With a new Gorgon. Do not bid me speak;
  See, and then speak yourselves.
                            Exeunt Macbeth and Lennox.
                      Awake, awake!
Ring the alarum-bell! Murther and treason!

---

50. The labor . . . physics pain: the pleasure we take in labor of some kinds
cures it of laboriousness (to **physic** = to heal). (KR) **52. limited:** appointed.
58. combustion: tumult. **59. obscure bird:** bird of darkness, i.e. owl.
61. feverous. Referring to the chills and fever of ague. **66. Confusion:** utter
ruin. **68. Lord's anointed temple:** i.e. body of the King. **72. Gorgon:** i.e.
Medusa, who turned to stone anyone who looked at her face.

Banquo and Donalbain! Malcolm, awake!   75
Shake off this downy sleep, death's counterfeit,
And look on death itself! Up, up, and see
The great doom's image! Malcolm! Banquo!
As from your graves rise up, and walk like sprites,
To countenance this horror! Ring the bell.   80
                                                    Bell rings.

Enter LADY [MACBETH].

LADY MACBETH What's the business,
That such a hideous trumpet calls to parley
The sleepers of the house? Speak, speak!
MACDUFF   O gentle lady,
'Tis not for you to hear what I can speak:
The repetition in a woman's ear   85
Would murder as it fell.

Enter BANQUO.

                        O Banquo, Banquo,
Our royal master's murther'd!
LADY MACBETH   Woe, alas!
What, in our house?
BANQUO   Too cruel any where.
Dear Duff, I prithee contradict thyself,
And say, it is not so.   90

Enter MACBETH, LENNOX, ROSSE

MACBETH Had I but died an hour before this chance,
I had liv'd a blessed time; for from this instant
There's nothing serious in mortality:
All is but toys: renown and grace is dead,
The wine of life is drawn, and the mere lees   95
Is left this vault to brag of.

Enter MALCOLM *and* DONALBAIN.

DONALBAIN What is amiss?
MACBETH   You are, and do not know't.

---

78. great doom's image: exact likeness of Doomsday.   **79. sprites:** spirits, ghosts.
(KR)   **80. countenance:** (1) accord with; (2) behold; (3) express it sympatheti-
cally on your own face. (KR)   **85. repetition:** report.   **93. serious in mortality:** worthwhile in human life.   **94. toys:** trifles.   **95. drawn...lees:** comparing a
corpse to a vessel emptied (*drawn*) of liquor (distillation, spirits), leaving only dregs,
or sediment (*lees*). (KR)

The spring, the head, the fountain of your blood
Is stopp'd, the very source of it is stopp'd.
MACDUFF Your royal father's murther'd.
MALCOLM   O, by whom?   100
LENNOX Those of his chamber, as it seem'd, had done't.
Their hands and faces were all badg'd with blood;
So were their daggers, which unwip'd we found
Upon their pillows. They star'd and were distracted;
No man's life was to be trusted with them.   105
MACBETH O, yet I do repent me of my fury,
That I did kill them.
MACDUFF   Wherefore did you so?
MACBETH Who can be wise, amaz'd, temp'rate, and furious,
Loyal, and neutral, in a moment? No man.
Th' expedition of my violent love   110
Outrun the pauser, reason. Here lay Duncan,
His silver skin lac'd with his golden blood,
And his gash'd stabs look'd like a breach in nature
For ruin's wasteful entrance; there, the murtherers,
Steep'd in the colors of their trade, their daggers   115
Unmannerly breech'd with gore. Who could refrain,
That had a heart to love, and in that heart
Courage to make 's love known?
LADY MACBETH   Help me hence, ho!
MACDUFF Look to the lady.
MALCOLM [Aside to Donalbain.] Why do we hold our tongues,
That most may claim this argument for ours?   120
DONALBAIN [Aside to Malcolm] What should be spoken here,
        where our fate,
Hid in an auger-hole, may rush and seize us?
Let's away,
Our tears are not yet brew'd.
MALCOLM [Aside to Donalbain.] Nor our strong sorrow
Upon the foot of motion.

---

96. vault: (1) wine vault; (2) world (for which the sky is a vaulted roof).
98. spring, head, fountain. All three words mean "source."   **102. badg'd:** marked.
108. amaz'd: bewildered.   **110. expedition:** haste.   **111. pauser:** i.e. more deliberate mover.   **113. breach in nature:** gap in the defenses of life, violation of
natural order. (KR)   **114. wasteful:** destructive.   **115. colors:** (1) badge, insignia;
(2) redness (of blood). (KR)   **116. Unmannerly:** immoderately, improperly. (KR)
breech'd: covered, as if with breeches.   **120. argument:** subject, topic.   **122. Hid
. . . auger-hole:** concealed in some unsuspected cranny.   **124. Our . . . brew'd:** i.e.
we haven't yet time for weeping.   **125. Upon . . . motion:** ready to act.

BANQUO   Look to the lady.   125
                           [*Lady Macbeth is carried out.*]
And when we have our naked frailties hid,
That suffer in exposure, let us meet
And question this most bloody piece of work,
To know it further. Fears and scruples shake us.
In the great hand of God I stand, and thence   130
Against the undivulg'd pretense I fight
Of treasonous malice.
MACDUFF   And so do I.
ALL   So all.
MACBETH Let's briefly put on manly readiness,
And meet i' th' hall together.
ALL   Well contented.
             Exeunt [*all but Malcolm and Donalbain*].
MALCOLM What will you do? Let's not consort with them;   135
To show an unfelt sorrow is an office
Which the false man does easy. I'll to England.
DONALBAIN To Ireland, I; our separated fortune
Shall keep us both the safer. Where we are,
There's daggers in men's smiles; the near in blood,   140
The nearer bloody.
MALCOLM   This murtherous shaft that's shot
Hath not yet lighted, and our safest way
Is to avoid the aim. Therefore to horse,
And let us not be dainty of leave-taking,
But shift away. There's warrant in that theft   145
Which steals itself, when there's no mercy left.
                           Exeunt.

SCENE 4

Enter ROSSE *with an* OLD MAN.

OLD MAN Threescore and ten I can remember well,
Within the volume of which time I have seen

---

126. frailties hid: bodies clothed. **128. question:** discuss. **129. scruples:** doubts, suspicions. **130. In . . . hand:** i.e. under . . . protection. **131. undivulg'd pretense:** secret design. **132. malice:** enmity. **133. briefly:** quickly. **readiness:** i.e. dress. **140. near:** nearer (an older comparative form than *nearer*). **141. The nearer bloody:** i.e. the greater the danger of murder. **142. lighted:** i.e. spent its force. **144. dainty of:** particular about. **145. shift away:** quietly disappear. **warrant:** justification. **146. steals itself:** goes away stealthily.

Hours dreadful and things strange; but this sore night
Hath trifled former knowings.
ROSSE   Ha, good father,
Thou seest the heavens, as troubled with man's act,   5
Threatens his bloody stage. By th' clock 'tis day,
And yet dark night strangles the travelling lamp.
Is't night's predominance, or the day's shame,
That darkness does the face of earth entomb,
When living light should kiss it?
OLD MAN   'Tis unnatural,   10
Even like the deed that's done. On Tuesday last,
A falcon, tow'ring in her pride of place,
Was by a mousing owl hawk'd at, and kill'd.
ROSSE And Duncan's horses (a thing most strange and certain),
Beauteous and swift, the minions of their race,   15
Turn'd wild in nature, broke their stalls, flung out,
Contending 'gainst obedience, as they would make
War with mankind.
OLD MAN   'Tis said, they eat each other.
ROSSE They did so—to th' amazement of mine eyes
That look'd upon't.

Enter MACDUFF.

                         Here comes the good Macduff.   20
How goes the world, sir, now?
MACDUFF   Why, see you not?
ROSSE Is't known who did this more than bloody deed?
MACDUFF Those that Macbeth hath slain.
ROSSE   Alas the day,
What good could they pretend?
MACDUFF   They were suborned.
Malcolm and Donalbain, the King's two sons,   25
Are stol'n away and fled, which puts upon them
Suspicion of the deed.
ROSSE   'Gainst nature still!

2.4. Location: Inverness. Outside Macbeth's castle.   **3. sore:** grievous, dreadful.   **4. trifled former knowings:** made earlier experiences seem trifling.
5. heavens. With play on the theatrical sense "roof over the stage," beginning
a figure continued in *act* and *stage*.   **7. lamp:** torch, i.e. sun.   **12. tow'ring . . .
place:** circling upward to the highest pitch of her flight.   **13. mousing:** i.e. whose
natural prey is small creatures on the ground.   **15. minions:** darlings, finest speci-
mens.   **18. eat:** ate (pronounced *et*).   **24. What . . . pretend:** i.e. what could they
have hoped to gain by it. **suborned:** bribed.

Thriftless ambition, that will ravin up
Thine own live's means! Then 'tis most like
The sovereignty will fall upon Macbeth.   30
MACDUFF He is already nam'd, and gone to Scone
   To be invested.
ROSSE   Where is Duncan's body?
MACDUFF Carried to Colmekill,
   The sacred store-house of his predecessors
   And guardian of their bones.
ROSSE   Will you to Scone?   35
MACDUFF No, cousin, I'll to Fife.
ROSSE   Well, I will thither.
MACDUFF Well, may you see things well done there: adieu,
   Lest our old robes sit easier than our new!
ROSSE Farewell, father.
OLD MAN God's benison go with you, and with those   40
   That would make good of bad, and friends of foes!

                                                     Exeunt omnes.

---

28. ravin: devour ravenously.   **29. live's:** life's.   **31. nam'd:** chosen. **Scone:** site of
the coronation of Scottish kings.   **33. Colmekill:** Iona, where Scottish kings were
then buried.   **36. Fife:** Macduff is Thane of Fife.   **40. benison:** blessing.

Act 3

SCENE I

Enter BANQUO.

BANQUO Thou hast it now: King, Cawdor, Glamis, all,
　As the weïrd women promis'd, and I fear
　Thou play'dst most foully for't; yet it was said
　It should not stand in thy posterity,
　But that myself should be the root and father　　　　5
　Of many kings. If there come truth from them—
　As upon thee, Macbeth, their speeches shine—
　Why, by the verities on thee made good,
　May they not be my oracles as well,
　And set me up in hope? But hush, no more.　　　　10

　　　Sennet sounded. Enter MACBETH *as King*, LADY
　　[MACBETH *as Queen*], LENNOX, ROSSE, LORDS, *and*
　　　　　　ATTENDANTS.

MACBETH Here's our chief guest.
LADY MACBETH　　　　　　　If he had been forgotten,
　It had been as a gap in our great feast,
　And all-thing unbecoming.
MACBETH To-night we hold a solemn supper, sir,
　And I'll request your presence.
BANQUO　　　　　　　　Let your Highness　　　15
　Command upon me, to the which my duties
　Are with a most indissoluble tie
　For ever knit.
MACBETH　　　　Ride you this afternoon?
BANQUO　　　　　　　　　　　Ay, my good lord.
MACBETH We should have else desir'd your good advice　　20

3.1. Location: Forres. The palace.　**4. posterity:** descendants. (KR)　**7. As:** i.e. as
may well be since. **shine:** i.e. are brilliantly fulfilled.　**10 s.d. Sennet:** trumpet call.
13. all-thing: wholly.　**14. solemn:** formal.　**16. to the which:** i.e. to which
command.

(Which still hath been both grave and prosperous)
In this day's council; but we'll take to-morrow.
Is't far you ride?
BANQUO As far, my lord, as will fill up the time
'Twixt this and supper. Go not my horse the better,   25
I must become a borrower of the night
For a dark hour or twain.
MACBETH   Fail not our feast.
BANQUO My lord, I will not.
MACBETH We hear our bloody cousins are bestow'd
In England and in Ireland, not confessing   30
Their cruel parricide, filling their hearers
With strange invention. But of that to-morrow,
When therewithal we shall have cause of state
Craving us jointly. Hie you to horse; adieu,
Till you return at night. Goes Fleance with you?   35
BANQUO Ay, my good lord. Our time does call upon 's.
MACBETH I wish your horses swift and sure of foot;
And so I do command you to their backs.
Farewell.   *Exit Banquo.*
Let every man be master of his time   40
Till seven at night. To make society
The sweeter welcome, we will keep ourself
Till supper-time alone; while then, God be with you!
                    Exeunt Lords [with Lady Macbeth and others.
                    Manent Macbeth and a Servant].
Sirrah, a word with you. Attend those men
Our pleasure?   45
SERVANT They are, my lord, without the palace gate.
MACBETH Bring them before us.   *Exit Servant.*
                    To be thus is nothing,
But to be safely thus. Our fears in Banquo
Stick deep, and in his royalty of nature
Reigns that which would be fear'd. 'Tis much he dares,   50
And to that dauntless temper of his mind,
He hath a wisdom that doth guide his valor

21. **still:** ever. **grave and prosperous:** weighty and profitable.   25. **Go . . . better:**
if my horse go not faster (than I expect).   29. **are bestow'd:** have taken up resi-
dence.   31. **parricide:** one who murders a relative or ruler. (KR)   33-34. **cause . . .
jointly:** official business requiring our joint attention.   38. **commend:** commit,
entrust.   43. **while:** until.   44. **Sirrah:** term of address used to inferiors.
47. **thus:** i.e. king.   48. **in:** concerning.   49. **royalty of nature:** natural kingli-
ness.   50. **would:** must.   51. **to:** in addition to.

To act in safety. There is none but he
Whose being I do fear; and under him
My Genius is rebuk'd, as it is said   55
Mark Antony's was by Caesar. He chid the sisters
When first they put the name of king upon me,
And bade them speak to him; then prophet-like
They hail'd him father to a line of kings.
Upon my head they plac'd a fruitless crown,   60
And put a barren sceptre in my gripe,
Thence to be wrench'd with an unlineal hand,
No son of mine succeeding. If't be so,
For Banquo's issue have I fil'd my mind,
For them the gracious Duncan have I murther'd,   65
Put rancors in the vessel of my peace
Only for them, and mine eternal jewel
Given to the common enemy of man,
To make them kings—the seeds of Banquo kings!
Rather than so, come fate into the list,   70
And champion me to th' utterance! Who's there?

      Enter SERVANT *and two* MURTHERERS.

Now go to the door, and stay there till we call.

                                Exit Servant.
Was it not yesterday we spoke together?
[BOTH] MURDERERS It was, so please your Highness.
MACBETH   Well then, now
Have you consider'd of my speeches?—know   75
That it was he in the times past which held you
So under fortune, which you thought had been
Our innocent self? This I made good to you
In our last conference, pass'd in probation with you:
How you were borne in hand, how cross'd, the instruments,   80
Who wrought with them, and all things else that might
To half a soul and to a notion craz'd
Say, "Thus did Banquo."

---

55. Genius: guardian spirit. **rebuk'd:** daunted. **56. Caesar:** Octavius Caesar. See *Antony and Cleopatra,* 2.3.19–38. **chid:** chided. **61. gripe:** grip, grasp. **62. with:** by. **unlineal:** from another family line. **64. fil'd:** defiled. **65. gracious:** good. **67. eternal jewel:** i.e. immortal soul. **68. common . . . man:** the devil. **70. list:** lists, arena. **71. champion me:** contend with me as an opposing champion. **to th' utterance:** to the end (French *a outrance*), i.e. until I perish or fate is thwarted. **77. under:** out of favor with. **79. pass'd in probation:** reviewed and proved true. **80. borne in hand:** deceived. **cross'd:** thwarted. **82. To:** even to. **notion:** mind.

1. MURDERER   You made it known to us.

MACBETH I did so; and went further, which is now
Our point of second meeting. Do you find   85
Your patience so predominant in your nature
That you can let this go? Are you so gospell'd,
To pray for this good man, and for his issue,
Whose heavy hand hath bow'd you to the grave,
And beggar'd yours for ever?

1. MURDERER   We are men, my liege.

MACBETH Ay, in the catalogue ye go for men,   91
As hounds and greyhounds, mungrels, spaniels, curs,
Shoughs, water-rugs, and demi-wolves are clipt
All by the name of dogs; the valued file
Distinguishes the swift, the slow, the subtle,   95
The house-keeper, the hunter, every one,
According to the gift which bounteous nature
Hath in him clos'd; whereby he does receive
Particular addition, from the bill
That writes them all alike: and so of men.   100
Now, if you have a station in the file,
Not i' th' worst rank of manhood, say't,
And I will put that business in your bosoms,
Whose execution takes your enemy off,
Grapples you to the heart and love of us,   105
Who wear our health but sickly in his life,
Which in his death were perfect.

2. MURDERER   I am one, my liege,
Whom the vile blows and buffets of the world
Hath so incens'd that I am reckless what
I do to spite the world.

1. MURDERER   And I another,   110
So weary with disasters, tugg'd with fortune,
That I would set my life on any chance,
To mend it, or be rid on't.

MACBETH   Both of you
Know Banquo was your enemy.

---

87. gospell'd: under the spell of the Gospel.   **91. catalogue:** comprehensive listing.
go for: are entered as.   **93. Shoughs:** shaggy lap-dogs. **water-rugs:** long-haired
water-dogs. **demi-wolves:** hybrids bred of dogs and wolves. **clipt:** called.   **94. valued file:** list which specifies values.   **96. house-keeper:** watchdog.   **98. clos'd:**
enclosed.   **99. addition:** title, description. **from:** in contrast with.   **100. writes . . .
alike:** lists them all together indiscriminately.   **106. in his life:** while he lives.
111. tugg'd with: pulled about by.   **112. set:** stake.

[BOTH] MURDERERS   True, my lord.
MACBETH So is he mine; and in such bloody distance,   115
  That every minute of his being thrusts
  Against my near'st of life; and though I could
  With barefac'd power sweep him from my sight,
  And bid my will avouch it, yet I must not,
  For certain friends that are both his and mine,   120
  Whose loves I may not drop, but wail his fall
  Who I myself struck down. And thence it is
  That I to your assistance do make love,
  Masking the business from the common eye
  For sundry weighty reasons.
2. MURDERER   We shall, my lord,   125
  Perform what you command us.
1. MURDERER   Though our lives—
MACBETH Your spirits shine through you. Within this hour, at most,
  I will advise you where to plant yourselves,
  Acquaint you with the perfect spy o' th' time,
  The moment on't, for't must be done to-night,   130
  And something from the palace; always thought
  That I require a clearness: and with him—
  To leave no rubs nor botches in the work—
  Fleance his son, that keeps him company,
  Whose absence is no less material to me   135
  Than is his father's, must embrace the fate
  Of that dark hour. Resolve yourselves apart,
  I'll come to you anon.
[BOTH] MURDERERS   We are resolv'd, my lord.
MACBETH I'll call upon you straight; abide within.
                                        [*Exeunt Murderers.*]
  It is concluded: Banquo, thy soul's flight,   140
  If it find heaven, must find it out to-night.   *Exit.*

---

115. distance: enmity (in fencing, the space maintained between combat-
ants).   **117. near'st of life:** most vital part, i.e. heart.   **119. avouch:** justify.
120. For: on account of.   **121. wail:** i.e. must wail.   **123. to . . . love:** woo
your aid.   **128. advise:** instruct.   **129. perfect spy:** probably, precise information (*spy* = espial, i.e. intelligence). Some see here a reference to the Third Murderer, who appears in 3.3.   **131. something from:** some distance away from.
thought: borne in mind.   **132. require a clearness:** must remain free of suspicion.
133. rubs: rough spots, imperfections.   **137. Resolve yourselves apart:** go off and
make up your minds.

SCENE 2

Enter MACBETH'S LADY *and a* SERVANT.

LADY MACBETH Is Banquo gone from court?

SERVANT Ay, madam, but returns again to-night.

LADY MACBETH Say to the King, I would attend his leisure
For a few words.

SERVANT   Madam, I will.   *Exit.*

LADY MACBETH   Nought's had, all's spent,
Where our desire is got without content;   5
'Tis safer to be that which we destroy
Than by destruction dwell in doubtful joy.

Enter MACBETH.

How now, my lord, why do you keep alone,
Of sorriest fancies your companions making,
Using those thoughts which should indeed have died   10
With them they think on? Things without all remedy
Should be without regard: what's done, is done.

MACBETH We have scorch'd the snake, not kill'd it;
She'll close and be herself, whilest our poor malice
Remains in danger of her former tooth.   15
But let the frame of things disjoint, both the worlds suffer,
Ere we will eat our meal in fear, and sleep
In the affliction of these terrible dreams
That shake us nightly. Better be with the dead,
Whom we, to gain our peace, have sent to peace,   20
Than on the torture of the mind to lie
In restless ecstasy. Duncan is in his grave;
After life's fitful fever he sleeps well.
Treason has done his worst; nor steel, nor poison,
Malice domestic, foreign levy, nothing,   25
Can touch him further.

LADY MACBETH   Come on;
Gentle my lord, sleek o'er your rugged looks,

3.2. Location: Forres. The palace. **5. content:** happiness, satisfaction. **7. doubt-ful:** apprehensive, uncertain. (KR) **9. sorriest:** most wretched. **10. Using:** entertaining. **11. without all:** beyond any possible. **12. without regard:** i.e. not thought about. **13. scorch'd:** slashed, i.e. merely wounded. **14. close:** heal. **poor malice:** feeble enmity. **15. her former tooth:** her poison fang exactly as before. **16. disjoint:** fall apart. **both . . . suffer:** heaven and earth suffer destruction. **17. Ere we will:** rather than that we should. **21. torture:** i.e. rack. **22. restless ecstasy:** a frenzy of agitation. **23. fitful:** intermittent. **27. Gentle my lord:** my noble lord. **sleek:** smooth. **rugged:** rough.

Be bright and jovial among your guests to-night.
MACBETH So shall I, love, and so, I pray, be you.
 Let your remembrance apply to Banquo,   30
 Present him eminence both with eye and tongue:
 Unsafe the while, that we
 Must lave our honors in these flattering streams,
 And make our faces vizards to our hearts,
 Disguising what they are.
LADY MACBETH   You must leave this.   35
MACBETH O, full of scorpions is my mind, dear wife!
 Thou know'st that Banquo and his Fleance lives.
LADY MACBETH But in them nature's copy not eterne.
MACBETH There's comfort yet, they are assailable.
 Then be thou jocund; ere the bat hath flown   40
 His cloister'd flight, ere to black Hecat's summons
 The shard-borne beetle with his drowsy hums
 Hath rung night's yawning peal, there shall be done
 A deed of dreadful note.
LADY MACBETH   What's to be done?
MACBETH Be innocent of the knowledge, dearest chuck, 45
 Till thou applaud the deed. Come, seeling night,
 Scarf up the tender eye of pitiful day,
 And with thy bloody and invisible hand
 Cancel and tear to pieces that great bond
 Which keeps me pale! Light thickens, and the crow 50
 Makes wing to th' rooky wood;
 Good things of day begin to droop and drowse,
 Whiles night's black agents to their preys do rouse.
 Thou marvel'st at my words, but hold thee still:
 Things bad begun make strong themselves by ill.   55
 So prithee go with me.   *Exeunt.*

---

30. apply: be given. **31. eminence:** special favor. **32–33. Unsafe . . . streams:** for the time we are unsafe, so that we must make our honors look clean by washing them in these streams of flattery. **34. vizards:** masks. **38. copy:** (1) copyhold, a lease subject to cancellation; (2) casting (from the mould used by Nature to form men). **eterne:** everlasting. **39. There's:** i.e. in that thought there is.
40. jocund: cheerful. (KR) **41. cloister'd:** circumscribed, restricted (?) or through cloisters (?). **42. shard-borne:** carried on scaly wings (?) or a variant spelling of *shard-born*, i.e. dung-bred (?). (In F1 modern *born* is usually spelled *borne*).
45. chuck: a term of endearment (from *chick*). **46. seeling:** blinding. The eyelids of falcons were sewn together (seeled) in order to tame them. **47. Scarf up:** cover. **pitiful:** compassionate. **49. bond:** Banquo's lease on life. **50. crow:** rook.
51. rooky: frequented by rooks.

SCENE 3

Enter three MURTHERERS.

1. MURDERER But who did bid thee join with us?
3. MURDERER   Macbeth.
2. MURDERER He needs not our mistrust, since he delivers
Our offices, and what we have to do,
To the direction just.
1. MURDERER   Then stand with us.
The west yet glimmers with some streaks of day;   5
Now spurs the lated traveller apace
To gain the timely inn, [and] near approaches
The subject of our watch.
3. MURDERER   Hark, I hear horses.
BANQUO (*Within.*) Give us a light there, ho!
2. MURDERER Then 'tis he; the rest
That are within the note of expectation   10
Already are i' th' court.
1. MURDERER   His horses go about.
3. MURDERER Almost a mile; but he does usually,
So all men do, from hence to th' palace gate
Make it their walk.

Enter BANQUO, *and* FLEANCE *with a torch.*

2. MURDERER   A light, a light!
3. MURDERER   'Tis he.
1. MURDERER Stand to't.   15
BANQUO It will be rain to-night.
1. MURDERER   Let it come down.
                              [*They assault Banquo.*]
BANQUO O, treachery! Fly, good Fleance, fly, fly, fly!
Thou mayst revenge. O slave!   [*Dies. Fleance escapes.*]
3. MURDERER Who did strike out the light?
1. MURDERER   Was't not the way?
3. MURDERER There's but one down; the son is fled.
2. MURDERER   We have lost   20
Best half of our affair.
1. MURDERER Well, let's away, and say how much is done.
                                              Exeunt.

3.3. Location: Forres. A park near the palace.   **2. He . . . mistrust:** we need feel
no suspicion of him (the Third Murderer).   **3. offices:** duties.   **4. To . . . just:**
precisely according to Macbeth's instructions.   **6. lated:** belated.   **10. within . . .**
expectation: on the list of expected guests.

SCENE 4

Banquet prepar'd. Enter MACBETH, LADY [MACBETH], ROSSE,
LENNOX, LORDS, *and* ATTENDANTS.

MACBETH You know your own degrees, sit down. At first
And last, the hearty welcome.
LORDS   Thanks to your Majesty.
MACBETH Ourself will mingle with society,
And play the humble host.
Our hostess keeps her state, but in best time   5
We will require her welcome.
LADY MACBETH Pronounce it for me, sir, to all our friends,
For my heart speaks they are welcome.

Enter FIRST MURTHERER [*to the door*].

MACBETH See, they encounter thee with their hearts' thanks.
Both sides are even; here I'll sit i' th' midst.   10
Be large in mirth; anon we'll drink a measure
The table round.—   [*Goes to the door.*]
There's blood upon thy face.
MURDERER   'Tis Banquo's then.
MACBETH 'Tis better thee without than he within.
Is he dispatch'd?
MURDERER   My lord, his throat is cut;   15
That I did for him.
MACBETH   Thou art the best o' th' cut-throats,
Yet he's good that did the like for Fleance.
If thou didst it, thou art the nonpareil.
MURDERER Most royal sir, Fleance is scap'd.
MACBETH Then comes my fit again. I had else been perfect,   20
Whole as the marble, founded as the rock,
As broad and general as the casing air;
But now I am cabin'd, cribb'd, confin'd, bound in
To saucy doubts and fears. But Banquo's safe?
MURDERER Ay, my good lord; safe in a ditch he bides,   25
With twenty trenched gashes on his head,
The least a death to nature.

3.4. Location: Forres. The palace.   **1. degrees:** ranks and hence order of seating.   **1–2. At . . . last:** once for all.   **5. state:** chair of state.   **6. require:** request.
9. encounter: respond to.   **11. large:** free, unrestrained.   **measure:** bumper.
14. thee . . . within: i.e. on your face than in his body.   **18. nonpareil:** best.
(KR)   **21. founded:** immovable.   **22. broad and general:** free and unconfined.
casing: enveloping.   **24. saucy:** importunate.

MACBETH   Thanks for that:
There the grown serpent lies; the worm that's fled
Hath nature that in time will venom breed,
No teeth for th' present. Get thee gone; to-morrow   30
We'll hear ourselves again.   *Exit Murderer.*
LADY MACBETH   My royal lord,
You do not give the cheer. The feast is sold
That is not often vouch'd, while 'tis a-making,
'Tis given with welcome. To feed were best at home;
From thence, the sauce to meat is ceremony,   35
Meeting were bare without it.

        Enter the GHOST OF BANQUO *and sits in Macbeth's place.*

MACBETH   Sweet remembrancer!
Now good digestion wait on appetite,
And health on both!
LENNOX   May 't please your Highness sit.
MACBETH Here had we now our country's honor roof'd,
Were the grac'd person of our Banquo present,   40
Who may I rather challenge for unkindness
Than pity for mischance.
ROSSE   His absence, sir,
Lays blame upon his promise. Please 't your Highness
To grace us with your royal company?
MACBETH The table's full.
LENNOX   Here is a place reserv'd, sir.   45
MACBETH Where?
LENNOX Here, my good lord. What is 't that moves your
        Highness?
MACBETH Which of you have done this?
LORDS   What, my good lord?
MACBETH Thou canst not say I did it; never shake
Thy gory locks at me.   50
ROSSE Gentlemen, rise, his Highness is not well.
LADY MACBETH Sit, worthy friends; my lord is often thus,
And hath been from his youth. Pray you keep seat.
The fit is momentary, upon a thought

---

28. worm: here, young serpent.   **31. hear ourselves:** confer.   **32. give the cheer:**
play the convivial host, toast the company. (KR)   **32–34. The feast . . . welcome:**
unless the guests are frequently assured of their welcome, a feast is no better than a
meal that one pays for.   **34. To feed:** i.e. simply to eat.   **35. From thence:** away
from home.   **39. honor:** nobility, nobles. **roof'd:** all under one roof.   **41. challenge
for:** charge with.   **54. upon a thought:** in a moment.

He will again be well. If much you note him, 55
You shall offend him and extend his passion.
Feed, and regard him not.—Are you a man?
MACBETH Ay, and a bold one, that dare look on that
Which might appall the devil.
LADY MACBETH   O proper stuff!
This is the very painting of your fear; 60
This is the air-drawn dagger which you said
Led you to Duncan. O, these flaws and starts
(Impostors to true fear) would well become
A woman's story at a winter's fire,
Authoriz'd by her grandam. Shame itself, 65
Why do you make such faces? When all's done,
You look but on a stool.
MACBETH   Prithee see there!
Behold! look! lo! how say you?
Why, what care I? if thou canst nod, speak too.
If charnel-houses and our graves must send 70
Those that we bury back, our monuments
Shall be the maws of kites.   [*Exit Ghost.*]
LADY MACBETH   What? quite unmann'd in folly?
MACBETH If I stand here, I saw him.
LADY MACBETH   Fie, for shame!
MACBETH Blood hath been shed ere now, i' th' olden time,
Ere humane statute purg'd the gentle weal; 75
Ay, and since too, murthers have been perform'd
Too terrible for the ear. The [time] has been,
That when the brains were out, the man would die,
And there an end; but now they rise again
With twenty mortal murthers on their crowns, 80
And push us from our stools. This is more strange
Than such a murther is.
LADY MACBETH   My worthy lord,

---

56. offend him: make him worse. **extend his passion:** prolong his attack.
59. proper: fine. **61. air-drawn:** drawn on the air (a sense supported by *painting* in line 60) or drawn through the air (supported by line 62). **62. flaws:** sudden bursts of passion (properly used of gusty winds). **63. to:** compared with. **become:** befit. **65. Authoriz'd:** told on the authority of. **67. You look...stool:** you are only looking at a stool. **70. charnel-houses:** houses for bodies. (KR). **71–72. our . . . kites:** our tombs had better be the stomachs of birds of prey, i.e. there is no point in burying the dead. **75. humane.** Elizabethan spelling did not distinguish between *human* and *humane;* many editors read *human* here, perhaps rightly. **statute:** laws. (KR) **purg'd . . . weal:** cleansed the commonwealth (weal) and made it gentle, or civilized. **80. mortal murthers:** deadly wounds. **crowns:** heads.

Your noble friends do lack you.

MACBETH   I do forget.
Do not muse at me, my most worthy friends,
I have a strange infirmity, which is nothing   85
To those that know me. Come, love and health to all,
Then I'll sit down. Give me some wine, fill full.

Enter GHOST.

I drink to th' general joy o' th' whole table,
And to our dear friend Banquo, whom we miss;
Would he were here! to all, and him, we thirst,   90
And all to all.

LORDS   Our duties, and the pledge.

MACBETH Avaunt, and quit my sight! let the earth hide thee!
Thy bones are marrowless, thy blood is cold;
Thou hast no speculation in those eyes
Which thou dost glare with!

LADY MACBETH   Think of this, good peers,   95
But as a thing of custom. 'Tis no other;
Only it spoils the pleasure of the time.

MACBETH What man dare, I dare.
Approach thou like the rugged Russian bear,
The arm'd rhinoceros, or th' Hyrcan tiger,   100
Take any shape but that, and my firm nerves
Shall never tremble. Or be alive again,
And dare me to the desert with thy sword;
If trembling I inhabit then, protest me
The baby of a girl. Hence, horrible shadow!   105
Unreal mock'ry, hence!   [*Exit Ghost.*]
                    Why, so; being gone,
I am a man again. Pray you sit still.

LADY MACBETH You have displac'd the mirth, broke the good
          meeting,
With most admir'd disorder.

MACBETH   Can such things be,

---

84. **muse:** wonder.   90. **thirst:** i.e. drink eagerly.   91. **all to all:** all good to all (?)
or let everyone drink to all (?). **the pledge:** i.e. we drink the toast you have proposed.   94. **speculation:** sight.   99. **like:** in the likeness of.   100. **arm'd:** armored.
Hyrcan: of Hyrcania, near the Caspian Sea.   101. **nerves:** sinews.   103. **the desert:**
i.e. some uninhabited place (where nobody would intervene).   104. **If . . . inhabit:**
if the body I inhabit feels fear. **protest:** proclaim.   105. **The baby . . . girl:** a baby
girl. **shadow:** ghost, imitation. (KR)   109. **admir'd:** wondered at.

And overcome us like a summer's cloud,   110
Without our special wonder? You make me strange
Even to the disposition that I owe,
When now I think you can behold such sights,
And keep the natural ruby of your cheeks,
When mine is blanch'd with fear.
ROSSE   What sights, my lord?   115
LADY MACBETH I pray you speak not. He grows worse and worse,
Question enrages him. At once, good night.
Stand not upon the order of your going,
But go at once.
LENNOX   Good night, and better health
Attend his Majesty!
LADY MACBETH   A kind good night to all!   120
                                Exeunt Lords [and Attendants].
MACBETH It will have blood, they say; blood will have blood.
Stones have been known to move and trees to speak;
Augures and understood relations have
By maggot-pies and choughs and rooks brought forth
The secret'st man of blood. What is the night?   125
LADY MACBETH Almost at odds with morning, which is which.
MACBETH How say'st thou, that Macduff denies his person
At our great bidding?
LADY MACBETH   Did you send to him, sir?
MACBETH I hear it by the way; but I will send.
There's not a one of them but in his house   130
I keep a servant fee'd. I will to-morrow
(And betimes I will) to the weïrd sisters.
More shall they speak; for now I am bent to know,
By the worst means, the worst. For mine own good
All causes shall give way. I am in blood   135
Stepp'd in so far that, should I wade no more,
Returning were as tedious as go o'er.

110. **overcome:** pass over. **like . . . cloud:** i.e. suddenly. **111–12. strange
. . . owe:** i.e. feel a stranger to the courageous man I supposed myself to be.
117. **Question enrages him:** talk aggravates his condition. **At once:** to you
all. 119. **at once:** all together. 123. **Augures:** auguries, omens. **understood
relations:** occult significances and relationships perceived. 124. **By:** by means
of. **maggot-pies and choughs:** magpies and jackdaws (which, like rooks, could
be taught to speak) **brought forth:** revealed. 125. **man of blood:** murderer.
127. **How say'st thou:** what do you think of the fact. 129. **by the way:** indirectly. 132. **betimes:** very early. 133. **bent:** determined. 135. **causes:** (other)
considerations. 136. **should I:** even if I were to. **more:** farther. 137. **were:** would
be. **go:** going.

Strange things I have in head, that will to hand,
Which must be acted ere they may be scann'd.
LADY MACBETH You lack the season of all natures, sleep.   140
MACBETH Come, we'll to sleep. My strange and self-abuse
Is the initiate fear that wants hard use:
We are yet but young in deed.   *Exeunt.*

SCENE 5

Thunder. Enter the three WITCHES, *meeting* HECAT.

1. WITCH Why, how now, Hecat? you look angerly.
HECAT Have I not reason, beldams as you are?
Saucy and overbold, how did you dare
To trade and traffic with Macbeth
In riddles and affairs of death;   5
And I, the mistress of your charms,
The close contriver of all harms,
Was never call'd to bear my part,
Or show the glory of our art?
And which is worse, all you have done   10
Hath been but for a wayward son,
Spiteful and wrathful, who (as others do)
Loves for his own ends, not for you.
But make amends now. Get you gone,
And at the pit of Acheron   15
Meet me i' th' morning; thither he
Will come to know his destiny.
Your vessels and your spells provide,
Your charms and every thing beside.
I am for th' air; this night I'll spend   20
Unto a dismal and a fatal end.
Great business must be wrought ere noon:
Upon the corner of the moon
There hangs a vap'rous drop profound,

139. ere . . . scann'd: without being properly studied.   140. season: preservative.
141. strange and self-abuse: strange self-delusion, self-estrangement (?) (KR)
142. initiate . . . use: fear felt by the beginner who lacks the experience that hardens one.   143. deed: i.e. crime.   3.5. This scene is probably spurious; see Textual Notes and Note on the Text. (KR)   Location: An open place.   2. beldams: hags.
7. close: secret.   11. wayward son: i.e. a disciple who is untrue to our teaching.   15. Acheron: a river in Hades; here, hell itself.   21. dismal: ill-boding, sinister.   24. profound: low-hanging, i.e. ready to drop off.

I'll catch it ere it come to ground;   25
And that, distill'd by magic sleights,
Shall raise such artificial sprites
As by the strength of their illusion
Shall draw him on to his confusion.
He shall spurn fate, scorn death, and bear   30
His hopes 'bove wisdom, grace, and fear;
And you all know, security
Is mortals' chiefest enemy.
Music, and a song. Sing within: "Come away, come away, etc."
Hark, I am call'd; my little spirit, see,
Sits in a foggy cloud, and stays for me.   [*Exit.*]
1. WITCH Come, let's make haste, she'll soon be back again.   36
                                                       Exeunt

SCENE 6

Enter LENNOX *and another* LORD.

LENNOX My former speeches have but hit your thoughts,
Which can interpret farther; only I say
Things have been strangely borne. The gracious Duncan
Was pitied of Macbeth; marry, he was dead.
And the right valiant Banquo walk'd too late,   5
Whom you may say (if't please you) Fleance kill'd,
For Fleance fled. Men must not walk too late.
Who cannot want the thought, how monstrous
It was for Malcolm and for Donalbain
To kill their gracious father? Damned fact!   10
How it did grieve Macbeth! Did he not straight
In pious rage the two delinquents tear,
That were the slaves of drink and thralls of sleep?
Was not that nobly done? Ay, and wisely too;
For 'twould have anger'd any heart alive   15
To hear the men deny't. So that, I say,

---

26. sleights: skills, artifice, trickery. (KR)   **27. artificial sprites:** spirits produced by magic arts.   **29. confusion:** ruin.   **32. security:** overconfidence.
33. s.d. "Come . . . etc." For this song see the Textual Notes.   3.6. Location:
Somewhere in Scotland.   **1. My former speeches:** what I have been saying.
hit: coincided with.   **2. interpret farther:** draw further inferences.   **3. borne:**
managed, carried on. **gracious:** good.   **4. of:** by. **marry . . . dead:** to be sure, that
was after he died (not before).   **8. cannot . . . thought:** i.e. can help thinking.
10. fact: deed, crime.   **12. pious:** loyal.

He has borne all things well, and I do think
That had he Duncan's sons under his key
(As, and't please heaven, he shall not), they should find
What 'twere to kill a father; so should Fleance.   20
But peace! for from broad words, and 'cause he fail'd
His presence at the tyrant's feast, I hear
Macduff lives in disgrace. Sir, can you tell
Where he bestows himself?

LORD   The [son] of Duncan
(From whom this tyrant holds the due of birth)   25
Lives in the English court, and is receiv'd
Of the most pious Edward with such grace
That the malevolence of fortune nothing
Takes from his high respect. Thither Macduff
Is gone to pray the holy king, upon his aid   30
To wake Northumberland and warlike Siward,
That by the help of these (with Him above
To ratify the work) we may again
Give to our tables meat, sleep to our nights;
Free from our feasts and banquets bloody knives;   35
Do faithful homage and receive free honors;
All which we pine for now. And this report
Hath so exasperate [the] King that he
Prepares for some attempt of war.

LENNOX   Sent he to Macduff?

LORD He did; and with an absolute "Sir, not I,"   40
The cloudy messenger turns me his back,
And hums, as who should say, "You'll rue the time
That clogs me with this answer."

LENNOX   And that well might
Advise him to a caution, t' hold what distance
His wisdom can provide. Some holy angel   45

---

19. and: if.   **21. from broad words:** because of his outspokenness.   **24. bestows himself:** has taken refuge.   **25. holds . . . birth:** withholds his birthright (the crown).   **27. pious:** saintly. **Edward:** Edward the Confessor. **grace:** favor. **28–29. That . . . respect:** i.e. that he is held in as high respect as if ill fortune had not deprived him of the kingship.   **30. upon his aid:** on Malcolm's behalf.   **34. Give . . . meat:** hold our usual feasts.   **35. Free from . . . knives:** free . . . from knives. **36. faithful:** sincere (not pretended, as now). **free:** freely given (not bought by acquiescence in evildoing).   **38. the King:** i.e. Macbeth.   **41. cloudy:** scowling. **turns me:** turns (a colloquialism).   **42. hums:** says humph. **as who:** as one who. (KR)   **43. clogs:** encumbers.   **44–45. Advise . . . provide:** warn him to keep as far out of Macbeth's way as he can contrive.

Fly to the court of England, and unfold
His message ere he come, that a swift blessing
May soon return to this our suffering country
Under a hand accurs'd!

LORD   I'll send my prayers with him.   *Exeunt.*

48–49. suffering country Under: country suffering under.

Act 4

SCENE I

Thunder. Enter the three WITCHES.

1. WITCH Thrice the brinded cat hath mew'd.
2. WITCH Thrice, and once the hedge-pig whin'd.
3. WITCH Harpier cries, "'Tis time, 'tis time."
1. WITCH Round about the cauldron go;
    In the poison'd entrails throw;   5
    Toad, that under cold stone
    Days and nights has thirty-one
    Swelt'red venom sleeping got,
    Boil thou first i' th' charmed pot.
ALL Double, double, toil and trouble;   10
    Fire burn, and cauldron bubble.
2. WITCH Fillet of a fenny snake,
    In the cauldron boil and bake;
    Eye of newt and toe of frog,
    Wool of bat and tongue of dog,   15
    Adder's fork and blind-worm's sting,
    Lizard's leg and howlet's wing,
    For a charm of pow'rful trouble,
    Like a hell-broth boil and bubble.
ALL Double, double, toil and trouble;   20
    Fire burn, and cauldron bubble.
3. WITCH Scale of dragon, tooth of wolf,
    Witch's mummy, maw and gulf
    Of the ravin'd salt-sea shark,
    Root of hemlock digg'd i' th' dark,   25
    Liver of blaspheming Jew,

4.1. Location: A cave; in the middle, a boiling cauldron. **1. brinded:** brindled, streaked. **2. hedge-pig:** hedgehog. (KR) **3. Harpier.** See note on 1.1.9–10. **8. Swelt'red:** exuded in sweaty drops. **10. Double:** (1) two-fold, twice; (2) deceive; here an incantation as important for its sound as its sense. (KR) **12. Fillet:** slice. **fenny:** inhabiting swamps. **16. fork:** forked tongue. **17. howlet's:** owlet's. **23. mummy:** medicinal substance made from a mummy. **maw and gulf:** stomach and gullet. **24. ravin'd:** glutted with prey (?) or voracious (?).

Gall of goat, and slips of yew
Sliver'd in the moon's eclipse,
Nose of Turk and Tartar's lips,
Finger of birth-strangled babe   30
Ditch-deliver'd by a drab,
Make the gruel thick and slab.
Add thereto a tiger's chawdron,
For th' ingredience of our ca'dron.
ALL Double, double, toil and trouble;   35
Fire burn, and cauldron bubble.
2. WITCH Cool it with a baboon's blood,
Then the charm is firm and good.

     Enter HECAT *and the other three* WITCHES.

HECAT O, well done! I commend your pains,
And every one shall share i' th' gains.   40
And now about the cauldron sing,
Like elves and fairies in a ring,
Enchanting all that you put in.
    Music and a song: "Black spirits, etc."   [*Exit Hecat.*]
2. WITCH By the pricking of my thumbs,
Something wicked this way comes.   [*Knocking.*]
        Open, locks,   46
        Whoever knocks!

     Enter MACBETH.

MACBETH How now, you secret, black, and midnight hags?
What is't you do?
ALL   A deed without a name.
MACBETH I conjure you, by that which you profess   50
(How e'er you come to know it), answer me:
Though you untie the winds, and let them fight
Against the churches; though the yesty waves
Confound and swallow navigation up;
Though bladed corn be lodg'd, and trees blown down; 55

---

28. Sliver'd: cut off. **29. Tartar:** Moslem inhabitant of central Asia, descended
from the Turks and Mongols; also strolling vagabond. With *blaspheming Jew* and
Turk the reference suggests archetypal foreign opponents to Christian European
culture. (KR) **31. drab:** whore. **32. slab:** sticky. **33. chawdron:** entrails.
39–43. Probably spurious. See Textual Notes. **43 s.d. "Black spirits, etc."** For
this song see the Textual Notes. **50. that . . . profess:** i.e. the demonic arts.
52. untie the winds: cf. I.3.II. (KR) **53. yesty:** yeasty, foamy. **55. bladed corn:**
ripe wheat. **lodg'd:** beaten down.

Though castles topple on their warders' heads;
Though palaces and pyramids do slope
Their heads to their foundations; though the treasure
Of nature's [germains] tumble all together,
Even till destruction sicken; answer me   60
To what I ask you.
1. WITCH   Speak.
2. WITCH   Demand.
3. WITCH   We'll answer.
1. WITCH Say, if th' hadst rather hear it from our mouths,
Or from our masters'?
MACBETH   Call 'em; let me see 'em.
1. WITCH Pour in sow's blood, that hath eaten
Her nine farrow; grease that's sweaten   65
From the murderer's gibbet throw
Into the flame.
ALL   Come high or low;
Thyself and office deftly show!

Thunder. FIRST APPARITION, *an armed Head.*

MACBETH Tell me, thou unknown power—
1. WITCH   He knows thy thought:
Hear his speech, but say thou nought.   70
1. APPARITION Macbeth! Macbeth! Macbeth! Beware Macduff,
Beware the Thane of Fife. Dismiss me. Enough.
                                                        He descends.
MACBETH What e'er thou art, for thy good caution, thanks;
Thou hast harp'd my fear aright. But one word more—
1. WITCH He will not be commanded. Here's another,   75
More potent than the first.

Thunder. SECOND APPARITION, *a bloody Child.*

2. APPARITION Macbeth! Macbeth! Macbeth!
MACBETH Had I three ears, I'ld hear thee.
2. APPARITION Be bloody, bold, and resolute: laugh to scorn
The pow'r of man; for none of woman born   80
Shall harm Macbeth.   *Descends.*

---

57. slope: bend. **59. germains:** germens, seeds; the *semines* existing in nature from which all, including man, is created. **60. sicken:** be satiated. **65. nine farrow:** litter of nine. **68 s.d. an armed Head.** Perhaps signifying the rebellion of Macduff. **74. harp'd . . . aright:** hit upon the tune my fear has been playing. **76. s.d. a bloody Child.** Recalling Macduff, "untimely ripped" from his mother's womb (see 5.8.15–16).

MACBETH Then live, Macduff; what need I fear of thee?
But yet I'll make assurance double sure,
And take a bond of fate: thou shalt not live,
That I may tell pale-hearted fear it lies,   85
And sleep in spite of thunder.

Thunder. THIRD APPARITION, *a Child crowned,
with a tree in his hand.*

What is this
That rises like the issue of a king,
And wears upon his baby-brow the round
And top of sovereignty?
ALL   Listen, but speak not to't.
3. APPARITION Be lion-mettled, proud, and take no care   90
Who chafes, who frets, or where conspirers are:
Macbeth shall never vanquish'd be until
Great Birnan wood to high Dunsinane hill
Shall come against him.   *Descend.*
MACBETH   That will never be.
Who can impress the forest, bid the tree   95
Unfix his earth-bound root? Sweet bodements! good!
Rebellious dead, rise never till the wood
Of Birnan rise, and our high-plac'd Macbeth
Shall live the lease of nature, pay his breath
To time and mortal custom. Yet my heart   100
Throbs to know one thing: tell me, if your art
Can tell so much, shall Banquo's issue ever
Reign in this kingdom?
ALL   Seek to know no more.
MACBETH I will be satisfied. Deny me this,
And an eternal curse falls on you! Let me know.   105
Why sinks that cauldron? and what noise is this?

Hoboys.

1. WITCH Show!
2. WITCH Show!

---

84. take ... fate: i.e. bind Fate to its contract by killing Macduff.   **86. s.d. a Child crowned.** Perhaps signifying Malcolm. (KR) **tree.** Foreshadowing the action of Malcolm's soldiers in cutting down and carrying boughs to Dunsinane.   **87. like:** in the likeness of. **issue:** child. (KR)   **88–89. round And top:** crown.   **95. impress:** force into service.   **96. bodements:** prophecies.   **97. Rebellious dead.** Referring, presumably, to Banquo. Many editors adopt Theobald's emendation *Rebellious head* or his conjecture *Rebellion's head*.   **99. the lease of nature:** his full span of life (i.e. he will die a natural death).   **100. mortal custom:** i.e. death that comes to everyone.   **106. noise:** music (a frequent meaning).

3. WITCH Show!
ALL Show his eyes, and grieve his heart;   110
Come like shadows, so depart.

A show of eight KINGS, *[the eighth] with a glass in his hand,*
and BANQUO *last.*

MACBETH Thou art too like the spirit of Banquo; down!
Thy crown does sear mine eyeballs. And thy hair,
Thou other gold-bound brow, is like the first.
A third is like the former. Filthy hags,   115
Why do you show me this?—A fourth? Start, eyes!
What, will the line stretch out to th' crack of doom?
Another yet? A seventh? I'll see no more.
And yet the eight appears, who bears a glass
Which shows me many more; and some I see   120
That twofold balls and treble sceptres carry.
Horrible sight! Now I see 'tis true,
For the blood-bolter'd Banquo smiles upon me,
And points at them for his.   [*Apparitions vanish.*]
What? is this so?
1. WITCH   Ay, sir, all this is so. But why   125
Stands Macbeth thus amazedly?
Come, sisters, cheer we up his sprites,
And show the best of our delights.
I'll charm the air to give a sound,
While you perform your antic round;   130
That this great king may kindly say
Our duties did his welcome pay.
                Music. The Witches dance and vanish.
MACBETH Where are they? Gone? Let this pernicious hour
Stand aye accursed in the calendar!
Come in, without there!

---

111. shadows: ghosts, shades, fictions, imitations. (KR) **111. s.d. glass:** mirror
(here, a magic one). **119. eight:** eighth. **121. twofold . . . sceptres.** James I of
England and VI of Scotland was twice crowned, at Scone and Westminster. Thus
the orb, part of the regalia, is here called "twofold." The English coronation uses
two sceptres, the Scottish, one; hence *treble sceptres,* though this may refer to the title
"King of Great Britain, France, and Ireland." Banquo was the legendary founder
of the Stuart dynasty: see Introduction. **123. blood-bolter'd:** with his hair mat-
ted with blood. **125–32.** Probably spurious. **126. amazedly:** as in a trance.
127. sprites: spirits. **130. antic round:** fantastic circular dance. **131. this great
king:** perhaps a compliment to the monarch (James I) in the audience. (KR)
132. Our . . . pay: our attentions repaid the welcome he gave us.

Enter LENNOX.

LENNOX   What's your Grace's will?   135
MACBETH   Saw you the weïrd sisters?
LENNOX   No, my lord.
MACBETH   Came they not be you?
LENNOX   No indeed, my lord.
MACBETH   Infected be the air whereon they ride,
And damn'd all those that trust them! I did hear
The galloping of horse. Who was't came by?   140
LENNOX 'Tis two or three, my lord, that bring you word
Macduff is fled to England.
MACBETH   Fled to England!
LENNOX   Ay, my good lord.
MACBETH [*Aside.*] Time, thou anticipat'st my dread exploits:
The flighty purpose never is o'ertook   145
Unless the deed go with it. From this moment
The very firstlings of my heart shall be
The firstlings of my hand. And even now,
To crown my thoughts with acts, be it thought and done:
The castle of Macduff I will surprise,   150
Seize upon Fife, give to th' edge o' th' sword
His wife, his babes, and all unfortunate souls
That trace him in his line. No boasting like a fool;
This deed I'll do before this purpose cool.
But no more sights!—Where are these gentlemen?   155
Come bring me where they are.   *Exeunt.*

SCENE 2

Enter MACDUFF'S WIFE, *her* SON, *and* ROSSE.

LADY MACDUFF   What had he done, to make him fly the land?
ROSSE   You must have patience, madam.
LADY MACDUFF   He had none;
His flight was madness. When our actions do not,
Our fears do make us traitors.

140. **horse:** horses (a common plural) or horsemen.   144. **thou anticipat'st:** you forestall. (KR)   145. **The flighty purpose:** i.e. a purpose, always fleeting. 146. **unless . . . it:** unless it is performed as soon as conceived.   147–48. **The very . . . hand:** i.e. intention shall coincide with performance. **firstlings:** first-born. 150. **surprise:** seize upon.   153. **trace:** follow.   4.2. Location: Fife. Macduff's castle.   2. **have patience:** exercise self-control.

ROSSE You know not
Whether it was his wisdom or his fear. 5
LADY MACDUFF Wisdom? to leave his wife, to leave his babes,
His mansion and his titles, in a place
From whence himself does fly? He loves us not,
He wants the natural touch; for the poor wren,
The most diminutive of birds, will fight, 10
Her young ones in her nest, against the owl.
All is the fear, and nothing is the love;
As little is the wisdom, where the flight
So runs against all reason.
ROSSE My dearest coz,
I pray you school yourself. But for your husband, 15
He is noble, wise, judicious, and best knows
The fits o' th' season. I dare not speak much further,
But cruel are the times when we are traitors,
And do not know ourselves; when we hold rumor
From what we fear, yet know not what we fear, 20
But float upon a wild and violent sea
Each way, and move. I take my leave of you;
'Shall not be long but I'll be here again.
Things at the worst will cease, or else climb upward
To what they were before. My pretty cousin, 25
Blessing upon you!
LADY MACDUFF Father'd he is, and yet he's fatherless.
ROSSE I am so much a fool, should I stay longer,
It would be my disgrace and your discomfort.
I take my leave at once. *Exit Rosse.*
LADY MACDUFF Sirrah, your father's dead, 30
And what will you do now? How will you live?
SON As birds do, mother.
LADY MACDUFF What, with worms and flies?
SON With what I get, I mean, and so do they.
LADY MACDUFF Poor bird, thou'dst never fear the net nor lime,

---

7. titles: title deeds, hence estates. **9. wants:** lacks. **natural touch:** i.e. the feeling natural to a husband and father. **14. coz:** cousin, i.e. kinswoman. **15. school:** control. **17. fits . . . season:** disturbances of the time (another use of the figure of a recurrent fever). **19. know ourselves:** recognize ourselves as such. **hold:** credit (?) or interpret (?). **20. From what we fear:** because of (or in accordance with) our fears. **22. Each . . . move.** Probably corrupt, unless Rosse in his haste breaks off his sentence (some editors read *move—*). Proposed emendations include *And each way move, And move each way, Each way it moves;* most editors adopt Dover Wilson's reading, *Each way and none.* **23. but:** before. **29. It . . . discomfort:** i.e. I should weep. **34. lime:** birdlime, a sticky substance spread to catch birds.

The pitfall nor the gin.   35
SON Why should I, mother? Poor birds they are not set for.
My father is not dead, for all your saying.
LADY MACDUFF Yes, he is dead. How wilt thou do for a father?
SON Nay, how will you do for a husband?
LADY MACDUFF Why, I can buy me twenty at any market.   40
SON Then you'll buy 'em to sell again.
LADY MACDUFF Thou speak'st with all thy wit, and yet, i' faith,
With wit enough for thee.
SON Was my father a traitor, mother?
LADY MACDUFF Ay, that he was.   45
SON What is a traitor?
LADY MACDUFF Why, one that swears and lies.
SON And be all traitors that do so?
LADY MACDUFF Every one that does so is a traitor, and
must be hang'd.   50
SON And must they all be hang'd that swear and
lie?
LADY MACDUFF Every one.
SON Who must hang them?
LADY MACDUFF Why, the honest men.   55
SON Then the liars and swearers are fools; for
there are liars and swearers enow to beat the honest
men and hang up them.
LADY MACDUFF Now God help thee, poor monkey! But
how wilt thou do for a father?   60
SON If he were dead, you'ld weep for him; if you
would not, it were a good sign that I should quickly
have a new father.
LADY MACDUFF Poor prattler, how thou talk'st!

Enter a MESSENGER.

MESSENGER Bless you, fair dame! I am not to you known,   65
Though in your state of honor I am perfect.
I doubt some danger does approach you nearly.
If you will take a homely man's advice,
Be not found here; hence with your little ones.

---

35. **pitfall. . . gin:** trap . . . snare.   **36. Poor:** little, insubstantial. (KR)   **43. With
. . . thee:** i.e. you are quite clever enough for a child.   **47. swears and lies:** swears
an oath and breaks it (doubtless with another allusion to the "equivocation" of
Father Garnet and others; cf. 2.3.8).   **51. swear:** use profanity (as lines 56–58
make clear).   **66. in . . . perfect:** I know well your honored position.   **67. doubt:**
fear.   **68. homely:** plain.

To fright you thus, methinks I am too savage;   70
To do worse to you were fell cruelty,
Which is too nigh your person. Heaven preserve you!
I dare abide no longer.   *Exit Messenger.*
LADY MACDUFF   Whither should I fly?
I have done no harm. But I remember now
I am in this earthly world—where to do harm   75
Is often laudable, to do good sometime
Accounted dangerous folly. Why then, alas,
Do I put up that womanly defense,
To say I have done no harm?

                    Enter MURTHERERS.

                    What are these faces?
[1.] MURDERER Where is your husband?   80
LADY MACDUFF I hope, in no place so unsanctified
Where such as thou mayst find him.
[1.] MURDERER   He's a traitor.
SON Thou li'st, thou shag-ear'd villain!
[1.] MURDERER   What, you egg! [*Stabbing him.*]
Young fry of treachery!
SON   He has kill'd me, mother: 84
Run away, I pray you!   [*Dies.*]

        Exit [*Lady Macduff*] *crying "Murther!"*
        [*and pursued by the Murderers*].

                SCENE 3

            Enter MALCOLM *and* MACDUFF.

MALCOLM Let us seek out some desolate shade, and there
Weep our sad bosoms empty.
MACDUFF   Let us rather
Hold fast the mortal sword, and like good men
Bestride our downfall birthdom. Each new morn
New widows howl, new orphans cry, new sorrows   5

---

70. To fright: i.e. even to frighten.   **71. To do worse:** i.e. to do you actual harm.
fell: savage.   **72. Which:** i.e. such cruelty.   **78. womanly:** womanish.   **83. shag-
ear'd:** with shaggy hair about your ears. Some editors prefer Steevens' conjecture
shag-hair'd.   **84. fry:** spawn.   4.3. Location: England. Before King Edward's palace.
3. mortal: deadly.   **4. Bestride:** stand over protectively. **downfall:** downfallen.
birthdom: native land.

Strike heaven on the face, that it resounds
As if it felt with Scotland, and yell'd out
Like syllable of dolor.
MALCOLM   What I believe, I'll wail,
What know, believe; and what I can redress,
As I shall find the time to friend, I will.   10
What you have spoke, it may be so perchance.
This tyrant, whose sole name blisters our tongues,
Was once thought honest; you have lov'd him well;
He hath not touch'd you yet. I am young, but something
You may discern of him through me, and wisdom   15
To offer up a weak, poor, innocent lamb
T' appease an angry god.
MACDUFF I am not treacherous.
MALCOLM   But Macbeth is.
A good and virtuous nature may recoil
In an imperial charge. But I shall crave your pardon;   20
That which you are, my thoughts cannot transpose:
Angels are bright still, though the brightest fell.
Though all things foul would wear the brows of grace,
Yet grace must still look so.
MACDUFF   I have lost my hopes.
MALCOLM Perchance even there where I did find my doubts.   25
Why in that rawness left you wife and child,
Those precious motives, those strong knots of love,
Without leave-taking? I pray you,
Let not my jealousies be your dishonors,
But mine own safeties. You may be rightly just,   30
What ever I shall think.
MACDUFF   Bleed, bleed, poor country!
Great tyranny, lay thou thy basis sure,
For goodness dare not check thee; wear thou thy wrongs,

---

8. Like . . . dolor: a similar cry of pain.   **10. to friend:** favorable.   **12. sole:** mere.   **13. honest:** honorable.   **14. young:** i.e. inexperienced.   **14–15. something . . . me:** you may see a way of ingratiating yourself with him by betraying me. Most editors follow Theobald in emending *discern* to *deserve.*   **15. wisdom:** i.e. it would be the way of worldly wisdom.   **19. recoil:** give way, retrograde.   **20. crave:** demand, beg. (KR)   **In . . . charge:** at a king's command, or under pressure brought by a king.   **21. transpose:** change, translate. (KR)   **23–24. Though . . . so:** even if every wickedness assumes the appearance of virtue, virtue must still retain that appearance; i.e. even in these bad times an appearance of virtue must not be taken as a sure sign of villainy.   **24. hopes:** i.e. of Malcolm's cooperation.   **25. doubts:** i.e. of Macduff's loyalty.   **26. rawness:** unprotected state.   **27. motives:** persons moving you to love and protect them.   **29. jealousies:** suspicions.   **33. wrongs:** wrongful gains, usurped powers.

The title is affeer'd! Fare thee well, lord,
I would not be the villain that thou think'st   35
For the whole space that's in the tyrant's grasp,
And the rich East to boot.
MALCOLM   Be not offended;
I speak not as in absolute fear of you.
I think our country sinks beneath the yoke:
It weeps, it bleeds, and each new day a gash   40
Is added to her wounds. I think withal
There would be hands uplifted in my right;
And here from gracious England have I offer
Of goodly thousands. But, for all this,
When I shall tread upon the tyrant's head,   45
Or wear it on my sword, yet my poor country
Shall have more vices than it had before,
More suffer, and more sundry ways than ever,
By him that shall succeed.
MACDUFF   What should he be?
MALCOLM It is myself I mean; in whom I know   50
All the particulars of vice so grafted
That, when they shall be open'd, black Macbeth
Will seem as pure as snow, and the poor state
Esteem him as a lamb, being compar'd
With my confineless harms.
MACDUFF   Not in the legions   55
Of horrid hell can come a devil more damn'd
In evils to top Macbeth.
MALCOLM   I grant him bloody,
Luxurious, avaricious, false, deceitful,
Sudden, malicious, smacking of every sin
That has a name; but there's no bottom, none,   60
In my voluptuousness. Your wives, your daughters,
Your matrons, and your maids could not fill up
The cestern of my lust, and my desire
All continent impediments would o'erbear
That did oppose my will. Better Macbeth   65
Than such an one to reign.

---

34. affeer'd: confirmed, authoritatively settled. **37. to boot:** in addition.
38. absolute fear: complete distrust. **39. think:** am mindful that. **41. withal:**
besides. **43. England:** the King of England. **48. and more sundry:** and in
more diverse. **51. particulars:** varieties. **52. open'd:** disclosed. **57. top:** surpass.
58. Luxurious: lecherous, self-indulgent. (KR) **59. Sudden:** violently impulsive.
(KR) **63. cestern:** cistern. **64. continent:** (1) restraining; (2) chaste.

MACDUFF   Boundless intemperance
In nature is a tyranny; it hath been
Th' untimely emptying of the happy throne,
And fall of many kings. But fear not yet
To take upon you what is yours. You may   70
Convey your pleasures in a spacious plenty,
And yet seem cold, the time you may so hoodwink.
We have willing dames enough; there cannot be
That vulture in you to devour so many
As will to greatness dedicate themselves,   75
Finding it so inclin'd.
MALCOLM   With this, there grows
In my most ill-compos'd affection such
A stanchless avarice that, were I king,
I should cut off the nobles for their lands,
Desire his jewels, and this other's house,   80
And my more-having would be as a sauce
To make me hunger more, that I should forge
Quarrels unjust against the good and loyal,
Destroying them for wealth.
MACDUFF   This avarice
Sticks deeper, grows with more pernicious root   85
Than summer-seeming lust; and it hath been
The sword of our slain kings. Yet do not fear,
Scotland hath foisons to fill up your will
Of your mere own. All these are portable,
With other graces weigh'd.   90
MALCOLM But I have none. The king-becoming graces,
As justice, verity, temp'rance, stableness,
Bounty, perseverance, mercy, lowliness,
Devotion, patience, courage, fortitude,
I have no relish of them, but abound   95
In the division of each several crime,

---

67. nature: i.e. a man's nature. **is a tyranny.** Because its rule is absolute.
70. what is yours: i.e. the throne.   **71. Convey:** manage stealthily.   **72. cold:**
chaste, self-controlled, with calm, slow-moving humors (phlegmatic) rather than
hot, impulsive ones (choleric). (KR) **hoodwink:** blindfold.   **77. ill-compos'd:**
lacking self-control, composure. (KR) **affection:** emotion, internal state.
(KR) **78. stanchless:** insatiable.   **86. summer-seeming:** summer-beseeming, i.e.
appropriate to one's heyday (and hence tending to lessen with age, unlike avarice).
88. foisons: abundance, nourishment. (KR)   **89. Of . . . own:** i.e. in royal property
alone. **portable:** bearable.   **90. With . . . weigh'd:** balanced by virtuous qualities.   **93. lowliness:** humility.   **95. relish:** trace, taste. (KR)   **96. division:** subdi-
visions, various manifestations. **several crime:** separate sin.

Acting it many ways. Nay, had I pow'r, I should
Pour the sweet milk of concord into hell,
Uproar the universal peace, confound
All unity on earth.
MACDUFF   O Scotland, Scotland!   100
MALCOLM If such a one be fit to govern, speak.
I am as I have spoken.
MACDUFF   Fit to govern?
No, not to live. O nation miserable!
With an untitled tyrant bloody-sceptred,
When shalt thou see thy wholesome days again,   105
Since that the truest issue of thy throne
By his own interdiction stands accus'd,
And does blaspheme his breed? Thy royal father
Was a most sainted king; the queen that bore thee,
Oft'ner upon her knees than on her feet,   110
Died every day she liv'd. Fare thee well,
These evils thou repeat'st upon thyself
Hath banish'd me from Scotland. O my breast,
Thy hope ends here!
MALCOLM   Macduff, this noble passion,
Child of integrity, hath from my soul   115
Wip'd the black scruples, reconcil'd my thoughts
To thy good truth and honor. Devilish Macbeth
By many of these trains hath sought to win me
Into his power, and modest wisdom plucks me
From over-credulous haste. But God above   120
Deal between thee and me! for even now
I put myself to thy direction, and
Unspeak mine own detraction; here abjure
The taints and blames I laid upon myself,
For strangers to my nature. I am yet   125
Unknown to woman, never was forsworn,
Scarcely have coveted what was mine own,
At no time broke my faith, would not betray
The devil to his fellow, and delight

---

99. Uproar . . . peace: change into a tumult the orderliness of the universe. **confound:** utterly destroy.   **104. untitled:** unrightful, usurping.   **105. wholesome:** healthful, sound.   **107. interdiction:** ruling, sentence, declaration of incompetence (?). (KR)   **108. blaspheme:** defame.   **111. Died:** i.e. to the world (cf. 1 Corinthians 15:31).   **118. trains:** stratagems, devices.   **119. modest wisdom:** wise moderation, prudent caution.   **122. thy direction:** i.e., your counsel. (KR)   **125. For:** as.

No less in truth than life. My first false speaking 130
Was this upon myself. What I am truly
Is thine and my poor country's to command:
Whither indeed, before [thy] here-approach,
Old Siward, with ten thousand warlike men
Already at a point, was setting forth. 135
Now we'll together, and the chance of goodness
Be like our warranted quarrel! Why are you silent?
MACDUFF Such welcome and unwelcome things at once
'Tis hard to reconcile.

Enter a DOCTOR.

MALCOLM Well, more anon.—Comes the King forth, I pray you? 140
DOCTOR Ay, sir; there are a crew of wretched souls
That stay his cure. Their malady convinces
The great assay of art; but at his touch,
Such sanctity hath heaven given his hand, 144
They presently amend.
MALCOLM   I thank you, doctor.   *Exit [Doctor].*
MACDUFF What's the disease he means?
MALCOLM   'Tis call'd the evil:
A most miraculous work in this good king,
Which often, since my here-remain in England,
I have seen him do. How he solicits heaven,
Himself best knows; but strangely-visited people, 150
All swoll'n and ulcerous, pitiful to the eye,
The mere despair of surgery, he cures,
Hanging a golden stamp about their necks,
Put on with holy prayers, and 'tis spoken,
To the succeeding royalty he leaves 155
The healing benediction. With this strange virtue,
He hath a heavenly gift of prophecy,
And sundry blessings hang about his throne
That speak him full of grace.

Enter ROSSE.

MACDUFF   See who comes here.
MALCOLM My countryman; but yet I know him not. 160

---

135. at a point: completely prepared. 136. goodness: success. 137. like . . .
quarrel: as good as our cause is just. 142. stay: await. (KR) 142–43. convinces
. . . art: defeats the best medical skill. 145. presently: immediately. 146. evil:
scrofula ("the king's evil," supposedly cured by the royal touch). 150. strangely-
visited: afflicted in unusual ways. 152. mere: utter. 153. stamp: coin. 156. virtue:
power. 159. grace: God's grace. 160. know: recognize.

MACDUFF My ever gentle cousin, welcome hither.
MALCOLM I know him now. Good God betimes remove
The means that makes us strangers!
ROSSE Sir, amen.
MACDUFF Stands Scotland where it did?
ROSSE Alas, poor country,
Almost afraid to know itself! It cannot   165
Be call'd our mother, but our grave; where nothing,
But who knows nothing, is once seen to smile;
Where sighs, and groans, and shrieks that rent the air
Are made, not mark'd; where violent sorrow seems
A modern ecstasy. The dead man's knell   170
Is there scarce ask'd for who, and good men's lives
Expire before the flowers in their caps,
Dying or ere they sicken.
MACDUFF O relation!
Too nice, and yet too true.
MALCOLM What's the newest grief?
ROSSE That of an hour's age doth hiss the speaker;   175
Each minute teems a new one.
MACDUFF How does my wife?
ROSSE Why, well.
MACDUFF And all my children?
ROSSE Well too.
MACDUFF The tyrant has not batter'd at their peace?
ROSSE No, they were well at peace when I did leave 'em.
MACDUFF Be not a niggard of your speech; how goes't?   180
ROSSE When I came hither to transport the tidings,
Which I have heavily borne, there ran a rumor
Of many worthy fellows that were out,
Which was to my belief witness'd the rather,
For that I saw the tyrant's power afoot.   185
Now is the time of help; your eye in Scotland
Would create soldiers, make our women fight,
To doff their dire distresses.

---

161. gentle: noble. **166–67. nothing, But who:** no one except him who.
168. rent: rend. **169. mark'd:** noticed. **170. modern ecstasy:** i.e., violent sorrow has everyone in its grips, and is now so prevalent that extreme emotion seems
ordinary. (KR) **173. or ere:** before. **relation:** report. **174. nice:** precise, accurately detailed. **175. hiss the speaker:** cause the speaker to be hissed (for telling
stale news). **176. teems:** breeds, brings forth. **180. niggard:** stingy person. (KR)
182. heavily: sorrowfully. **183. out:** in arms. **184. witness'd the rather:** made the
more credible. **185. power:** forces. **186. time of help:** moment to apply the cure.

MALCOLM   Be't their comfort
We are coming thither. Gracious England hath
Lent us good Siward, and ten thousand men;   190
An older and a better soldier none
That Christendom gives out.
ROSSE   Would I could answer
This comfort with the like! But I have words
That would be howl'd out in the desert air,
Where hearing should not latch them.
MACDUFF   What concern they?   195
The general cause? or is it a fee-grief
Due to some single breast?
ROSSE   No mind that's honest
But in it shares some woe, though the main part
Pertains to you alone.
MACDUFF   If it be mine,
Keep it not from me, quickly let me have it.   200
ROSSE Let not your ears despise my tongue for ever,
Which shall possess them with the heaviest sound
That ever yet they heard.
MACDUFF   Humh! I guess at it.
ROSSE Your castle is surpris'd; your wife, and babes,
Savagely slaughter'd. To relate the manner,   205
Were on the quarry of these murther'd deer
To add the death of you.
MALCOLM   Merciful heaven!
What, man, ne'er pull your hat upon your brows;
Give sorrow words. The grief that does not speak
Whispers the o'er-fraught heart, and bids it break.   210
MACDUFF My children too?
ROSSE   Wife, children, servants, all
That could be found.
MACDUFF   And I must be from thence!
My wife kill'd too?
ROSSE   I have said.
MALCOLM   Be comforted.
Let's make us med'cines of our great revenge
To cure this deadly grief.   215

---

192. gives out: proclaims (?) or furnishes example of (?).   **194. would:** demand
to. **desert air:** air in some unpopulated spot.   **195. latch:** catch.   **196. fee-grief:**
private woe (*fee* = absolute ownership).   **197. Due to:** i.e. the property of.
206. quarry: heap of slaughtered bodies.   **210. o'er-fraught:** overburdened.
212. must. Past tense.

MACDUFF He has no children. All my pretty ones?
Did you say all? O hell-kite! All?
What, all my pretty chickens, and their dam,
At one fell swoop?
MALCOLM Dispute it like a man.
MACDUFF   I shall do so;   220
But I must also feel it as a man:
I cannot but remember such things were,
That were most precious to me. Did heaven look on,
And would not take their part? Sinful Macduff,
They were all strook for thee! naught that I am,   225
Not for their own demerits, but for mine,
Fell slaughter on their souls. Heaven rest them now!
MALCOLM Be this the whetstone of your sword, let grief
Convert to anger; blunt not the heart, enrage it.
MACDUFF O, I could play the woman with mine eyes,   230
And braggart with my tongue! But, gentle heavens,
Cut short all intermission. Front to front
Bring thou this fiend of Scotland and myself;
Within my sword's length set him; if he scape,
Heaven forgive him too!
MALCOLM   This [tune] goes manly.   235
Come go we to the King, our power is ready,
Our lack is nothing but our leave. Macbeth
Is ripe for shaking, and the pow'rs above
Put on their instruments. Receive what cheer you may,
The night is long that never finds the day.   240
                                        Exeunt.

---

219. swoop: i.e. swoop of the hell-kite.   **220. Dispute:** oppose, fight against.
225. for: on account of. **naught:** wicked.   **229. Convert:** be changed.
232. Front to front: face to face.   **235. too:** i.e. as I must have done, to let him
escape.   **237. Our . . . leave:** we need only take leave of the King.   **239. Put . . .
instruments:** arm themselves (?) or incite us, their agents (?).

Act 5

SCENE I

Enter a DOCTOR OF PHYSIC *and a* WAITING-GENTLEWOMAN.

DOCTOR I have two nights watch'd with you, but can
perceive no truth in your report. When was it she
last walk'd?

GENTLEWOMAN Since his Majesty went into the field, I have
seen her rise from her bed, throw her night-gown   5
upon her, unlock her closet, take forth paper, fold it,
write upon't, read it, afterwards seal it, and again
return to bed; yet all this while in a most fast sleep.

DOCTOR A great perturbation in nature, to receive at
once the benefit of sleep and do the effects of   10
watching! In this slumb'ry agitation, besides her walking and other actual performances, what, at any time,
have you heard her say?

GENTLEWOMAN That, sir, which I will not report after her.

DOCTOR You may to me, and 'tis most meet you   15
should.

GENTLEWOMAN Neither to you nor any one, having no witness to confirm my speech.

Enter LADY [MACBETH] *with a taper.*

Lo you, here she comes! This is her very guise, and
upon my life, fast asleep. Observe her, stand close.   20

DOCTOR How came she by that light?

GENTLEWOMAN Why, it stood by her. She has light by her
continually, 'tis her command.

DOCTOR You see her eyes are open.

GENTLEWOMAN Ay, but their sense are shut.   25

5.1. Location: Dunsinane. Macbeth's castle.   **9. perturbation:** technical term for
internal disorder of the affections, or emotions.   **10–11. do . . . watching:** perform
waking actions.   **11. agitation:** activity.   **19. her very guise:** exactly what she has
been doing.   **20. close:** out of sight.   **25. sense:** powers of sight.

DOCTOR What is it she does now? Look how she rubs
her hands.

GENTLEWOMAN It is an accustom'd action with her, to seem
thus washing her hands. I have known her continue
in this a quarter of an hour.   30

LADY MACBETH Yet here's a spot.

DOCTOR Hark, she speaks. I will set down what
comes from her, to satisfy my remembrance the more
strongly.

LADY MACBETH Out, damn'd spot! out, I say! One—   35
two—why then 'tis time to do't. Hell is murky. Fie,
my lord, fie, a soldier, and afeard? What need we fear
who knows it, when none can call our pow'r to
accompt? Yet who would have thought the old man
to have had so much blood in him?   40

DOCTOR Do you mark that?

LADY MACBETH The Thane of Fife had a wife; where is
she now? What, will these hands ne'er be clean? No
more o' that, my lord, no more o' that; you mar all
with this starting.   45

DOCTOR Go to, go to; you have known what you
should not.

GENTLEWOMAN She has spoke what she should not, I am sure
of that; heaven knows what she has known.

LADY MACBETH Here's the smell of the blood still. All   50
the perfumes of Arabia will not sweeten this little hand.
O, O, O!

DOCTOR What a sigh is there! The heart is sorely
charg'd.

GENTLEWOMAN I would not have such a heart in my bosom   55
for the dignity of the whole body.

DOCTOR Well, well, well.

GENTLEWOMAN Pray God it be, sir.

DOCTOR This disease is beyond my practice; yet I
have known those which have walk'd in their sleep   60
who have died holily in their beds.

LADY MACBETH Wash your hands, put on your night-
gown, look not so pale. I tell you yet again, Banquo's
buried; he cannot come out on 's grave.

---

33. satisfy: confirm. **39. accompt:** account. **45. this starting:** these
startled movements. **54. charg'd:** burdened. **59. practice:** professional skill.
64. on 's: of his.

DOCTOR Even so?   65
LADY MACBETH To bed, to bed; there's knocking at the
    gate. Come, come, come, come, give me your hand.
    What's done cannot be undone. To bed, to bed, to bed.
                                                      Exit Lady.
DOCTOR Will she go now to bed?
GENTLEWOMAN Directly.   70
DOCTOR Foul whisp'rings are abroad. Unnatural deeds
    Do breed unnatural troubles; infected minds
    To their deaf pillows will discharge their secrets.
    More needs she the divine than the physician.
    God, God, forgive us all! Look after her,   75
    Remove from her the means of all annoyance,
    And still keep eyes upon her. So good night.
    My mind she has mated, and amaz'd my sight.
    I think, but dare not speak.
GENTLEWOMAN   Good night, good doctor.   *Exeunt.*

SCENE 2

Drum and Colors. Enter MENTETH, CATHNESS,
                 ANGUS, LENNOX, SOLDIERS.

MENTETH The English pow'r is near, led on by Malcolm,
    His uncle Siward, and the good Macduff.
    Revenges burn in them; for their dear causes
    Would to the bleeding and the grim alarm
    Excite the mortified man.
ANGUS   Near Birnan wood   5
    Shall we well meet them; that way are they coming.
CATHNESS Who knows if Donalbain be with his brother?
LENNOX For certain, sir, he is not; I have a file
    Of all the gentry. There is Siward's son,
    And many unrough youths that even now   10
    Protest their first of manhood.
MENTETH   What does the tyrant?
CATHNESS Great Dunsinane he strongly fortifies.

---

76. annoyance: (self-)injury. 77. still: constantly. 78. mated: stupefied. amaz'd:
bewildered. 5.2. Location: The country near Dunsinane. 3. dear: heartfelt.
4. bleeding . . . alarm: i.e. bloody and grim battle. 5. mortified: moribund
(?) or paralyzed (?). 6. well: no doubt. 8. file: list. 10. unrough: unbearded.
11. Protest . . . manhood: assert their manhood for the first time.

Some say he's mad; others that lesser hate him
Do call it valiant fury; but for certain
He cannot buckle his distemper'd cause   15
Within the belt of rule.
ANGUS   Now does he feel
His secret murthers sticking on his hands;
Now minutely revolts upbraid his faith-breach;
Those he commands move only in command,
Nothing in love. Now does he feel his title   20
Hang loose about him, like a giant's robe
Upon a dwarfish thief.
MENTETH   Who then shall blame
His pester'd senses to recoil and start,
When all that is within him does condemn
Itself for being there?
CATHNESS   Well, march we on   25
To give obedience where 'tis truly ow'd.
Meet we the med'cine of the sickly weal,
And with him pour we, in our country's purge,
Each drop of us.
LENNOX   Or so much as it needs
To dew the sovereign flower and drown the weeds.   30
Make we our march towards Birnan.

                                        Exeunt marching.

SCENE 3

Enter MACBETH, DOCTOR, *and* ATTENDANTS

MACBETH Bring me no more reports, let them fly all.
Till Birnan wood remove to Dunsinane
I cannot taint with fear. What's the boy Malcolm?
Was he not born of woman? The spirits that know
All mortal consequences have pronounc'd me thus: 5
"Fear not, Macbeth, no man that's born of woman
Shall e'er have power upon thee." Then fly, false thanes,

---

15. distemper'd: swollen with disease, intemperate.   **16. rule:** self-control, temperate behavior.   **18. minutely revolts:** i.e. fresh revolts every minute.   **19. in
command:** because they are ordered to.   **23. pester'd senses:** tormented faculties.
start: move fitfully.   **27. med'cine:** i.e. Malcolm. **weal:** state.   **28. purge:** releas-
ing of diseased fluids.   **30. sovereign:** (1) royal; (2) supreme in curative power.
5.3. Location: Dunsinane. Macbeth's castle.   **1. them:** i.e. the thanes (see line 7).
fly: desert.   **3. taint:** be infected.   **5. mortal consequences:** human destinies.

And mingle with the English epicures!
The mind I sway by, and the heart I bear,
Shall never sag with doubt, nor shake with fear.   10

Enter SERVANT.

The devil damn thee black, thou cream-fac'd loon!
Where got'st thou that goose-look?
SERVANT There is ten thousand—
MACBETH   Geese, villain?
SERVANT   Soldiers, sir.
MACBETH Go prick thy face, and over-red thy fear,
Thou lily-liver'd boy. What soldiers, patch?   15
Death of thy soul! those linen cheeks of thine
Are counsellors to fear. What soldiers, whey-face?
SERVANT The English force, so please you.
MACBETH Take thy face hence. [*Exit Servant.*] Seyton!
—I am sick at heart
When I behold—Seyton, I say!—This push   20
Will cheer me ever, or [disseat] me now.
I have liv'd long enough: my way of life
Is fall'n into the sear, the yellow leaf,
And that which should accompany old age,
As honor, love, obedience, troops of friends,   25
I must not look to have; but in their stead,
Curses, not loud but deep, mouth-honor, breath,
Which the poor heart would fain deny, and dare not.
Seyton!

Enter SEYTON.

SEYTON What's your gracious pleasure?
MACBETH   What news more?   30
SEYTON All is confirm'd, my lord, which was reported.
MACBETH I'll fight, till from my bones my flesh be hack'd.
Give me my armor.

---

8. epicures: i.e. devotees of soft living, self-indulgence. **9. sway:** rule myself,
control my actions. **11. loon:** rascal. **15. lily-liver'd:** i.e. cowardly. **patch:** clown,
fool. **16. of:** on. **17. Are . . . fear:** will urge others to be fearful. **19. Seyton.**
May be pronounced the same as "Satan." **20. push:** effort. **21. disseat:** dethrone.
This is Jennens' conjecture for F1 *dis-eate,* and some argue that *cheer* should be
chair to match it. The later folios read *disease,* i.e. deprive of comfort and peace of
mind—a good guess, and appropriate to *cheer.* **22. way:** course. (Dr. Johnson's
famous conjecture *May* is unnecessary.) **23. sear:** dry, dessicated. **25. As:** such
as, namely. **27. mouth-honor:** false courtesies.

SEYTON   'Tis not needed yet.
MACBETH I'll put it on.
Send out moe horses, skirr the country round,   35
Hang those that talk of fear. Give me mine armor.
How does your patient, doctor?
DOCTOR   Not so sick, my lord,
As she is troubled with thick-coming fancies,
That keep her from her rest.
MACBETH   Cure [her] of that.
Canst thou not minister to a mind diseas'd,   40
Pluck from the memory a rooted sorrow,
Raze out the written troubles of the brain,
And with some sweet oblivious antidote
Cleanse the stuff'd bosom of that perilous stuff
Which weighs upon the heart?
DOCTOR   Therein the patient   45
Must minister to himself.
MACBETH Throw physic to the dogs, I'll none of it.
Come, put mine armor on; give me my staff.
Seyton, send out. Doctor, the thanes fly from me.—
Come, sir, dispatch.—If thou couldst, doctor, cast   50
The water of my land, find her disease,
And purge it to a sound and pristine health,
I would applaud thee to the very echo,
That should applaud again.—Pull't off, I say.—
What rhubarb, cyme, or what purgative drug,   55
Would scour these English hence? Hear'st thou of them?
DOCTOR Ay, my good lord; your royal preparation
Makes us hear something.
MACBETH   Bring it after me.—
I will not be afraid of death and bane,
Till Birnan forest come to Dunsinane.   60
                              [*Exeunt all but the Doctor.*]
DOCTOR Were I from Dunsinane away and clear,
Profit again should hardly draw me here.   *Exit.*

---

35. moe: more. **skirr:** scour.   **38. fancies:** fantasies, imaginings.   **42. Raze out:** erase. **written troubles of:** troubles written on.   **43. oblivious:** causing forgetfulness.   **48. staff:** lance.   **50. dispatch:** hurry up.   **50–51. cast The water:** analyze the urine, i.e. diagnose the disorder.   **52. pristine:** i.e. perfect, as formerly.   **54. Pull't off.** Referring to some part of the armor not properly adjusted.   **55. cyme:** possibly another word for *senna*, a cathartic or emetic.   **56. scour:** purge.   **62. Profit . . . here:** i.e. no fee would be large enough to bring me back.

SCENE 4

Drum and Colors. Enter MALCOLM, SIWARD, MACDUFF,
SIWARD'S SON, MENTETH, CATHNESS, ANGUS,
[LENNOX, ROSSE,] *and* SOLDIERS, *marching.*

MALCOLM Cousins, I hope the days are near at hand
That chambers will be safe.
MENTETH   We doubt it nothing.
SIWARD What wood is this before us?
MENTETH   The wood of Birnan.
MALCOLM Let every soldier hew him down a bough,
And bear't before him, thereby shall we shadow   5
The numbers of our host, and make discovery
Err in report of us.
SOLDIERS   It shall be done.
SIWARD We learn no other but the confident tyrant
Keeps still in Dunsinane, and will endure
Our setting down before't.
MALCOLM   'Tis his main hope;   10
For where there is advantage to be given,
Both more and less have given him the revolt,
And none serve with him but constrained things,
Whose hearts are absent too.
MACDUFF   Let our just censures
Attend the true event, and put we on   15
Industrious soldiership.
SIWARD   The time approaches
That will with due decision make us know
What we shall say we have, and what we owe.
Thoughts speculative their unsure hopes relate,
But certain issue strokes must arbitrate,   20
Towards which advance the war.   *Exeunt marching.*

5.4. Location: The country near Birnan wood. **2. chambers:** bedrooms (such
as Duncan's). **6. discovery:** reconnaissance. **9. Keeps:** remains. **10. setting
down before:** laying siege to. **11. advantage:** opportunity. **12. more and less:**
great and lowly. **14. our just censures:** i.e. our judgments, in order that they
may be just. **15. Attend . . . event:** await the actual outcome. **18. owe:** own.
19–20. Thoughts . . . arbitrate: talking about the event in advance is to deal in
mere hopes, uncertain of fulfillment; the real issue must be decided by action.

SCENE 5

Enter MACBETH, SEYTON, *and* SOLDIERS,
with Drum and Colors.

MACBETH Hang out our banners on the outward walls,
The cry is still, "They come!" Our castle's strength
Will laugh a siege to scorn; here let them lie
Till famine and the ague eat them up.
Were they not forc'd with those that should be ours,   5
We might have met them dareful, beard to beard,
And beat them backward home.
                                        A cry within of women.
                          What is that noise?
SEYTON It is the cry of women, my good lord.   [*Exit.*]
MACBETH I have almost forgot the taste of fears.
The time has been, my senses would have cool'd   10
To hear a night-shriek, and my fell of hair
Would at a dismal treatise rouse and stir
As life were in't. I have supp'd full with horrors;
Direness, familiar to my slaughterous thoughts,
Cannot once start me.

                          [*Enter* SEYTON.]

                          Wherefore was that cry?   15
SEYTON The Queen, my lord, is dead.
MACBETH She should have died hereafter;
There would have been a time for such a word.
To-morrow, and to-morrow, and to-morrow,
Creeps in this petty pace from day to day,   20
To the last syllable of recorded time;
And all our yesterdays have lighted fools
The way to dusty death. Out, out, brief candle!
Life's but a walking shadow, a poor player,
That struts and frets his hour upon the stage,   25
And then is heard no more. It is a tale
Told by an idiot, full of sound and fury,
Signifying nothing.

5.5. Location: Dunsinane. Macbeth's castle.   **4. ague:** fever.   **5. forc'd:** reinforced.   **6. dareful:** boldly.   **10. cool'd:** been chilled with terror.   **11. my . . .
hair:** the hair on my skin.   **12. treatise:** story.   **15. once start me:** ever make me
start.   **17. should . . . hereafter:** was bound to die later (if not to-day). *Should*
= would certainly.   **20. petty:** small, trivial.   **24. shadow:** shadow, shade, ghost,
imitation, fiction. **poor:** unskilled.

Enter a MESSENGER.

Thou com'st to use thy tongue;
Thy story quickly.

MESSENGER Gracious my lord,
I should report that which I say I saw,   30
But know not how to do't.

MACBETH Well, say, sir.

MESSENGER As I did stand my watch upon the hill,
I look'd toward Birnan, and anon methought
The wood began to move.

MACBETH Liar and slave!

MESSENGER Let me endure your wrath, if't be not so.   35
Within this three mile may you see it coming;
I say, a moving grove.

MACBETH If thou speak'st false,
Upon the next tree shall thou hang alive,
Till famine cling thee; if thy speech be sooth,
I care not if thou dost for me as much.   40
I pull in resolution, and begin
To doubt th' equivocation of the fiend
That lies like truth. "Fear not, till Birnan wood
Do come to Dunsinane," and now a wood
Comes toward Dunsinane. Arm, arm, and out!   45
If this which he avouches does appear,
There is nor flying hence, nor tarrying here.
I gin to be a-weary of the sun,
And wish th' estate o' th' world were now undone.
Ring the alarum-bell! Blow wind, come wrack,   50
At least we'll die with harness on our back.   *Exeunt.*

SCENE 6

Drum and Colors. Enter MALCOLM, SIWARD, MACDUFF,
and their army, with boughs.

MALCOLM Now near enough; your leavy screens throw down,
And show like those you are. You, worthy uncle,
Shall with my cousin, your right noble son,

39. **cling:** shrivel. **sooth:** truth.   41. **pull in:** rein in, check.   46. **avouches:**
asserts.   49. **estate:** settled order.   50. **wrack:** ruin.   51. **harness:** armor.
5.6. Location: Dunsinane. Plain before Macbeth's castle.   **sd. Colors:** flags, insignia.   2. **show . . . are:** appear in your own forms.

Lead our first battle. Worthy Macduff and we
Shall take upon 's what else remains to do,   5
According to our order.
SIWARD   Fare you well.
Do we but find the tyrant's power to-night,
Let us be beaten, if we cannot fight.
MACDUFF Make all our trumpets speak, give them all breath,
Those clamorous harbingers of blood and death.   10

Exeunt. Alarums continued.

SCENE 7

Enter MACBETH.

MACBETH They have tied me to a stake; I cannot fly,
But bear-like I must fight the course. What's he
That was not born of woman? Such a one
Am I to fear, or none.

Enter YOUNG SIWARD.

YOUNG SIWARD What is thy name?
MACBETH   Thou'lt be afraid to hear it.   5
YOUNG SIWARD No; though thou call'st thyself a hotter name
Than any is in hell.
MACBETH   My name's Macbeth.
YOUNG SIWARD The devil himself could not pronounce a title
More hateful to mine ear.
MACBETH   No; nor more fearful.
YOUNG SIWARD Thou liest, abhorred tyrant, with my sword   10
I'll prove the lie thou speak'st.

Fight, and Young Siward slain.
MACBETH   Thou wast born of woman.
But swords I smile at, weapons laugh to scorn,
Brandish'd by man that's of a woman born.   *Exit.*

Alarums. Enter MACDUFF.

MACDUFF That way the noise is. Tyrant, show thy face!
If thou beest slain and with no stroke of mine,   15
My wife and children's ghosts will haunt me still.
I cannot strike at wretched kerns, whose arms

---

4. battle: battalion.   **6. order:** plan of attack.   **10. harbingers:** omens, heralds.
5.7. Location: Scene continues.   **2. course:** round of bearbaiting.   **16. still:** always.

Are hir'd to bear their staves; either thou, Macbeth,
Or else my sword with an unbattered edge
I sheathe again undeeded. There thou shouldst be;   20
By this great clatter, one of greatest note
Seems bruited. Let me find him, Fortune!
And more I beg not.   *Exit. Alarums.*

Enter MALCOLM *and* SIWARD.

SIWARD This way, my lord, the castle's gently rend'red:
The tyrant's people on both sides do fight,   25
The noble thanes do bravely in the war,
The day almost itself professes yours,
And little is to do.
MALCOLM   We have met with foes
That strike beside us.
SIWARD   Enter, sir, the castle.

          Exeunt. Alarum.

SCENE 8

Enter MACBETH.

MACBETH Why should I play the Roman fool, and die
On mine own sword? Whiles I see lives, the gashes
Do better upon them.

Enter MACDUFF.

MACDUFF   Turn, hell-hound, turn!
MACBETH Of all men else I have avoided thee.
But get thee back, my soul is too much charg'd   5
With blood of thine already.
MACDUFF   I have no words,
My voice is in my sword, thou bloodier villain
Than terms can give thee out!   *Fight. Alarum.*
MACBETH   Thou losest labor.
As easy mayst thou the intrenchant air
With thy keen sword impress as make me bleed.   10
Let fall thy blade on vulnerable crests,

18. staves: spears. **20. undeeded:** having no deeds to its credit. **22. bruited:** announced. **24. gently rend'red:** surrendered without resistance. **29. strike beside us:** fight on our side (?) or deliberately avoid hitting us (?). 5.8. Location: Scene continues. **1. Roman fool:** i.e. noble suicide. **8. terms . . . out:** words can describe. **9. intrenchant:** incapable of being cut.

I bear a charmed life, which must not yield
To one of woman born.
MACDUFF   Despair thy charm,
And let the angel whom thou still hast serv'd
Tell thee, Macduff was from his mother's womb   15
Untimely ripp'd.
MACBETH Accursed be that tongue that tells me so,
For it hath cow'd my better part of man!
And be these juggling fiends no more believ'd,
That palter with us in a double sense,   20
That keep the word of promise to our ear,
And break it to our hope. I'll not fight with thee.
MACDUFF Then yield thee, coward,
And live to be the show and gaze o' th' time!
We'll have thee, as our rarer monsters are,   25
Painted upon a pole, and underwrit,
"Here may you see the tyrant."
MACBETH   I will not yield,
To kiss the ground before young Malcolm's feet,
And to be baited with the rabble's curse.
Though Birnan wood be come to Dunsinane,   30
And thou oppos'd, being of no woman born,
Yet I will try the last. Before my body
I throw my warlike shield. Lay on, Macduff,
And damn'd be him that first cries, "Hold, enough!"
                              Exeunt fighting. Alarums.

Enter fighting, and MACBETH *slain.*
[MACDUFF *carries off Macbeth's body.*]

SCENE 9

Retreat and flourish. Enter, with Drum and Colors, MALCOLM,
SIWARD, ROSSE, THANES, *and* SOLDIERS.

MALCOLM I would the friends we miss were safe arriv'd.
SIWARD Some must go off; and yet, by these I see,
So great a day as this is cheaply bought.
MALCOLM Macduff is missing, and your noble son.

---

13. Despair: despair of.   **14. angel:** bad angel, evil genius.   **16. Untimely:**
prematurely.   **18. better . . . man:** i.e. courage.   **20. palter:** equivocate.
26. Painted . . . pole: i.e. with your picture carried on a pole.   **29. baited:** harassed.
32. the last: i.e. his unaided strength and courage.   5.9. Location: Dunsinane.
Macbeth's castle.   **2. go off:** die.   **by:** to judge by.

ROSSE Your son, my lord, has paid a soldier's debt.   5
He only liv'd but till he was a man,
The which no sooner had his prowess confirm'd
In the unshrinking station where he fought,
But like a man he died.
SIWARD   Then he is dead?
ROSSE Ay, and brought off the field. Your cause of sorrow   10
Must not be measur'd by his worth, for then
It hath no end.
SIWARD   Had he his hurts before?
ROSSE Ay, on the front.
SIWARD   Why then, God's soldier be he!
Had I as many sons as I have hairs,
I would not wish them to a fairer death.   15
And so his knell is knoll'd.
MALCOLM   He's worth more sorrow,
And that I'll spend for him.
SIWARD   He's worth no more;
They say he parted well, and paid his score,
And so God be with him! Here comes newer comfort.

Enter MACDUFF *with Macbeth's head.*

MACDUFF Hail, King! for so thou art. Behold where stands   20
Th' usurper's cursed head: the time is free.
I see thee compass'd with thy kingdom's pearl,
That speak my salutation in their minds;
Whose voices I desire aloud with mine: 24
Hail, King of Scotland!
ALL   Hail, King of Scotland!   *Flourish.*
MALCOLM We shall not spend a large expense of time
Before we reckon with your several loves,
And make us even with you. My thanes and kinsmen,
Henceforth be earls, the first that ever Scotland
In such an honor nam'd. What's more to do,   30
Which would be planted newly with the time,
As calling home our exil'd friends abroad

8. **unshrinking . . . fought:** station where he fought without shrinking.
12. **before:** on the front of his body (i.e., he was fighting to the last, not fleeing, he died honorably).   16. **knoll'd:** tolled.   18. **parted:** departed.   20. **stands.** On a pole, according to Holinshed.   22. **compass'd . . . pearl:** surrounded by the noblest in your realm.   26. **We:** Malcolm speaks for the first time in the royal plural.   27. **reckon:** make an accounting.   28. **make . . . you:** i.e. reward you as you deserve.   31. **would . . . time:** should be performed as this new era begins.

That fled the snares of watchful tyranny,
Producing forth the cruel ministers
Of this dead butcher and his fiend-like queen,   35
Who (as 'tis thought) by self and violent hands
Took off her life; this, and what needful else
That calls upon us, by the grace of Grace,
We will perform in measure, time, and place.
So thanks to all at once and to each one,   40
Whom we invite to see us crown'd at Scone.

Flourish. Exeunt omnes.

34. Producing forth: bringing forward for trial.   **36. self and violent:** her own violent.   **39. in . . . place:** i.e. with due ceremony at the proper time and place.

NOTE ON THE TEXT

Our only authority for *Macbeth* is the First Folio (1623); all later texts are derived from that source. There is general agreement that the copy behind the F1 text was a promptbook, probably a scribal transcript based on Shakespeare's "foul papers." A quarto, printed from F1, was published in 1673.

The F1 text is felt to be on the whole a reasonably accurate reproduction of its manuscript copy, but there are a number of reasons for believing that the manuscript itself presented a shortened and somewhat adapted version of the play as Shakespeare originally wrote it. Among the reasons for this view are: the unusual brevity of the F1 text (it is the fifth shortest play in the canon and is at least a thousand lines shorter than any of the other tragedies written after *Julius Caesar* with the exception of *Timon of Athens*, itself a special case); the confusion arising apparently from cutting, possibly even of an entire scene or scenes, and rearrangement (note, for example, the implications of 1.7.46–54 and the raggedness and ambiguity of 1.2); and the intrusion, by a revising hand, most probably Thomas Middleton's, of the Hecate material in the witch scenes (3.5, 4.1.39–43, 125–32). See the Textual Notes for the texts of two songs from Middleton's *The Witch* (date uncertain, but probably c. 1615), which are called for in 3.5 and 4.1. These exceptional features, and the obviously interpolated compliment to James I in 4.3.140–59, point to the likelihood that the F1 *Macbeth* may represent a version specially prepared for court performance.

Simon Forman saw a performance of *Macbeth* at the Globe in 1611 (20 April); his account of the performance may be consulted in Sources and Contexts. Certain differences between Forman's account and the play as it appeared in F1 suggest that F1's text underwent some (probably, further) revision after 1611; critics have noticed, for example, that Forman makes no mention of Hecate.

For further information, see: J.D. Wilson, ed., New Shakespeare *Macbeth* (Cambridge, 1947); Kenneth Muir, ed., New Arden *Macbeth* (London, 1951); W.W. Greg, *The Shakespeare First Folio* (Oxford, 1955); D.A. Amnéus, "A Missing Scene in *Macbeth*," *JEGP,* LX (1961), 435–40; Christopher Spencer, *Davenant's "Macbeth" from the Yale Manuscript* (New Haven, 1961) and ed., *Five Restoration Adaptations of Shakespeare* (Urbana, 1965); J.M. Nosworthy, *Shakespeare's Occasional Plays* (London, 1965); G.K. Hunter, ed., New Penguin *Macbeth* (Harmondsworth, Middlesex, 1967); Stanley Wells, Gary Taylor, et al., *William Shakespeare: A Textual Companion* (Oxford, 1987); Nicholas Brooke, ed., New Oxford *Macbeth* (Oxford, 1990); John Jowett and Gary Taylor, "'With New Additions': Theatrical Interpolation in *Measure for Measure* [and *Macbeth*]," in Gary Taylor and John Jowett, *Shakespeare Reshaped, 1606–1623* (Oxford, 1993); Jacobson, Howard. "*Macbeth* I.v.48–52," *Notes and Queries* 47 (2000), 86; Holderness, Graham. "Notes and Queries: *Macbeth*," in *Textual Shakespeare: Writing and the Word* (Hatfield: University of Hertfordshire, 2003), 151–77; A.R. Braunmuller, ed., New Cambridge *Macbeth* (Updated JT, 2011).

TEXTUAL NOTES

Dramatis personae: *first given in Q (1673); expanded by Rowe and Capell*
Act-scene division: *from F1, with the exception of 5.8, 9, for which F1 indicates no break (see first notes to these scenes); present act-scene arrangement as a whole first established by Wilson*

I.I

Location: *Theobald*
1, 3, 5 s.pp. **1. Witch. . . . 2. Witch. . . . 3. Witch.**] *Rowe*; 1 . . . 2 . . . 3 *F1 (throughout)*
9–10 **2. Witch. . . . Anon!**] *Hunter conj.; All. Padock calls anon: F1*

I.2

Location: *Wilson (after Capell)*
o.s.d. **King Duncan, Malcolm**] *F2 (subs.);* King Malcome *F1*
o.s.d. **Sergeant**] *Globe;* Captaine *F1*
1 s.p. **Dun.**] *Capell;* King. *F1 (throughout)*
7, 25, 34 s.pp. **Serg.**] *Globe;* Cap. *F1*
13 **gallowglasses**] *F2 (subs.);* Gallowgrosses *F1*
14 **quarrel**] *Douai MS, Hanmer;* Quarry *F1*
26 **thunders break,**] *Pope;* Thunders: *F1;* Thunders breaking *F2*
32 **furbish'd**] *Rowe;* furbusht *F1*

33–4 **Dismay'd . . . Banquo?**] *as verse, Douai MS, Pope; as prose, F1*
34 **Banquo**] *F3;* Banquoh *F1 (the only appearance of this spelling, perhaps Shakespeare's; cf. Holinshed's Banquho)*
41 **tell—**] *Rowe;* tell: *F1*
44 s.d. **Exit Sergeant, attended.**] *Globe*
59 **Norways'**] *Steevens;* Norwayes *F1*

I.3

Location: *Rowe (subs.)*
32 **weïrd**] *Theobald;* weyward *F1 (F1 varies between weyward and weyard, the latter probably approximating the pronunciation)*
39 **Forres**] *Pope* (Foris); Soris *F1*
57 **rapt**] *Pope;* wrapt *F1*
91 **rebels'**] *Theobald;* Rebels *F1*
96 **make,**] *Rowe;* make *F1*
97 **death.**] *Rowe (subs.);* death, *F1*
98 **Came**] *Rowe;* Can *F1*
102 **herald**] *F2;* harrold *F1*
112 **did**] else did *F2*
116 s.d. **Aside.**] *Rowe*
117 s.d. **To . . . Angus.**] *White*
118 s.d. **Aside to Banquo.**] *Kittredge*
120 s.d. **Aside to Macbeth.**] *Kittredge*
127, 143 s.dd. **Aside.**] *Rowe*
130 s.d. **Aside.**] *Capell*

135 **hair**] *Rowe*; Heire *F1*
144 **him,**] *F4*; him *F1*
146 s.d. **Aside.**] *Hanmer*
153 s.d. **Aside to Banquo.**] *Kittredge*
154 **interim**] *Pope*; Interim *F1* (*in italics*)

1.4

Location: *Capell* (*after Rowe*)
1 **Are**] *F2*; Or *F1*
25 **throne . . . children**] *Rowe*; Throne, and State, Children, *F1*
42 **Enverness**] *ed.*; Envernes *F1*; Enuerns *Holinshed*
45 **harbinger**] *Rowe*; Herbenger *F1*
48 s.d. **Aside.**] *Douai MS, Rowe*
53 **done,**] *Q* (*1673*); done *F1*

1.5

Location: *Pope* (*after Rowe*)
1 s.p. **Lady M.**] *Capell*; Lady. *F1* (*throughout*)
1 s.d. **Reads.**] *Neilson* (*after Capell*)
8 **weïrd**] *Theobald*; weyward *F1*
17 **human**] *Rowe*; humane *F1*
23 **"Thus . . . do,"**] *quotes, Hunter conj.*
25 **Hie**] *F4*; High *F1*
28 **impedes thee**] *Pope*; impeides thee *F1*; thee hinders *F2*
47 **it**] *F3*; hit *F1*
63 **matters. To . . . time,**] *Theobald*; matters, to . . . time. *F1*

1.6

Location: *Theobald*
4 **marlet**] *Collier MS* (*after Rowe*); Barlet *F1*
5 **lov'd**] *Rowe*; loued *F1*
5 **mansionry**] *Theobald*; Mansonry *F1*
6 **jutty,**] *Steevens*; Iutty *F1*
8–9 **cradle. . . . haunt,**] *Rowe*; Cradle, . . . haunt: *F1*
9 **most**] *Rowe*; must *F1*
13 **God 'ield**] *Neilson* (*after Craig*); God-eyld *F1*
26 **theirs, in**] *Pope*; theirs in *F1*
29 **host,**] *F3*; Host *F1*

1.7

Location: *ed.* (*after Pelican*)
1 **well**] *Rowe*; well, *F1*
5 **be-all . . . end-all**] *hyphens, Pope*
5 **end-all—here,**] *Rowe* (*subs.*); end all. Heere, *F1*
6 **shoal**] *Theobald*; Schoole *F1* (*probably a variant spelling of* shoal)
20 **taking-off**] *hyphen, Capell*
21 **new-born babe**] *F4*; New-borne-Babe *F1*

28 **other—**] *Rowe*; other. *F1*
30 **not**] *Pope*; not, *F1*
47 **do**] *Rowe*; no *F1*
55 **me;**] *Capell* (*subs., after Rowe*); me, *F1*
68 **lies**] lye *F2*

2.1

Location: *ed.* (*after Capell*)
5 s.d. **Gives . . . dagger.**] *ed.* (*after Wilson*)
20 **weïrd**] *Theobald*; weyward *F1*
30 s.d. **with Fleance**] *Theobald* (*subs.*)
32 s.d. **Servant**] *Rowe*
52 **Hecat's**] *Johnson*; Heccats *F1*; Heccates *F2*
55 **strides**] *Pope*; sides *F1*
56 **sure**] *Pope conj.*; sowre *F1*
57 **way they**] *Rowe*; they may *F1*

2.2

Location: *ed.* (*after Wilson*)
4 **it:**] *Capell* (*after Rowe*); it, *F1*
8 s.d. **Within.**] *Steevens*
13 s.d. **Enter Macbeth.**] *placed as in Globe; after die. l. 8, F1*
15 **scream**] *F4*; schreame *F1*
18 s.d. **Looking . . . hands.**] *Pope*
32–3 **"Sleep . . . sleep"**] *quotes, Johnson*
34 **sleave**] *Seward conj.*; Sleeue *F1*
38 **more!"**] *Hanmer* (*subs.*); more *F1*
39–40 **"Glamis . . . more."**] *quotes, Hanmer*
59 **incarnadine**] *Rowe*; incarnardine *F1*
60 **one red**] *Q* (*1673*), *F4*; one, Red *F1*
70 s.d. **Knock.**] *placed as in Capell; after deed, l. 70, F1*

2.3

Location: *ed.* (*after Wilson*)
5 **time!**] *Kittredge*; time, *F1*
20 s.d. **Opens the gate.**] *Malone* (*after Capell; following l. 21*); *placed as in Kittredge*
34 **to . . . to**] *F2*; too . . . too *F1*
42 s.d. **Enter Macbeth.**] *placed as in Collier; after l. 41, F1*
56 **screams**] *F4*; Schreemes *F1*
73 s.d. **Exeunt . . . Lennox.**] *placed as in Dyce; after l. 73, F1*
119, 124 s.dd. **Aside to Donalbain.**] *Staunton*
121 s.d. **Aside to Malcolm.**] *Staunton*
125 s.d. **Lady . . .out.**] *Rowe*
134 s.d. **all . . . Donalbain**] *Hanmer*

2.4

Location: *Theobald*
7 **travelling**] *F3*; trauailing *F1*

16 **flung]** *F3*; flong *F1*
28 **ravin]** *Theobald*; rauen *F1*
37 **Well,]** *Theobald*; Well *F1*

3.1

Location: *Capell, Theobald*
2 **weïrd]** *Theobald*; weyard *F1*
10 s.d. **Lady . . . Queen, Lennox]**
  Capell (after Rowe); Lady Lenox *F1*
41–2 **night. . . . welcome,]** *Theobald*;
  Night, . . . welcome: *F1*
43 s.d. **with . . .others]** *ed. (after Rowe,*
  Pelican)
43 s.d. **Manent . . . Servant.]** *Kittredge*
55 **Genius]** *as Rowe; in italics, F1*
56 **Antony's]** *Douai MS (subs.), Pope*;
  Anthonies *F1*
74 s.p. **Both Mur.]** *ed.*; Murth. *F1*
75 **speeches?—know]** *Muir*; speeches:
  Know *F1*
78 **self?]** *Muir*; selfe. *F1*
105 **heart]** *Pope*; heart; *F1*
114, 138 s.pp. **Both Mur.]** *Dyce*; Murth. *F1*
134 **Fleance]** *F4 (so Holinshed)*; Fleans *F1*
  (*throughout rest of play*)
139 s.d. **Exeunt Murderers.]** *Theobald*
141 s.d. **Exit.]** *Theobald*; Exeunt. *F1*

3.2

Location: *Capell, Theobald (subs.)*
41 **Hecat's]** *F3*; Heccats *F1*
42 **shard-borne]** shard-born *F3*

3.3

Location: *Rowe (subs.)*
7 **and]** *F2*; end *F1*
16 s.d. **They assault Banquo.]**
  Theobald
18 s.d. **Dies. Fleance escapes.]** *Pope*

3.4

Location: *Pope (subs.)*
8 s.d. **to the door]** *Capell*
9 **thanks.]** *Pope*; thanks *F1*; thanks, *Q*
  (1673)
12 s.d. **Goes . . . door.]** *White (subs.)*
33 **a-making,]** *Dyce (comma, Pope)*; a
  making: *F1*
34 **given]** *F3*; giuen, *F1*
69 **I? if]** *Hanmer*; I, if *F1*
72 s.d. **Exit Ghost.]** *F2*
77 **time]** *White*; tiems *F1*
106 s.d. **Exit Ghost.]** *F2 (Exit.)*
120 s.d. **Exeunt]** *F2*; Exit *F1*
120 s.d. **and Attendants]** *Capell*
127 **thou,]** *Rowe*; thou *F1*
128 **bidding?]** *F3*; bidding. *F1*
132 **weïrd]** *Theobald*; weyard *F1*

134 **worst. For]** *Johnson*; worst, for *F1*
143 **in deed]** *Theobald*; indeed *F1*

3.5

Location: *Pelican*
2 **beldams]** *Douai MS (beldames),*
  Knight; (Beldams) *F1*
33 **mortals']** *Theobald*; Mortals *F1*
33 s.d. **Sing . . . etc.]** placed as in Capell;
  after l. 35, F1. The song here referred
  to occurs in Middleton's The Witch
  (written c. 1615), in Davenant's operatic
  adaptation of Macbeth (printed 1674,
  but produced as early as 1663–4), and in
  Q (1673). Since it seems highly probable
  that Davenant derived this song (and
  the one referred to at 4.1.43; see Textual
  Notes) from some earlier prompt-book
  of Shakespeare's Macbeth (Middleton's
  play was not printed until the late
  eighteenth century), the following text
  of the song is given from Davenant's
  version (3.8).

MUSICK AND SONG.
[*Sing within.*] Heccate, Heccate, Heccate!
  Oh come away:
[*Hec.*] Hark, I am call'd, my little
  Spirit see,
Sits in a foggy Cloud, and stays for me.
  [*Machine descends.*]
Sing within. Come away, Heccate,
  Heccate! Oh come away:
Hec. I come, I come, with all the speed
  I may,
With all the speed I may.
Where's *Stadling*?
2. Here.
Hec. Where's *Puckle*?
3. Here, and *Hopper* too, and *Helway* too.
1. We want but you, we want but you:
  Come away make up the Count.
Hec. I will but Noint, and then I
  mount,
  I will but, &c.
1. Here comes down one to fetch his
  due, a Kiss,
A Cull, a sip of blood.
And why thou staist so long, I muse,
Since th' Air's so sweet and good.
O art thou come; What News?
2. All goes fair for our delight,
  Either come, or else refuse,
  Now I'm furnish'd for the flight
  Now I go, and now I flye,
  Malking my sweet Spirit and I.
3. O what a dainty pleasure's this,
  To sail i'th' Air while the *Moon* shines
  fair;

To Sing, to Toy, to Dance and Kiss,
Over Woods, high Rocks and
  Mountains;
Over Hills, and misty Fountains:
Over Steeples, Towers, and Turrets:
We flye by night 'mongst troops of
  Spirits.
No Ring of Bells to our Ears sounds,
No howles of Wolves, nor Yelps of
  Hounds;
No, nor the noise of Waters breach,
Nor Cannons Throats our Height can
  reach.

The song in The Witch (*3.3*), *which
actually begins* Come away: Come away:
/ Heccat: Heccat, Come away *as the
s.d. in* Macbeth *suggests, differs in the
disposition of the singers (the whole song
being divided between Hecate and voices*
in the aire, *while* A Spirit like a Cat
descends *following* Ther's one comes
downe, *etc.*) *and in a few readings, notably
in the lines:* Ouer Seas, our Mistris
Fountaines, Ouer Steepe Towres, *and*
Turretts, (*cf.* Over Hills . . . Turrets:). Q
(*1673*), *which also contains two other songs
first appearing in Davenant (following 2.2,
from Davenant 2.5, and 2.3, from Davenant
2.5 [first 16 lines only]*), *offers an inferior
text of this song, derived almost certainly
from Davenant, and the whole song is sung
by three witches only (the line* Over Hills
. . . Fountains: *reading* Over misty Hills
and Fountains,).
35 s.d. **Exit.**] *Capell*

3.6

Location: *Muir*
21 **'cause**] *Pope*; cause *F1*
24 **son**] *Theobald*; Sonnes *F1*
31 **Siward**] *Theobald (from Holinshed)*;
  Seyward *F1 (throughout)*
38 **the**] *Hanmer*; their *F1*

4.1

Location: *Rowe (subs.); a "cave scene" was
actually used in the Smock Alley
(c. 1674–82) production, probably suggested
by Davenant's version of the play (1674),
and a* Cauldorne *is called for in the
Padua prompt-book (c. 1640)*
5 **throw;**] *Douai MS (subs.), Rowe
  (subs.);* throw *F1*
7 **thirty-one**] *Capell (subs.);*
  thirty one: *F1*
23 **Witch's**] *Singer;* Witches *F1*
24 **salt-sea**] *hyphen, Capell*

34 **cau'dron**] *ed.*; Cawdron *F1*
43 s.d. **song: "Black spirits, etc."**] *The
  song here referred to occurs in Middleton's*
  The Witch (*c. 1609*), *5.3, and in
  Davenant's adaptation of* Macbeth (*1674*),
  *4.1, but not in Q (1673). The following text
  of the song, like that printed in the note to
  3.4.33 s.d., is taken from Davenant, since
  it seems probable that he derived it from an
  earlier prompt-book of Shakespeare's play.*
    MUSICK AND SONG.
  Hec. Black Spirits, and white,
    Red Spirits and gray;
    Mingle, mingle, mingle,
    You that mingle may.
  1. *Witch. Tiffin, Tiffin,* keep it stiff in.
  2. Fire drake *Puckey,* make it luckey:
  Hec. Lyer *Robin,* you must bob in.
  Chor. A round, a round, a round, about,
    about,
    All ill come running in, all
    good keep out.
  1. Here's the blood of a Bat!
  Hec. O put in that, put in that.
  2. Here's Lizards brain.
  Hec. Put in a grain.
  1. Here's Juice of Toad, here's oyl of
    Adder
    That will make the Charm grow
    madder.
  2. Put in all these, 'twill raise the stanch.
  Hec. Nay here's three ownces of a
    redhair'd Wench.
  Chor. A round, a round, &c.

  The text in The Witch *is essentially the same,
  the most interesting variants being* Libbards
  Bane *for* Lizards brain, *the* yonker madder
  for the Charm grow madder, *and* rid the
  Stench *for* raise the stanch.
43 s.d. **Exit Hecat.**] *ed. (after Dyce)*
45 s.d. **Knocking.**] *Collier*
47 **Whoever**] *F3*; who euer *F1*
59 **nature's germains**] *Pope*; Natures
  Germaine *F1*
59 **all together**] *Pope*; altogether *F1*
63 **masters'**] *Capell*; Masters *F1*
65 **grease**] *Pope*; Greaze *F1*
68, 86 s.dd. **Apparition**] Apparation *F1*
69 **power—**] *Rowe*; power. *F1*
73 **thanks;**] *F3 (subs.)*; thanks *F1*
74 **more—**] *Rowe*; more. *F1*
83 **assurance**] *Pope*; assurance: *F1*
90 **lion-mettled**] *hyphen, Pope*
93 **Birnan**] *ed.*; Byrnam *F1 (the only
  occurrence of this form in F1; elsewhere*
  Byrnan(e) *or* Birnan(e); *Holinshed has*
  Bernane *and* Birnane)

93 Dunsinane] *Rowe;* Dunsmane *F1*
98 high-plac'd] *hyphen, F3*
111 s.d. the eighth] *Kittredge; F1 s.d. reads:*
A shew of eight Kings, and Banquo
last, with a glasse in his hand.
114 gold-bound brow] *Theobald;* Gold-
bound-brow *F1*
124 s.d. Apparitions vanish.] *Globe*
130 antic] *Theobald;* Antique *F1*
136 weïrd] *Theobald;* Weyard *F1*
144 s.d. Aside.] *Johnson*

4.2

Location: *Theobald (after Rowe)*
1 s.p. L. Macd.] *Rowe;* Wife. *F1*
(throughout scene)
10 diminutive] *F4;* diminitiue *F1*
23 'Shall] *ed.;* Shall *F1*
41 buy] *F3;* by *F1*
42 with all] *F2;* withall *F1*
49–50 Every . . . hang'd.] *as prose, Pope;*
as verse, F1
59–60 Now . . . father?] *as prose, Pope; as*
verse, F1
69–70 ones. . . . thus,] *F2 (subs.);* ones . .
. thus. *F1*
79 s.d. Enter Murtherers.] *placed as in*
Globe; after l. 79, F1
80, 82, 83 s.pp. 1. Mur.] *Capell*
83 s.d. Stabbing him.] *Rowe*
85 s.d. Dies.] *Capell*
85 s.d. Lady Macduff . . . and . . .
Murderers] *Theobald (subs.)*

4.3

Location: *Dyce (after Rowe)*
4 birthdom] *Johnson;* Birthdome *F1*
34 affeer'd] *Hanmer;* affear'd *F1*
72 cold,] *Theobald;* cold. *F1*
104 bloody-sceptred] *hyphen, Pope*
107 accus'd] *Wilson;* accust *F1;*
accurst *F2*
109 sainted king] *F4;* Sainted-King *F1*
127 own,] *F2;* owne. *F1*
133 thy] *F2;* they *F1*
133 here-approach] *hyphen, Pope*
145 s.d. Exit Doctor.] *Capell;* Exit. *F1*
(after amend. l. 145)
148 here-remain] *hyphen, Pope*
150 strangely-visited] *hyphen, Pope*
170 dead man's] *Johnson;* Deadmans *F1*
195–6 they? . . . cause?] *Theobald;*
they, . . . cause, *F1*
233 myself;] *Theobald;* my selfe *F1*
235 tune] *Rowe;* time *F1*

5.1

Location: *Capell (subs., after Rowe)*

26–7 What . . . hands.] *as prose, Douai*
MS, Pope; as verse, F1
37 fear] *Rowe;* feare? *F1*
46–7 Go . . . not.] *as prose, Douai MS,*
Pope; as verse, F1

5.2

Location: *Capell*
10 unrough] *Theobald;* vnruffe *F1*
28 we,] *Rowe;* we *F1*

5.3

Location: *Capell (after Rowe)*
1 two] *F2;* too *F1*
19 s.d. Exit Servant.] *Dyce*
19–20 Seyton!— . . . say!—] *Rowe;*
Seyton, I am sick at hart, / When I
behold: Seyton, I say, *F1*
21 disseat] *Jennens conj.;* dis-eate *F1;*
disease *F2*
24 old age] *F2;* Old-Age *F1*
39 her] *F2*
52 pristine] *F2;* pristiue *F1*
60 s.d. Exeunt . . . Doctor.] *Dyce*
(after Steevens)
62 s.d. Exit.] *Steevens;* Exeunt *F1*

5.4

Location: *Globe (after Pope)*
o.s.d. Lennox, Rosse] *Malone*
7 s.p. Soldiers.] *Dyce;* Sold. *F1*
14–5 just censures Attend] *best*
Censures / Before *F2*

5.5

Location: *Theobald (subs., after Pope)*
7 s.d. A . . . women.] *placed as in Dyce;*
after l. 7, F1
8 s.d. Exit.] *Collier MS*
15 s.d. Enter Seyton.] *Collier MS*
37 false] *F2;* fhlse *F1*

5.6

Location: *Capell (after Rowe)*

5.7

Location: *ed. (after Wilson)*
20 be;] *Pope (subs.);* be, *F1*

5.8

5.8] *Dyce*
Location: *ed. (after Ridley)*
34 s.d. Macduff . . . body.] *ed.*

5.9

5.9] *Wilson (after Kittredge conj.)*
Location: *ed. (after Wilson)*
41 s.d. Exeunt omnes.] Exeunt
Omnes. / FINIS. *F1*

Sources and Contexts

"An English Man" and
"A Scottish Man"

Andrew Boorde

*Andrew Boorde's the fyrst boke of the introduction of knowledge
(London, 1555), is one of the earliest guidebooks in English. A physician,
Boorde traveled widely. His description of the known nations of the world
was popular enough to be reprinted. Each chapter includes a woodcut figure,
with a monologue dramatizing contemporary notions of what the country-
men and women were thought to be like. A description of the country's geography follows, with a conversion table of coins in local denominations. The
presence of these tables implies that the guide was designed for practical use.*

*Why would an Englishman want to carry around a travel guide with this
goofy, half-naked stereotype of himself on the first page? The figure that capers
here seems designed to caution the reader about contemporary preconceptions of
Englishness he might encounter in other countries. We can assume stereotypes
had the same potency in Renaissance culture that they have today: at once
trivial and also cutting, connected to contemporary anxieties about national
and personal identity. Note the effeminacy of this figure, its ambiguous class,
and the rustic setting. As the monologue tells us, this Englishman is strong and
could be faithful and wise, if he would only make up his mind, educate himself
and be true to himself – instead of giddily chasing new fashions.*

AN ENGLISH MAN

THE FIRST chapter treateth of the natural disposition of an English man, and of the noble realm of England, & of the money
that there is used.

I am an English man, and naked I stand here
Musing in my minde, what raiment I shall wear
For now I will wear this and now I will wear that;
Now I will wear I cannot tell what.

Andrew Boorde, "An English man," and "A Scottish man," from *The Fyrst Book of
the Introduction of Knowledge*. (1547; ed. F. J. Furnivall.) Early English Text Society.
10. London: Trübner, 1870.

All new fashions be pleasant to me;   5
I will have them, whether I thrive or thee.
Now I am a frisker, all men doth on me look
What would I do, but set cock on the hoop
What do I care, if all the world me fail?
I will get a garment, shall reach to my tail.   10
Then I am a minion, for I wear the new guise.
The next year after this I trust to be wise,
Not only in wearing my gorgeous array;
For I will go to learning a whole summer's day
I will learn Latin, Hebrew, Greek and French   15
And I will learn Duty, sitting on my bench.
I do fear no man, all men feareth me;
I overcome my adversaries, by land and by see.
I had no peer, if to my self I were true;
Because I am not so, divers times I do rue.   20
Yet I lack nothing, I have all thing at will
If I were wise and would hold my self still,
And meddle with no matters, to me pertaining
But ever to be true, to god and my king.
But I have such matters rolling in my pate   25
That I will speak and do I cannot tell what;
No man shall let me, but I will have my mind,
And to father, mother and friend, I will be unkind;
I will follow mine own mind and mine old trade
Who shall let me, the devil's nails unpared: 30
Yet above all things, new fashions I love well,
And to wear them my thrift I will sell.
In all this world, I shall have but a time,
Hold the cup good fellow, here is thine and mine.

---

6. thee: prosper. **8. set cocke:** &etc.: goof, clown, screw up. **11. min-ion:** male favorite or lover; perhaps alluding to a rude etymology of the word "English" from "ingle," or catamite. **13. array:** clothing, outfit.
20. rue: regret it. **25. pate:** head. **27. let:** hinder. **28. friend:** friend, lover.
30. the devil's . . . unpared: screw whoever tries to get in my way.

Fig. 5. Woodcut portrait of an English man, Andrew Boorde, *The Fyrst Boke of the Introduction of Knowledge*, Chapter 1.

Fig. 6. Woodcut portrait of a Scottish man, Andrew Boorde, *The Fyrst Boke of the Introduction of Knowledge*, Chapter 4.

A SCOTTISH MAN

Andrew Boorde's Scottish man stands arm akimbo (elbow toward the viewer), an "in your face" pose that signifies status in Renaissance portraiture. Well dressed but boasting that fashions hold no power over him, he poses indoors — a location that suggests a cultured man. His reference to Scotland's historical alliance with France underscores the longstanding hostilities between England and its northern neighbor. The same stereotype can sometimes appear in both negative and positive forms. Here we see a version of native Scottish hardiness and ferocity that contemporary historians, such as John Bellenden and William Harrison, often admired (see Floyd-Wilson's discussion in the Critical Essays section of this volume). Yet Boorde presents those qualities in negative terms, associating this Scot's fierceness with duplicity, enmity and murder.

THE FOURTH chapter treateth of Scotland and the natural disposition of a Scotish man. And of their money, and of their speech.

I am a Scotishman and true I am to France
In every country, myself I do advance
I will boast myself, I will crake and face
I love to be exalted, here and in every place
An Englishman I cannot naturally love 5
Wherefore I offend them, and my lord above
He that will double with any man
He may speed well, but I cannot tell when
I am a Scotyshman and have dissembled much
And in my promise I have not kept touch 10
Great murder and theft in times past I have used
I trust to god herafter, such things shall be refused
And what word I do speak, be it in mirth or in borde
The foul evil shall be, at the end of my word
Yet will I not change my apparel nor array 15
Although the frenchmen go never so gay.

---

3. crake: var. of "crack"—boast, brag; also the harsh sound of a crow; **face:** swagger, bluff, confront.   **7. double with:** deceive.   **8. speed well:** get on well, do well.   **13. borde:** jest, game, mockery.   **16. gay:** fashionably dressed.

PERFORMANCE OF *MACBETH*
AT THE GLOBE

Simon Forman, 1611

The following manuscript jottings by Dr. Simon Forman (1552–1611) are bound up as part (fols. 200–207ᵛ) of a substantial volume (Bodleian Ashm. MS. 208), containing, in Forman's holograph, astrological, alchemical, and biographical materials. They record [a performance] seen by Forman at the Globe in 1611 of Macbeth. (The date 1610 assigned by Forman to the performance of Macbeth that he attended on Saturday April 20, is presumably a slip for 1611, since April 20 fell on a Saturday in 1611 but not in 1610.) Some of his details are especially interesting because they suggest possible differences between the play as performed at the Globe and the text as preserved in F1. In the present text, extra minim strokes in m and n have been silently regularized. (GBE, 1974) In addition, other orthographic elements have been lightly modernized consistent with the conventions Evans used for the playtext. The exception is names, which here retain Forman's spellings to give a sense of the variability of Renaissance English writing and possible puns. The title itself seems to pun on Forman's name, as the Latinate "per formane" might mean either "performance" or "by Forman" or both. (KR, 2011)

The Book of Plays and Notes therof performane for Common Policy.

IN MACKBETH, at the glod [Globe], 1610 [1611] the 20 of April [Saturday], there was to be observed first how Mackbeth and Bancko, two noblemen of Scotland, riding through a wood, there stood before them three women, fairies or nymphs, and saluted Mackbeth saying three times unto him, Hail Mackbeth, King of Codon [Cawdor], for thou shalt be a king, but shalt beget no kings, etc. Then said Bancko, What all to Mackbeth and nothing to me? Yes, said the nymphs, Hail to thee Banko, thou shalt beget kings, yet be no king. And so they departed and came to the court of Scotland to Dunkin, king of Scots, and it was in the days of Edward the Confessor. And Dunkin bade them both kindly welcome. And made Mackbeth forthwith Prince of Northumberland, and sent him home to his own castle, and appointed Mackbeth to provide for him, for he would sup with him the next day at night, and did so. And Mackebeth contrived to kill

Dunkin, and through the persuasion of his wife did that night murder the king in his own castle, being his guest. And there were many prodigies seen that night and the day before. And when Mack Beth had murdered the king, the blood on his hands could not be washed off by any means, nor from his wife's hands, which handled the bloody daggers in hiding them, by which means they became both much amazed and affronted. The murder being known, Dunkin's two sons fled, the one to England and the [other to] Wales, to save themselves. They being fled, they were supposed guilty of the murder of their father, which was nothing so. Then was Mackbeth crowned king, and then he, for fear of Banko his old companion, that he should beget kings but be no king himself, he contrived the death of Banko and caused him to be murdered on the way, as he rode. The next night, being at supper with his noblemen whom he had bid to a feast (to the which also Banco should have come) he began to speak of noble Banco, and to wish that he were there. And as he thus did, standing up to drink a carouse to him, the ghost of Banco came and sat down in his chair behind him. And he, turning about to sit down again, saw the ghost of Banco, which fronted him so that he fell into a great passion of fear and fury, uttering many words about his murder, by which, when they heard that Banco was murdered, they suspected Mackbet.

Then Mack Dove fled to England to the king's son. And so they raised an army and came into Scotland, and at Dunston Anyse overthrew Mackbet. In the meantime, while Macdovee was in England, Mackbet slew Mack Dove's wife and children, and after in the battle Mackdove slew Mackbet.

Observe also how Mackbete's queen did rise in the night in her sleep and walk, and talked and confessed all, and the doctor noted her words.

"MACBETH"

Jorge Luis Borges

Jorge Luis Borges (1899–1986), an Argentine writer known for his poems, es-
says, and short stories, has been widely read and translated around the world.
Throughout his career, Borges returned frequently to Shakespeare's life, char-
acters, works and art, engaging them as an artist and a critic. This compact,
evocative poem "Macbeth" imagines Shakespeare and his main character as
collaborators. The poem touches down in the language of the play in a number
of registers and even imitates Shakespearean patterns of diction. In his 1970
prologue to a Spanish edition of Macbeth, *Borges (who was multilingual)*
observes that Shakespeare regularly exploits the fact that Renaissance English
evolved from both Anglo-Germanic and Latinate languages. This "least Eng-
lish of English poets" frequently alternates words from different language fami-
lies, balancing long and "luminous" Latinate words with "brief" and "direct"
Anglo-Saxon ones.[1] We can hear this subtle play of tongues in Shakespeare's
"The multitudinous seas incarnadine, /Making the green one, red" and in
Borges's "destined way."

MACBETH
Nuestros actos prosiguen su camino,
que no conoce término.
Maté a mi rey para que Shakespeare
urdiera su tragedia.

MACBETH
Our acts continue on their destined way
which does not know an end.
I slew my sovereign so that Shakespeare
might plot his tragedy.

1. Jorge Luis Borges, "Macbeth." *Obras Completas*. Ed. Sarah Luisa Del Carril. 3rd ed. Vol. 4. Buenos Aires: Emecé Editores, 2005, 146.

CRITICAL ESSAYS

ON THE KNOCKING AT THE GATE
IN *MACBETH*
Thomas De Quincey

Thomas De Quincey (1785-1859), Victorian journalist and essayist, puzzles here over his intense reaction to the strange moment when a knocking sound echoes on stage immediately after Duncan's murder. His meditation on the experience of this moment (Act 2 scenes 2 and 3) illustrates the complex emotional and cognitive affects that Macbeth *can produce in performance.*

FROM MY boyish days I had always felt a great perplexity on one point in Macbeth: it was this: the knocking at the gate, which succeeds to the murder of Duncan, produced to my feelings an effect for which I never could account: the effect was—that it reflected back upon the murder a peculiar awfulness and a depth of solemnity: yet, however obstinately I endeavoured with my understanding to comprehend this, for many years I never could see *why* it should produce such an effect.—

Here I pause for one moment to exhort the reader never to pay any attention to his understanding when it stands in opposition to any other faculty of his mind. The mere understanding, however useful and indispensable, is the meanest faculty in the human mind, and the most to be distrusted: and yet the great majority of people trust to nothing else; which may do for ordinary life, but not for philosophic purposes. Of this, out of ten thousand instances that I might produce, I will cite one. Ask of any person whatsoever, who is not previously prepared for the demand by a knowledge of perspective, to draw in the rudest way the commonest appearance which depends upon the laws of that science—as for instance, to represent the effect of two walls standing at right angles to each other, or the appearance of the houses on each side of a street, as seen by a person looking down the street from one extremity. Now in all cases, unless the person has happened to observe in pictures how it is that artists produce these effects, he will be utterly unable to make the smallest approximation to it. Yet

Thomas De Quincey, "On Knocking at the Gate." The London Magazine, 1823.

why?—For he has actually seen the effect every day of his life. The reason is—that he allows his understanding to overrule his eyes. His understanding, which includes no intuitive knowledge of the laws of vision, can furnish him with no reason why a line which is known and can be proved to be a horizontal line, should not *appear* a horizontal line: a line, that made any angle with the perpendicular less than a right angle, would seem to him to indicate that his houses were all tumbling down together. Accordingly he makes the line of his houses a horizontal line, and fails of course to produce the effect demanded. Here then is one instance out of many, in which not only the understanding is allowed to overrule the eyes, but where the understanding is positively allowed to obliterate the eyes as it were: for not only does the man believe the evidence of his understanding in opposition to that of his eyes, but (what is monstrous!) the idiot is not aware that his eyes ever gave such evidence. He does not know that he has seen (and therefore *quoad* his consciousness has *not* seen) that which he *has* seen every day of his life.

But, to return from this digression,—my understanding could furnish no reason why the knocking at the gate in Macbeth should produce any effect direct or reflected: in fact, my understanding said positively that it could *not* produce any effect. But I knew better: I felt that it did: and I waited and clung to the problem until further knowledge should enable me to solve it.—At length, in 1812, Mr Williams made his *début* on the stage of Rateliffe Highway, and executed those unparalleled murders which have procured for him such a brilliant and undying reputation. On which murders, by the way, I must observe, that in one respect they have had an ill effect, by making the connoisseur in murder very fastidious in his taste, and dissatisfied with any thing that has been since done in that line. All other murders look pale by the deep crimson of his; and, as an amateur once said to me in a querulous tone, 'There has been absolutely nothing *doing* since his time, or nothing that's worth speaking of.' But this is wrong: for it is unreasonable to expect all men to be great artists, and born with the genius of Mr. Williams.—Now it will be remembered that in the first of these murders (that of the Marrs), the same incident (of a knocking at the door soon after the work of extermination was complete) did actually occur, which the genius of Shakespeare had invented: and all good judges, and the most eminent dilettanti acknowledged the felicity of Shakespeare's suggestion as soon as it was actually realized. Here then was a fresh proof that I had been right in relying on my own feeling in opposition to my understanding; and again I set myself to study the problem: at length I solved it to my own satisfaction; and my solution is this. Murder in ordinary cases, where the sympathy is wholly directed to the case of the murdered person, is an incident of coarse and vulgar horror; and for this reason—that it flings the interest exclusively upon the natural but ignoble instinct by which we cleave to life; an instinct which, as being indispensable to the primal law of self-preservation, is the same in kind (though different in degree) amongst all living creatures; this instinct therefore, because it annihilates all distinctions, and degrades the greatest of men to the level of 'the poor beetle that we tread on,' exhibits human nature in its most abject and humiliating attitude. Such an attitude would little suit the purposes of the poet. What then must he do? He must throw the interest on the murderer: our sympathy must be with *him*; (of course I mean a sympathy of comprehension, a sympathy by which we enter into his feelings, and are made to understand them,—not a sympathy[1] of pity or approbation:) in the murdered person all strife of thought, all flux and reflux of passion and of purpose, are crushed by one over-whelming panic: the fear of instant death smites him 'with its petrific mace.' But in the murderer, such a murderer as a poet will condescend to, there must be raging some great storm of passion,—jealousy, ambition, vengeance, hatred, —which will create a hell within him; and into this hell we are to look.

In Macbeth, for the sake of gratifying his own enormous and teeming faculty of creation, Shakespeare has introduced two murderers: and, as usual in his hands, they are remarkably discriminated: but, though in Macbeth the strife of mind is greater than in his wife, the tiger spirit not so awake, and his feelings caught chiefly by contagion from her,—yet, as both were finally involved in the guilt of murder, the murderous mind of necessity is finally to be presumed in both. This was to be expressed; and on its own account, as well as to make it a more proportionable antagonist to the unoffending nature of their victim, 'the gracious Duncan,' and adequately to expound 'the deep damnation of his taking off,' this was to be expressed with peculiar energy. We were to be made to feel that the human nature, *i.e.* the divine nature of love and mercy, spread through the hearts of all creatures, and seldom utterly withdrawn from man,— was gone, vanished, extinct; and that the fiendish nature had taken

---

1. It seems almost ludicrous to guard and explain my use of a word in a situation where it should naturally explain itself. But it has become necessary to do so, in consequence of the unscholarlike use of the word sympathy, at present so general, by which, instead of taking it in its proper sense, as the act of reproducing in our minds the feelings of another, whether for hatred, indignation, love, pity, or approbation, it is made a mere synonyme of the word *pity*; and hence, instead of saying, 'sympathy *with* another,' many writers adopt the monstrous barbarism of 'sympathy *for* another.'

its place. And, as this effect is marvellously accomplished in the dia-
logues and soliloquies themselves, so it is finally consummated by the
expedient under consideration; and it is to this that I now solicit the
reader's attention. If the reader has ever witnessed a wife, daughter,
or sister, in a fainting fit, he may chance to have observed that the
most affecting moment in such a spectacle, is *that* in which a sigh
and a stirring announce the recommencement of suspended life. Or,
if the reader has ever been present in a vast metropolis on the day
when some great national idol was carried in funeral pomp to his
grave, and chancing to walk near the course through which it passed,
has felt powerfully, in the silence and desertion of the streets and in
the stagnation of ordinary business, the deep interest which at that
moment was possessing the heart of man,—if all at once he should
hear the death-like stillness broken up by the sound of wheels rattling
away from the scene, and making known that the transitory vision
was dissolved, he will be aware that at no moment was his sense of
the complete suspension and pause in ordinary human concerns so
full and affecting as at that moment when the suspension ceases, and
the goings-on of human life are suddenly resumed. All action in any
direction is best expounded, measured, and made apprehensible, by
reaction. Now apply this to the case in Macbeth. Here, as I have said,
the retiring of the human heart and the entrance of the fiendish heart
was to be expressed and made sensible. Another world has stepped
in; and the murderers are taken out of the region of human things,
human purposes, human desires. They are transfigured: Lady Macbeth
is 'unsexed;' Macbeth has forgot that he was born of woman; both are
conformed to the image of devils; and the world of devils is suddenly
revealed. But how shall this be conveyed and made palpable? In order
that a new world may step in, this world must for a time disappear.
The murderers, and the murder, must be insulated—cut off by an
immeasurable gulph from the ordinary tide and succession of human
affairs—locked up and sequestered in some deep recess: we must be
made sensible that the world of ordinary life is suddenly arrested—
laid asleep—tranced—racked into a dread armistice: time must be
annihilated; relation to things without abolished; and all must pass
self-withdrawn into a deep syncope and suspension of earthly passion.
Hence it is that when the deed is done—when the work of darkness
is perfect, then the world of darkness passes away like a pageantry in
the clouds: the knocking at the gate is heard; and it makes known
audibly that the reaction has commenced: the human has made its
reflux upon the fiendish: the pulses of life are beginning to beat again:
and the re-establishment of the goings-on of the world in which we

live, first makes us profoundly sensible of the awful parenthesis that had suspended them.

Oh! mighty poet!—Thy works are not as those of other men, simply and merely great works of art; but are also like the phenomena of nature, like the sun and the sea, the stars and the flowers,—like frost and snow, rain and dew, hail-storm and thunder, which are to be studied with entire submission of our own faculties, and in the perfect faith that in them there can be no too much or too little, nothing useless or inert—but that, the further we press in our discoveries, the more we shall see proofs of design and self-supporting arrangement where the careless eye had seen nothing but accident!

N.B. In the above specimen of psychological criticism, I have purposely omitted to notice another use of the knocking at the gate, viz. the opposition and contrast which it produces in the porter's comments to the scenes immediately preceding; because this use is tolerably obvious to all who are accustomed to reflect on what they read. A third use also, subservient to the scenical illusion, has been lately noticed by a critic in the LONDON MAGAZINE: I fully agree with him; but it did not fall in my way to insist on this.

X.Y.Z.

"BORN OF WOMAN"
FANTASIES OF MATERNAL POWER
IN *MACBETH*

Janet Adelman

In an essay that has become a classic of modern literary criticism, teacher and scholar Janet Adelman illuminates the twin themes that define the psychological world of Macbeth: *masculine vulnerability and maternal threat.*

IN THE last moments of any production of *Macbeth*, as Macbeth feels himself increasingly hemmed in by enemies, the stage will resonate hauntingly with variants of his repeated question, "What's he/That was not born of woman?" (5.7.2–3; for variants, see 5.3.4,6; 5.7.11,13; 5.8.13, 31).[1] Repeated seven times, Macbeth's allusion to the witches' prophecy—"none of woman born/Shall harm Macbeth" (4.1.80–81)—becomes virtually a talisman to ward off danger; even after he has begun to doubt the equivocation of the fiend (5.5.43), mere repetition of the phrase seems to Macbeth to guarantee his invulnerability. I want in this essay to explore the power of these resonances, particularly to explore how Macbeth's assurance seems to turn itself inside out, becoming dependent not on the fact that all men are, after all, born of woman but on the fantasy of escape from this universal condition. The duplicity of Macbeth's repeated question–its capacity to mean both itself and its opposite–carries such weight at the end of the play, I think, because the whole of the play represents in very powerful form both the fantasy of a virtually absolute and destructive maternal power and the fantasy of absolute escape from this power; I shall argue in fact that the peculiar texture of the end of the play is generated partly by the tension between these two fantasies.

Maternal power in *Macbeth* is not embodied in the figure of a particular mother (as it is, for example, in *Coriolanus*); it is instead diffused throughout the play, evoked primarily by the figures of the witches and Lady Macbeth. Largely through Macbeth's relationship to them, the play becomes (like *Coriolanus*) a representation of primitive fears about male identity and autonomy itself,[2] about those loom-

Janet Adelman, "'Born of Woman': Fantasies of Maternal Power in *Macbeth*." In *Cannibals, Witches, and Divorce: Estranging the Renaissance*. Selected papers from the English Institute, 1985. Ed. Marjorie Garber. Baltimore: Johns Hopkins UP, 1985. 90–121. © 1987 The English Institute. Reprinted with permission of The Johns Hopkins University Press.

ing female presences who threaten to control one's actions and one's mind, to constitute one's very self, even at a distance. When Macbeth's first words echo those we have already heard the witches speak—"So fair and foul a day I have not seen" (1.3.38); "Fair is foul, and foul is fair" (1.1.11)—we are in a realm that questions the very possibility of autonomous identity. The play will finally reimagine autonomous male identity, but only through the ruthless excision of all female presence, its own peculiar satisfaction of the witches' prophecy.

In 1600, after the Earl of Gowrie's failed attempt to kill James VI, one James Weimis of Bogy, testifying about the earl's recourse to necromancy, reported that the earl thought it "possible that the seed of man and woman might be brought to perfection otherwise then by the *matrix* of the woman."[3] Whether or not Shakespeare deliberately recalled Gowrie in his portrayal of the murderer of James's ancestor,[4] the connection is haunting: the account of the conspiracy hints that, for Gowrie at least, recourse to necromancy seemed to promise at once invulnerability and escape from the maternal matrix.[5] The fantasy of such escape in fact haunts Shakespeare's plays. A few years after Macbeth, Posthumus will make the fantasy explicit: attributing all ills in man to the "woman's part," he will ask, "Is there no way for men to be, but women/Must be half-workers?" (*Cymbeline*, 2.5.1–2).[6] The strikingly motherless world of *The Tempest* and its potent image of absolute male control answers Posthumus' questions affirmatively: there at least, on that bare island, mothers and witches are banished and creation belongs to the male alone.

Even in one of Shakespeare's earliest plays, male autonomy is ambivalently portrayed as the capacity to escape the maternal matrix that has misshaped the infant man.[7] The man who will become Richard III emerges strikingly as a character for the first time as he watches his brother Edward's sexual success with the Lady Grey. After wishing syphilis on him so that he will have no issue (a concern that anticipates Macbeth's), Richard constructs his own desire for the crown specifically as compensation for his failure at the sexual game. Unable to "make [his] heaven in a lady's lap," he will "make [his] heaven to dream upon the crown" (*3 Henry VI*, 3.2.148,169). But his failure to make his heaven in a lady's lap is itself understood as the consequence of his subjection to another lady's lap, to the misshaping power of his mother's womb:

Why, love forswore me in my Mother's womb;
And, for I should not deal in her soft laws,
She did corrupt frail nature with some bribe
To shrink mine arm up like a withered shrub;
To make an envious mountain on my back.
[3.2.153–57]

Richard blames his deformity on a triad of female powers: Mother, Love, and Nature all fuse, conspiring to deform him as he is being formed in his mother's womb. Given this image of female power, it is no wonder that he turns to the compensatory heaven of the crown. But the crown turns out to be an unstable compensation. Even as he shifts from the image of the misshaping womb to the image of the crown, the terrifying enclosure of the womb recurs, shaping his attempt to imagine the very political project that should free him from dependence on ladies' laps:

> I'll make my heaven to dream upon the crown
> And, whiles I live, t'account this world but hell
> Until my misshaped trunk that bears this head
> Be round impalèd with a glorious crown.
> And yet I know not how to get the crown,
> For many lives stand between me and home;
> And I–like one lost in a thorny wood,
> That rents the thorns and is rent with the thorns,
> Seeking a way and straying from the way,
> Not knowing how to find the open air
> But toiling desperately to find it out–
> Torment myself to catch the English crown;
> And from that torment I will free myself
> Or hew my way out with a bloody axe.
>
> [3.2.168–81]

The crown for him is "home," the safe haven. But through the shifting meaning of "impalèd," the crown as safe haven is itself transformed into the dangerous enclosure: the stakes that enclose him protectively turn into the thorns that threaten to impale him.[8] Strikingly, it is not his head but the trunk that bears his head that is so impaled by crown and thorns: the crown compensatory for ladies' laps fuses with the image of the dangerous womb in an imagistic nightmare in which the lap/womb/home/crown become the thorny wood from which he desperately seeks escape into the open air. Through this imagistic transformation, these lines take on the configuration of a birth fantasy, or more precisely a fantasy of impeded birth, a birth that the man-child himself must manage by hewing his way out with a bloody axe.[9] Escape from the dangerous female is here achieved by recourse to the exaggeratedly masculine bloody axe. This, I will argue, is precisely the psychological configuration of *Macbeth*, where dangerous female presences like Love, Nature, Mother are given embodiment in Lady Macbeth and the witches, and where Macbeth wields the bloody axe in an attempt to escape their dominion over him.

At first glance, Macbeth seems to wield the bloody axe to comply with, not to escape, the dominion of women. The play constructs Macbeth as terrifyingly pawn to female figures. Whether or not he is rapt by the witches' prophecies because the horrid image of Duncan's murder has already occurred to him, their role as gleeful prophets constructs Macbeth's actions in part as the enactments of their will. And he is impelled toward murder by Lady Macbeth's equation of masculinity and murder: in his case, the bloody axe seems not an escape route but the tool of a man driven to enact the ferociously masculine strivings of his wife.[10] Nonetheless, the weight given the image of the man not born of woman at the end suggests that the underlying fantasy is the same as in Richard's defensive construction of his masculinity: even while enacting the wills of women, Macbeth's bloody masculinity enables an escape from them in fantasy—an escape that the play itself embodies in dramatic form at the end. I will discuss first the unleashing of female power and Macbeth's compliance with that power, and then the fantasy of escape.

In the figures of Macbeth, Lady Macbeth, and the witches, the play gives us images of a masculinity and a femininity that are terribly disturbed; this disturbance seems to me both the cause and the consequence of the murder of Duncan. In *Hamlet*, Shakespeare had reconstructed the Fall as the death of the ideal father; here, he constructs a revised version in which the Fall is the death of the ideally androgynous parent. For Duncan combines in himself the attributes of both father and mother: he is the center of authority, the source of lineage and honor, the giver of name and gift; but he is also the source of all nurturance, planting the children to his throne and making them grow. He is the father as androgynous parent from whom, singly, all good can be imagined to flow, the source of a benign and empowering nurturance the opposite of that imaged in the witches' poisonous cauldron and Lady Macbeth's gall-filled breasts. Such a father does away with any need for a mother: he is the image of both parents in one, threatening aspects of each controlled by the presence of the other.[11] When he is gone, "The wine of life is drawn, and the mere lees/Is left this vault to brag of" (2.3.93–94): nurturance itself is spoiled, as all the play's imagery of poisoned chalices and interrupted feasts implies. In his absence male and female break apart, the female becoming merely helpless or merely poisonous and the male merely bloodthirsty; the harmonious relation of the genders imaged in Duncan fails.

In *Hamlet*, the absence of the ideal protecting father brings the son face to face with maternal power. The absence of Duncan similarly unleashes the power of the play's malevolent mothers. But this father-king seems strikingly absent even before his murder. Heavily idealized, he is nonetheless largely ineffectual: even while he is alive, he is unable to hold his kingdom together, reliant on a series of bloody men to suppress an increasingly successful series of rebellions.[12] The witches are already abroad in his realm; they in fact constitute our introduction to that realm. Duncan, not Macbeth, is the first person to echo them ("When the battle's lost and won" [1.1.4]; "What he hath lost, noble Macbeth hath won" [1.2.69]). The witches' sexual ambiguity terrifies: Banquo says of them, "You should be women,/And yet your beards forbid me to interpret/That you are so" (1.3.45–47). Is their androgyny the shadow-side of the King's, enabled perhaps by his failure to maintain a protective masculine authority? Is their strength a consequence of his weakness? (This is the configuration of *Cymbeline*, where the power of the witch-queen-stepmother is so dependent on the failure of Cymbeline's masculine authority that she obligingly dies when that authority returns to him.) Banquo's question to the witches may ask us to hear a counterquestion about Duncan, who should be man. For Duncan's androgyny is the object of enormous ambivalence: idealized for his nurturing paternity, he is nonetheless killed for his womanish softness, his childish trust, his inability to read men's minds in their faces, his reliance on the fighting of sons who can rebel against him. Macbeth's description of the dead Duncan—"his silver skin lac'd with his golden blood" (2.3.110)—makes him into a virtual icon of kingly worth; but other images surrounding his death make him into an emblem not of masculine authority, but of female vulnerability. As he moves toward the murder, Macbeth first imagines himself the allegorical figure of murder, as though to absolve himself of the responsibility of choice. But the figure of murder then fuses with that of Tarquin:

> wither'd Murther,
> . . . thus with his stealthy pace,
> With Tarquin's ravishing strides, towards his design
> Moves like a ghost.
>
> [2.1.52–56]

These lines figure the murder as a display of male sexual aggression against a passive female victim: murder here becomes rape; Macbeth's victim becomes not the powerful male figure of the king, but the helpless Lucrece.[13] Hardened by Lady Macbeth to regard maleness and violence as equivalent, that is, Macbeth responds to Duncan's idealized milky gentleness as though it were evidence of his femaleness. The horror of this gender transformation, as well as the horror of the murder, is implicit in Macduff's identification of the king's body as a new Gorgon ("Approach the chamber, and destroy your sight/With a new Gorgon" [2.3.70–71]). The power of this image lies partly in its suggestion that Duncan's bloodied body, with its multiple wounds, has been revealed as female and hence blinding to his sons: as if the threat all along was that Duncan would be revealed as female and that this revelation would rob his sons of his masculine protection and hence of their own masculinity.[14]

In *King Lear*, the abdication of protective paternal power seems to release the destructive power of a female chaos imaged not only in Goneril and Regan, but also in the storm on the heath. Macbeth virtually alludes to Lear's storm as he approaches the witches in act 4, conjuring them to answer though they "untie the winds, and let them fight/Against the Churches," though the "waves/Confound and swallow navigation up," though "the treasure/Of Nature's germens tumble all together/Even till destruction sicken" (4.1.52–60; see *King Lear*, 3.2.1–9). The witches merely implicit on Lear's heath have become in *Macbeth* embodied agents of storm and disorder,[15] and they are there from the start. Their presence suggests that the absence of the father that unleashes female chaos (as in *Lear*) has already happened at the beginning of *Macbeth*; that absence is merely made literal in Macbeth's murder of Duncan at the instigation of female forces. For this father-king cannot protect his sons from powerful mothers, and it is the son's—and the play's—revenge to kill him, or, more precisely, to kill him first and love him after, paying him back for his excessively "womanish" trust and then memorializing him as the ideal androgynous parent.[16] The reconstitution of manhood becomes a central problem of the play in part, I think, because the vision of manhood embodied in Duncan has already failed at the play's beginning.

The witches constitute our introduction to the realm of maternal malevolence unleashed by the loss of paternal protection; as soon as Macbeth meets them, he becomes (in Hecate's probably non-Shakespearean words) their "wayward son" (3.5.11). This maternal malevolence is given its most horrifying expression in Shakespeare in the image through which Lady Macbeth secures her control over Macbeth:

> I have given suck, and know
> How tender 'tis to love the babe that milks me:
> I would, while it was smiling in my face,
> Have pluck'd my nipple from his boneless gums,
> And dash'd the brains out, had I so sworn
> As you have done to this.
>
> [1.7.54–59]

This image of murderously disrupted nurturance is the psychic equivalence of the witches' poisonous cauldron; both function to subject Macbeth's will to female forces.[17] For the play strikingly constructs the fantasy of subjection to maternal malevolence in two parts, in the witches and in Lady Macbeth, and then persistently identifies the two parts as one. Through this identification, Shakespeare in effect locates the source of his culture's fear of witchcraft in individual human history, in the infant's long dependence on female figures felt as all-powerful: what the witches suggest about the vulnerability of men to female power on the cosmic plane, Lady Macbeth doubles on the psychological plane.

Lady Macbeth's power as a female temptress allies her in a general way with the witches as soon as we see her. The specifics of that implied alliance begin to emerge as she attempts to harden herself in preparation for hardening her husband: the disturbance of gender that Banquo registers when he first meets the witches is played out in psychological terms in Lady Macbeth's attempt to unsex herself. Calling on spirits ambiguously allied with the witches themselves, she phrases this unsexing as the undoing of her own bodily maternal function:

> Come, you Spirits
> That tend on mortal thoughts, unsex me here,
> And fill me, from the crown to the toe, top-full
> Of direst cruelty! make thick my blood,
> Stop up th'access and passage to remorse;
> That no compunctious visitings of Nature
> Shake my fell purpose, nor keep peace between
> Th'effect and it! Come to my woman's breasts,
> And take my milk for gall, you murth'ring ministers.
>   [1.5.40–48]

In the play's context of unnatural births, the thickening of the blood and the stopping up of access and passage to remorse begin to sound like attempts to undo reproductive functioning and perhaps to stop the menstrual blood that is the sign of its potential.[18] The metaphors in which Lady Macbeth frames the stopping up of remorse, that is, suggest that she imagines an attack on the reproductive passages of her own body, on what makes her specifically female. And as she invites the spirits to her breasts, she reiterates the centrality of the attack specifically on maternal function: needing to undo the "milk of human kindness" (1.5.18) in Macbeth, she imagines an attack on her own literal milk, its transformation into gall. This imagery locates the horror of the scene in Lady Macbeth's unnatural abrogation of her maternal function. But latent within this image of unsexing is the horror of the maternal function itself. Most modern editors follow Johnson in glossing "take my milk for gall" as "take my milk in exchange for gall," imagining in effect that the spirits empty out the natural maternal fluid and replace it with the unnatural and poisonous one.[19] But perhaps Lady Macbeth is asking the spirits to take her milk *as* gall, to nurse from her breast and find in her milk their sustaining poison. Here the milk itself is the gall; no transformation is necessary. In these lines Lady Macbeth focuses the culture's fear of maternal nursery—a fear reflected, for example, in the common worries about the various ills (including female blood itself) that could be transmitted through nursing and in the sometime identification of colostrum as witch's milk.[20] Insofar as her milk itself nurtures the evil spirits, Lady Macbeth localizes the image of maternal danger, inviting the identification of her maternal function itself with that of the witch. For she here invites precisely that nursing of devil-imps so central to the current understanding of witchcraft that the presence of supernumerary teats alone was often taken as sufficient evidence that one was a witch.[21] Lady Macbeth and the witches fuse at this moment, and they fuse through the image of perverse nursery.

It is characteristic of the play's division of labor between Lady Macbeth and the witches that she, rather than they, is given the imagery of perverse nursery traditionally attributed to the witches. The often noted alliance between Lady Macbeth and the witches constructs malignant female power both in the cosmos and in the family; it in effect adds the whole weight of the spiritual order to the condemnation of Lady Macbeth's insurrection.[22] But despite the superior cosmic status of the witches, Lady Macbeth seems to the finally the more frightening figure. For Shakespeare's witches are an odd mixture of the terrifying and the near comic. Even without consideration of the Hecate scene (3.5) with its distinct lightening of tone and its incipient comedy of discord among the witches, we may begin to feel a shift toward the comic in the presentation of the witches: the specificity and predictability of the ingredients in their dire recipe pass over toward grotesque comedy even while they create a (partly pleasurable) shiver of horror.[23] There is a distinct weakening of their power after their first appearances: only halfway through the play, in 4.1, do we hear that they themselves have masters (4.1.63). The more Macbeth claims for them, the less their actual power seems: by the time Macbeth evokes the cosmic damage they can wreak (4.1.50–60), we have already felt the presence of such damage, and felt it moreover not as issuing from the witches but as a divinely sanctioned nature's expressions of outrage at the disruption of patriarchal order. The witches' displays of thunder and lightning, like their apparitions, are mere theatrics compared to what we have already heard; and the serious disruptions of natural order—the storm that toppled the chimneys and made the earth shake (2.3.53–60), the unnatural darkness in day (2.4.5–10), the cannibalism of Duncan's horses (2.4.14–18)–seem the horrifying but reassuringly familiar signs of God's displeasure, firmly under His–not their–control. Partly because their power is thus circumscribed, nothing the witches say or do conveys the presence of awesome and unexplained malevolence in the way that Lear's storm does. Even the process of dramatic representation itself may diminish their power: embodied, perhaps, they lack full power to terrify: "Present fears"–even of witches–"are less than horrible imaginings" (1.3.137–38). They tend thus to become as much containers for as expressions of nightmare; to a certain extent, they help to exorcise the terror of female malevolence by localizing it.

The witches may of course have lost some of their power to terrify through the general decline in witchcraft belief. Nonetheless, even when that belief was in full force, these witches would have been less frightening than their Continental sisters, their crimes less sensational. For despite their numinous and infinitely suggestive indefinability,[24] insofar as they are witches, they are distinctly English witches; and most commentators on English witchcraft note how tame an affair it was in comparison with witchcraft belief on the Continent.[25] The most sensational staples of Continental belief from the *Malleus Maleficarum* (1486) on–the ritual murder and eating of infants, the attacks specifically on the male genitals, the perverse sexual relationship with demons–are missing or greatly muted in English witchcraft belief, replaced largely by a simpler concern with retaliatory wrongdoing of exactly the order Shakespeare points to when one of his witches announces her retaliation for the sailor's wife's refusal to share her chestnuts.[26] We may hear an echo of some of the Continental beliefs in the hint of their quasi-sexual attack on the sailor with the uncooperative wife (the witches promise to "do and do and do," leaving him drained "dry as hay") and in the infanticidal contents of the cauldron, especially the "finger of birth-strangled babe" and the blood of the sow "that hath eaten/Her nine farrow." The cannibalism that is a staple of Continental belief may be implicit in the contents of that grim cauldron; and the various eyes, toes, tongues, legs, teeth, livers, and noses (indiscriminately human and animal) may evoke primitive fears of dismemberment close to the center of witchcraft belief. But these terrors remain largely implicit. For Shakespeare's witches are both smaller and greater than their Continental sisters: on the one hand, more the representation of English homebodies with relatively small concerns; on the other, more the incarnation of literary or mythic fates or sybils, given the power not only to predict but to enforce the future. But the staples of Continental witchcraft belief are not altogether missing from the play: for the most part, they are transferred away from the witches and recur as the psychological issues evoked by Lady Macbeth in her relation to Macbeth. She becomes the inheritor of the realm of primitive relational and bodily disturbance: of infantile vulnerability to maternal power, of dismemberment and its developmentally later equivalent, castration. Lady Macbeth brings the witches' power home: they get the cosmic apparatus, she gets the psychic force. That Lady Macbeth is the more frightening figure–and was so, I suspect, even before belief in witchcraft had declined–suggests the firmly domestic and psychological basis of Shakespeare's imagination.[27]

The fears of female coercion, female definition of the male, that are initially located cosmically in the witches thus find their ultimate locus in the figure of Lady Macbeth, whose attack on Macbeth's virility is the source of her strength over him and who acquires that strength, I shall argue, partly because she can make him imagine himself as an infant vulnerable to her. In the figure of Lady Macbeth, that is, Shakespeare rephrases the power of the witches as the wife/mother's power to poison human relatedness at its source; in her, their power of cosmic coercion is rewritten as the power of the mother to misshape or destroy the child. The attack on infants and on the genitals characteristic of Continental witchcraft belief is thus in her returned to its psychological source: in the play these beliefs are localized not in the witches but in the great central scene in which Lady Macbeth persuades Macbeth to the murder of Duncan. In this scene, Lady Macbeth notoriously makes the murder of Duncan the test of Macbeth's virility; if he cannot perform the murder, he is in effect reduced to the helplessness of an infant subject to her rage. She begins by attacking his manhood, making her love for him contingent on the murder that she identifies as equivalent to his male potency: "From this time/Such I account thy love" (1.7.38–39); "When you durst do it, then you were a man" (1.7.49). Insofar as his drunk hope is now "green and pale" (1.7.37), he is identified as emasculated, exhibiting the symptoms not only of hangover, but also of the greensickness, the typical disease of timid young virgin women. Lady Macbeth's argument is, in effect, that any signs of the "milk of human kindness" (1.5.17) mark him as more womanly than she; she proceeds to enforce his masculinity by demonstrating her willingness to dry up that milk in herself, specifically by destroying her nursing infant in fantasy: "I would, while it was smiling in my face,/Have pluck'd my nipple from his boneless gums,/And dash'd the brains out" (1.7.56–58). That this image has no place in the plot, where the Macbeths are strikingly childless, gives some indication of the inner necessity through which it appears. For Lady Macbeth expresses here not only the hardness she imagines to be male, not only her willingness to unmake the most essential maternal relationship; she expresses also a deep fantasy of

Macbeth's utter vulnerability to her. As she progresses from questioning Macbeth's masculinity to imagining herself dashing out the brains of her infant son,[28] she articulates a fantasy in which to be less than a man is to become interchangeably a woman or a baby,[29] terribly subject to the wife/mother's destructive rage.

By evoking this vulnerability, Lady Macbeth acquires a power over Macbeth more absolute than any the witches can achieve. The play's central fantasy of escape from woman seems to me to unfold from this moment; we can see its beginnings in Macbeth's response to Lady. Macbeth's evocation of absolute maternal power. Macbeth first responds by questioning the possibility of failure ("If we should fail?" [1.7.59]). Lady Macbeth counters this fear by inviting Macbeth to share in her fantasy of omnipotent malevolence: "What cannot you and I perform upon/Th'unguarded Duncan?" (1.7.70–71). The satiated and sleeping Duncan takes on the vulnerability that Lady Macbeth has just invoked in the image of the feeding, trusting infant;[30] Macbeth releases himself from the image of this vulnerability by sharing in the murder of this innocent. In his elation at this transfer of vulnerability from himself to Duncan, Macbeth imagines Lady Macbeth the mother to infants sharing her hardness, born in effect without vulnerability; in effect, he imagines her as male and then reconstitutes himself as the invulnerable male child of such a mother:

> Bring forth men-children only!
> For thy undaunted mettle should compose
> Nothing but males.
>
> [1.7.73–75]

Through the double pun on *mettle/metal* and *male/mail*, Lady Macbeth herself becomes virtually male, composed of the hard metal of which the armored male is made.[31] Her children would necessarily be men, composed of her male mettle, armored by her mettle, lacking the female inheritance from the mother that would make them vulnerable. The man-child thus brought forth would be no trusting infant; the very phrase *men-children* suggests the presence of the adult man even at birth, hence the undoing of childish vulnerability.[32] The mobility of the imagery—from male infant with his brains dashed out to Macbeth and Lady Macbeth triumphing over the sleeping, trusting Duncan, to the all-male invulnerable man-child, suggests the logic of the fantasy: only the child of an all-male mother is safe. We see here the creation of a defensive fantasy of exemption from the woman's part: as infantile vulnerability is shifted to Duncan, Macbeth creates in himself the image of Lady Macbeth's hardened all-male man-child; in committing the murder, he thus becomes like Richard III, using the bloody axe to free himself in fantasy from the dominion of women, even while apparently carrying out their will.

Macbeth's temporary solution to the infantile vulnerability and maternal malevolence revealed by Lady Macbeth is to imagine Lady Macbeth the all-male mother of invulnerable infants. The final solution, both for Macbeth and for the play itself, though in differing ways, is an even more radical excision of the female: it is to imagine a birth entirely exempt from women, to imagine in effect an all-male family, composed of nothing but males, in which the father is fully restored to power. Overtly, of course, the play denies the possibility of this fantasy: Macduff carries the power of the man not born of woman only through the equivocation of the fiends, their obstetrical joke that quibbles with the meaning of *born* and thus confirms circuitously that all men come from women after all. Even Macbeth, in whom, I think, the fantasy is centrally invested, knows its impossibility: his false security depends exactly on his commonsense assumption that everyone is born of woman. Nonetheless, I shall argue, the play curiously enacts the fantasy that it seems to deny: punishing Macbeth for his participation in a fantasy of escape from the maternal matrix, it nonetheless allows the audience the partial satisfaction of a dramatic equivalent to it. The dual process of repudiation and enactment of the fantasy seems to me to shape the ending of *Macbeth* decisively; I will attempt to trace this process in the rest of this essay.

The witches' prophecy has the immediate force of psychic relevance for Macbeth partly because of the fantasy constructions central to 1.7:

Be bloody, bold, and resolute: laugh to scorn
The power of man, for none of woman born
Shall harm Macbeth.

[4.1.79–81]

The witches here invite Macbeth to make himself into the bloody and invulnerable man-child he has created as a defense against maternal malevolence in 1.7: the man-child ambivalently recalled by the accompanying apparition of the Bloody Child. For the apparition alludes at once to the bloody vulnerability of the infant destroyed by Lady Macbeth and to the bloodthirsty masculinity that seems to promise escape from this vulnerability, the bloodiness the witches urge Macbeth to take on. The doubleness of the image epitomizes exactly the doubleness of the prophecy itself: the prophecy constructs Macbeth's invulnerability in effect from the vulnerability of all other men, a vulnerability dependent on their having been born of woman. Macbeth does not question this prophecy, even after the experience of Birnam Wood should have taught him better, partly because it so perfectly meets his needs: in encouraging him to "laugh to scorn/The power of men," the prophecy seems to grant him exemption from the condition of all men, who bring with them the liabilities inherent in their birth. As Macbeth carries the prophecy as a shield onto the battlefield, his confidence in his own invulnerability increasingly reveals his sense of his own exemption from the universal human condition. Repeated seven times, the phrase *born to woman* with its variants begins to carry for Macbeth the meaning "vulnerable," as though vulnerability itself is the taint deriving from woman; his own invulnerability comes therefore to stand as evidence for his exemption from that taint. This is the subterranean logic of Macbeth's words to Young Siward immediately after Macbeth has killed him:

> Thou wast born of woman:–
> But swords I smile at, weapons laugh to scorn,
> Brandish'd by man that's of a woman born.
> [5.7.11–13]

Young Siward's death becomes in effect proof that he was born of woman; in the logic of Macbeth's psyche, Macbeth's invulnerability is the proof that he was not. The *but* records this fantasied distinction: it constructs the sentence "You, born of woman, are vulnerable; but I, not born of woman, am not."[33]

Insofar as this is the fantasy embodied in Macbeth at the play's end, it is punished by the equivocation of the fiends: the revelation that Macduff derives from woman, though by unusual means, musters against Macbeth all the values of ordinary family and community that Macduff carries with him. Macbeth, "cow'd" by the revelation (5.8.18),[34] is forced to take on the taint of vulnerability; the fantasy of escape from the maternal matrix seems to die with him. But although this fantasy is punished in Macbeth, it does not quite die with him; it continues to have a curious life of its own in the play, apart from its embodiment in him. Even from the beginning of the play, the fantasy has not been Macbeth's alone: as the play's most striking bloody man, he is in the beginning the bearer of this fantasy for the all-male community that depends on his bloody prowess. The opening scenes strikingly construct male and female as realms apart; and the initial descriptions of Macbeth's battles construe his prowess as a consequence of his exemption from the taint of woman.

In the description of his battle with Macdonwald, what looks initially like a battle between loyal and disloyal sons to establish primacy in the father's eyes is oddly transposed into a battle of male against female:

> Doubtful it stood;
> As two spent swimmers, that do cling together
> And choke their art. The merciless Macdonwald

(Worthy to be a rebel, for to that
The multiplying villainies of nature
Do swarm upon him) from the western isles
Of Kernes and Gallowglasses is supplied;
And Fortune, on his damned quarrel smiling,
Show'd like a rebel's whore: but all's too weak;
For brave Macbeth (well he deserves that name),
Disdaining Fortune, with his brandish'd steel,
Which smok'd with bloody execution,
Like Valour's minion, carv'd out his passage,
Till he fac'd the slave;
Which ne'er shook hands, nor bade farewell to him,
Till he unseam'd him from the nave to th' chops,
And fix'd his head upon our battlements.

[1.2.7–23]

The two initially indistinguishable figures metaphorized as the swim-mers eventually sort themselves out into victor and victim, but only by first sorting themselves out into male and female, as though Macbeth can be distinguished from Macdonwald only by making Macdonwald functionally female. The "merciless Macdonwald" is initially firmly identified; but by the time Macbeth appears, Macdonwald has tem-porarily disappeared, replaced by the female figure of Fortune, against whom Macbeth seems to fight ("brave Macbeth, . . . Disdaining For-tune, with his brandish'd steel"). The metaphorical substitution of Fortune for Macdonwald transforms the battle into a contest between male and female; it makes Macbeth's deserving of his name contingent on his victory over the female. We are prepared for this transformation by Macdonwald's sexual alliance with the tainting female, the whore Fortune;[35] Macbeth's identification as valor's minion redefines the bat-tle as a contest between the half-female couple Fortune/Macdonwald and the all–male couple Valor/Macbeth. Metaphorically, Macdonwald and Macbeth take on the qualities of the unreliable female and the heroic male; Macbeth's battle against Fortune turns out to be his battle against Macdonwald because the two are functionally the same. Macdonwald, tainted by the female, becomes an easy mark for Macbeth, who demonstrates his own untainted manhood by unseam-ing Macdonwald from the nave to the chops. Through its allusions both to castration and to Caesarian section, this unseaming furthermore remakes Macdonwald's body as female, revealing what his alliance with Fortune has suggested all along.

In effect, then, the battle that supports the father's kingdom plays out the creation of a conquering all-male erotics that marks its conquest by its triumph over a feminized body, simultaneously that of Fortune and Macdonwald. Hence, in the double action of the passage, the victorious unseaming happens twice: first on the body of Fortune and then on the body of Macdonwald. The lines descriptive of Macbeth's approach to Macdonwald–"brave Macbeth . . . Disdaining Fortune, with his brandish'd steel. . . carved out his passage"–make that approach contingent on Macbeth's first carving his passage through a female body, hewing his way out. The language here perfectly antici-pates Macduff's birth by Caesarian section, revealed at the end of the play: if Macduff is ripped untimely from his mother's womb, Macbeth here manages in fantasy his own Caesarian section,[36] carving his pas-sage out from the unreliable female to achieve heroic male action, in effect carving up the female to arrive at the male. Only after this rite of passage can Macbeth meet Macdonwald: the act of aggression toward the female body, the fantasy of self-birth, marks his passage to the contest that will be definitive of his maleness partly insofar as it is definitive of Macdonwald's tainted femaleness. For the all-male community surrounding Duncan, then, Macbeth's victory is allied with his triumph over femaleness; for them, he becomes invulnerable, "lapp'd in proof" (1.2.55) like one of Lady Macbeth's armored men-children.[37] Even before his entry into the play, that is, Macbeth is the bearer of the shared fantasy that secure male community depends on the prowess of the man in effect not born of woman, the man who can carve his own passage out, the man whose very maleness is the mark of his exemption from female power.[38]

Ostensibly, the play rejects the version of manhood implicit in the shared fantasy of the beginning. Macbeth himself is well aware that his capitulation to Lady Macbeth's definition of manhood entails his abandonment of his own more inclusive definition of what becomes a man (1.7.46); and Macduff's response to the news of his family's destruction insists that humane feeling is central to the definition of manhood (4.3.221). Moreover, the revelation that even Macduff had a mother sets a limiting condition on the fantasy of a bloody masculine escape from the female and hence on the kind of manhood defined by that escape. Nonetheless, even at the end, the play enables one version of the fantasy that heroic manhood is exemption from the female even while it punishes that fantasy in Macbeth. The key figure in whom this double movement is vested in the end of the play is Macduff; the unresolved contradictions that surround him are, I think, marks of ambivalence toward the fantasy itself. In insisting that mourning for his family is his right as a man, he presents family feeling as central to the definition of manhood; and yet he conspicuously leaves his family vulnerable to destruction when he goes off to offer his services to Malcolm. The play moreover insists on reminding us that he has inexplicably abandoned his family: both Lady Macduff and Malcolm question the necessity of this abandonment (4.2.6–14; 4.3.26–28); and the play never allows Macduff to explain himself. This unexplained abandonment severely qualifies Macduff's force as the play's central exemplar of a healthy manhood that can include the possibility of relationship to women: the play seems to vest diseased familial relations in Macbeth and the possibility of healthy ones in Macduff; and yet we discover dramatically that Macduff has a family only when we hear that he has abandoned it. Dramatically and psychologically, he takes on full masculine power only as he loses his family and becomes energized by the loss, converting his grief into the more "manly" tune of vengeance (4.3.235); the loss of his family here enables his accession to full masculine action even while his response to that loss insists on a more humane definition of manhood.[39] The play here pulls in two directions. It reiterates this doubleness by vesting in Macduff its final fantasy of exemption from woman. The ambivalence that shapes the portrayal of Macduff is evident even as he reveals to Macbeth that he "was from his mother's womb/Untimely ripp'd" (5.8.15–16): the emphasis on untimeliness and the violence of the image suggest that he has been prematurely deprived of a nurturing maternal presence; but the prophecy construes just this deprivation as the source of Macduff's strength.[40] The prophecy itself both denies and affirms the fantasy of exemption from women: in affirming that Macduff has indeed had a mother, it denies the fantasy of male self-generation; but in attributing his power to his having been untimely ripped from that mother, it sustains the sense that violent separation from the mother is the mark of the successful male. The final battle between Macbeth and Macduff thus replays the initial battle between Macbeth and Macdonwald. But Macduff has now taken the place of Macbeth: he carries with him the male power given him by the Caesarian solution, and Macbeth is retrospectively revealed as Macdonwald, the woman's man.

The doubleness of the prophecy is less the equivocation of the fiends than Shakespeare's own equivocation about the figure of Macduff and about the fantasy vested in him in the end. For Macduff carries with him simultaneously all the values of family and the claim that masculine power derives from the unnatural abrogation of family, including escape from the conditions of one's birth. Moreover, the ambivalence that shapes the figure of Macduff similarly shapes the dramatic structure of the play itself. Ostensibly concerned to restore natural order at the end,[41] the play bases that order upon the radical exclusion of the female. Initially construed as all-powerful, the women virtually disappear at the end, Lady Macbeth becoming so diminished a character that we scarcely trouble to ask ourselves whether the report of her suicide is accurate or not, the witches literally gone from the stage and so diminished in psychic power that Macbeth never mentions them and blames his defeat only on the equivocation of their male masters, the fiends; even Lady Macduff exists only to disappear. The bogus fulfillment of the Birnam Wood prophecy suggests the extent to which the natural order of the end depends on the exclusion of the female. Critics sometimes see in the march of Malcolm's soldiers bearing their green branches an allusion to the Maying festivals in which participants returned from the woods bearing branches, or to the ritual scourging of a hibernal figure by the forces of the oncoming spring.[42] The allusion seems to me clearly present; but it serves, I think, to mark precisely what the moving of Birnam Wood is not. Malcolm's use of Birnam Wood is a military maneuver. His drily worded command (5.4.4–7) leaves little room for suggestions of natural fertility or for the deep sense of the generative world rising up to expel its winter king; nor does the play later enable these associations except in a scattered and partly ironic way.[43] These trees have little resemblance to those in the Forest of Arden; their branches, like those carried by the apparition of the "child crowned, with a tree in his hand" (4.1.86), are little more than the emblems of a strictly patriarchal family tree.[44] This family tree, like the march of Birnam Wood itself, is relentlessly male: Duncan and sons, Banquo and son, Siward and son. There are no daughters and scarcely any mention of mothers in these family trees. We are brought as close as possible here to the fantasy of family without women.[45] In that sense, Birnam Wood is the perfect emblem of the nature that triumphs at the end of the play: nature without generative possibility, nature without women. Malcolm tells his men to carry the branches to obscure themselves, and that is exactly their function: insofar as they seem to allude to the rising of the natural order against Macbeth, they obscure the operations of male power, disguising them as a natural force; and they simultaneously obscure the extent to which natural order itself is here reconceived as purely male.[46]

If we can see the fantasy of escape from the female in the play's fulfillment of the witches' prophecies–in Macduff's birth by Caesarian section and in Malcolm's appropriation of Birnam Wood–we can see it also in the play's psychological geography. The shift from Scotland to England is srikingly the shift from the mother's to the father's terrain.[47] Scotland "cannot/Be call'd our mother, but our grave" (4.3.165–66), in Rosse's words to Macduff: it is the realm of Lady Macbeth and the witches, the realm in which the mother *is* the grave, the realm appropriately ruled by their bad son Macbeth. The escape to England is an escape from their power into the realm of the good father-king and his surrogate son Malcolm, "unknown to woman" (4.3.126). The magical power of this father to cure clearly balances the magical power of the witches to harm, as Malcolm (the father's son) balances Macbeth (the mother's son). That Macduff can cross from one realm into the other only by abandoning his family suggests the rigidity of the psychic geography separating England from Scotland. At the end of the play, Malcolm returns to Scotland mantled in the power England gives him, in effect bringing the power of the fathers with him: bearer of his father's line, unknown to woman, supported by his agent Macduff (empowered by his own special immunity from birth), Malcolm embodies utter separation from women and as such triumphs easily over Macbeth, the mother's son.

The play that begins by unleashing the terrible threat of destructive maternal power and demonstrates the helplessness of its central male figure before that power thus ends by consolidating male power, in effect solving the problem of masculinity by eliminating the female. In the psychological fantasies that I am tracing, the play portrays the failure of the androgynous parent to protect his son, that son's consequent fall into the dominion of the bad mothers, and the final victory of a masculine order in which mothers no longer threaten because they no longer exist. In that sense, *Macbeth* is a recuperative consolidation of male power, a consolidation in the face of the threat unleashed in *Hamlet* and especially in *King Lear* and never fully contained in those plays. In *Macbeth,* maternal power is given its most virulent sway and then abolished; at the end of the play we are in a purely male realm. We will not be in so absolute a male realm again until we are in Prospero's island-kingdom, similarly based firmly on the exiling of the witch Sycorax.

NOTES

1. All references to *Macbeth* are to the new Arden edition, edited by Kenneth Muir, (London: Methuen, 1972).
2. I have written elsewhere about Coriolanus' doomed attempts to create a self that is independent of his mother's will; see my "'Anger's My Meat': Feeding, Dependency, and Aggression in *Coriolanus,*" in *Representing Shakespeare: New Psychoanalytic Essays*, ed. Murray M. Schwartz and Coppélia Kahn (Baltimore: Johns Hopkins University Press, 1980), 129–49. Others have noted the extent to which both *Macbeth* and *Coriolanus* deal with the construction of a rigid male identity felt as a defense against overwhelming maternal power; see particularly Coppélia Kahn, *Man's Estate: Masculine Identity in Shakespeare* (Berkeley & Los Angeles: University of California Press, 1981), 151–92, whose chapter title–"The Milking Babe and the Bloody Man in *Coriolanus* and *Macbeth*"–indicates the similarity of

our concerns. Linda Bamber argues, however, that the absence of a feminine Other in *Macbeth* and *Coriolanus* prevents the development of manliness in the heroes, since true manliness "involves a detachment from the feminine" (*Comic Women, Tragic Men: A Study of Gender and Genre in Shakespeare* [Stanford: Stanford University Press, 1982], 20, 91–107).

3. "Gowries Conspiracie: A Discoverie of the unnaturall and vyle Conspiracie, attempted against the Kings Maiesties Person at Sanct-Iohnstoun, upon Twysday the Fifth of August, 1600," in *A Selection from the Harleian Miscellany* (London: C. &. G. Kearsley, 1793), 196.

4. Stanley J. Kozikowski argues strenuously that Shakespeare knew either the pamphlet cited above ("Gowries Conspiracie," printed in Scotland and London in 1600) or the abortive play on the conspiracy, apparently performed twice by the King's Men and then canceled in 1604 ("The Gowrie Conspiracy against James VI: A New Source for Shakespeare's *Macbeth*," *Shakespeare Studies* 13 [1980]: 197–211). Although I do not find his arguments entirely persuasive, it seems likely that Shakespeare knew at least the central facts of the conspiracy, given both James's annual celebration of his escape from it and the apparent involvement of the King's Men in a play on the subject. See also Steven Mullaney's suggestive use of the Gowrie material as an analogue for *Macbeth* in its link between treason and magical riddle ("Lying Like Truth: Riddle, Representation and Treason in Renaissance England," *ELH* 47 [1980]: 32, 38).

5. After the failure of the conspiracy, James searched the dead earl's pockets, finding nothing in them "but a little close parchment bag, full of magicall characters, and words of inchantment, wherin, it seemed, that he had put his confidence, thinking him selfe never safe without them, and therfore ever carried them about with him; beeing also observed, that, while they were uppon him, his wound whereof he died, bled not, but, incontinent after the taking of them away, the blood gushed out in great aboundance, to the great admiration of al the beholders" ("Gowries Conspiracie," 196). The magical stopping up of the blood and the sudden return of its natural flow seem to me potent images for the progress of Macbeth as he is first seduced and then abandoned by the witches' prophecies; that Gowrie's necromancer, like the witches, seemed to dabble in alternate modes of generation increases the suggestiveness of this association for *Macbeth*.

6. All references to Shakespeare's plays other than *Macbeth* are to the revised Pelican edition, *William Shakespeare: The Complete Works*, ed. Alfred Harbage (Baltimore, Penguin Books, 1969).

7. Richard Wheeler, Michael Neill, and Coppélia Kahn similarly understand Richard III's self-divided and theatrical masculinity as a defensive response to real or imagined maternal deprivation.

See Wheeler, "History, Character and Conscience in *Richard III*," *Comparative Drama* 5 (1971–72): 301–21, esp. 314–15; Neill, "Shakespeare's Halle of Mirrors: Play, Politics, and Psychology in *Richard III*," *Shakespeare Studies* 8 (1975): 99–129, esp. 104–6; and Kahn, *Man's Estate*, 63–66.

8. *Impale* in the sense of "to enclose with pales, stakes or posts; to surround with a pallisade" (*OED's* first meaning) is of course the dominant usage contemporary with *Macbeth*. But the word was in the process of change, *OED's* meaning 4, "to thrust a pointed stake through the body of, as a form of torture or capital punishment," although cited first in 1613, clearly seems to stand behind the imagistic transformation here. The shift in meaning perfectly catches Richard's psychological process, in which any protective enclosure is ambivalently desired and threatens to turn into a torturing impalement.

9. Robert N. Watson notes the imagery of Caesarian birth here and in *Macbeth* (*Shakespeare and the Hazards of Ambition* [Cambridge, Mass.: Harvard University Press, 1984], esp. 19–20, 99–105); the metaphors of Caesarian section and Oedipal rape are central to his understanding of ambitious self-creation insofar as both imagine a usurpation of the defining parental acts of generation (see, for example, pp. 3–5). Though it is frequently very suggestive, Watson's account tends too easily to blur the distinction between matricide and patricide: in fantasies of rebirth, the hero may symbolically replace the father to re-create himself, but he does so by means of an attack specifically on the maternal body. In Shakespeare's images of Caesarian birth, the father tends to be conspicuously absent; indeed, I shall argue, precisely his absence—not his defining presence—creates the fear of the engulfing maternal body to which the fantasy of Caesarian section is a response. This body tends to be missing in Watson's account, as it is missing in his discussion of Richard's Caesarian fantasy here.

10. In an early essay that has become a classic, Eugene Waith established the centrality of definitions of manhood and Lady Macbeth's role in enforcing Macbeth's particularly bloodthirsty version, a theme that has since become a major topos of *Macbeth* criticism ("Manhood and Valor in Two Shakespearean Tragedies," *ELH* 17 [1950]: 262–73). Among the ensuing legions, see, for example, Matthew N. Proser, *The Heroic Image in Five Shakespearean Tragedies.* (Princeton: Princeton University Press, 1965), 51–91; Michael Taylor, "Ideals of Manhood in *Macbeth*," *Etudes Anglaises* 21 (1968): 337–48 (unusual in its early emphasis on the extent to which the culture is complicit in defining masculinity as aggression); D. W. Harding, "Women's Fantasy of Manhood: A Shakespearean Theme," *Shakespeare Quarterly* 20 (1969): 245–53 (significant especially in its stress on women's responsibility for committing men to their false fantasy of manhood); Paul A. Jorgensen, *Our Naked Frailties: Sensational Art and Meaning in*

"Macbeth" (Berkeley & Los Angeles: University of California Press, 1971), esp. 147 ff.; Jarold Ramsey, "The Perversion of Manliness in *Macbeth*," *SEL* 13 (1973): 285–300; Carolyn Asp, "'Be bloody, bold, and resolute': Tragic Action and Sexual Stereotyping in *Macbeth*," *Studies in Philology* 25 (1981): 153–69 (significant especially for associating Macbeth's pursuit of masculinity with his pursuit of omnipotence); Harry Berger, Jr., "Text Against Performance in Shakespeare; The Example of *Macbeth*," in *The Forms of Power and the Power of Forms in the Renaissance*, ed. Stephen Greenblatt, special issue of *Genre* (15 [1982]), esp. 67–75; and Robert Kimbrough, "Macbeth: The Prisoner of Gender," *Shakespeare Studies* 16 (1983): 175–90. Virtually all these essays recount the centrality of 1.7 to this theme; most see Macbeth's willingness to murder as his response to Lady Macbeth's nearly explicit attack on his male potency. Dennis Biggins and James J. Greene note particularly the extent to which the murder itself is imagined as a sexual act through which the union of Macbeth and Lady Macbeth is consummated; see Biggins, "Sexuality, Witchcraft, and Violence in *Macbeth*," *Shakespeare Studies* 8 (1975): 255– 77; Greene, "Macbeth: Masculinity as Murder," *American Imago* 41 (1984): 155–80; see also Watson, *Shakespeare and the Hazards of Ambition*, 90. My account differs from most of these largely in stressing the infantile components of Macbeth's susceptibility to Lady Macbeth. The classic account of these pre-Oedipal components in the play is David B. Barron's brilliant early essay "The Babe That Milks: An Organic Study of *Macbeth*," originally published in 1960 and reprinted in *The Design Within*, ed. M. D. Faber (New York: Science House, 1970), 253–79. For similar readings, see Marvin Rosenberg, *The Masks of Macbeth* (Berkeley & Los Angeles: University of California Press, 1978), 81–82, 270–72, and especially Kahn, *Man's Estate,* 151–55, 172–92, and Richard P. Wheeler, *Shakespeare's Development and the Problem Comedies* (Berkeley & Los Angeles: University of California Press, 1981), 144–49; as always, I am deeply and minutely indebted to the two last named.

11. Harry Berger, Jr., associates both Duncan's vulnerability and his role in legitimizing the bloody masculinity of his thanes with his status as the androgynous supplier of blood and milk ("The Early Scenes of *Macbeth*: Preface to a New Interpretation," *ELH* 47 [1980]: 26–28). Murray M. Schwartz and Richard Wheeler note specifically the extent to which the male claim to androgynous possession of nurturant power reflects a fear of maternal power outside male control (Schwartz, "Shakespeare through Contemporary Psychoanalysis," in *Representing Shakespeare*, 29. Wheeler, *Shakespeare's Development*, 146. My discussion of Duncan's androgyny is partly a consequence of my having heard Peter Erickson's rich account of the Duke's taking on of nurturant function in *As You Like It* at MLA in 1979; this account

is now part of his *Patriarchal Structures in Shakespeare's Drama* (Berkeley & Los Angeles: University of California Press, 1985); see esp. pp. 27–37.

12. Many commentators note that Shakespeare's Duncan is less ineffectual than Holingshed's; others note the continuing signs of his weakness. See especially Harry Berger's brilliant account of the structural effect of Duncan's weakness in defining his (and Macbeth's) society ("The Early Scenes," 1–31).

13. Many note the appropriateness of Macbeth's conflation of himself with Tarquin, given the play's alliance of sexuality and murder. See, for example, Ian Robinson, "The Witches and Macbeth," *Critical Review* 11 (1968): 104; Biggins, "Sexuality, Witchcraft, and Violence," 269; and Watson, *Shakespeare and the Hazards of Ambition*, 100. Arthur Kirsch works extensively with the analogy, seeing the Tarquin of *The Rape of Lucrece* as a model for Macbeth's ambitious desire ("Macbeth's Suicide," *ELH* 51 [1984]: 269–96). Commentators on the analogy do not in general note that it transforms Macbeth's kingly victim into a woman; Norman Rabkin is the exception (*Shakespeare and the Problem of Meaning* [Chicago: Chicago University Press, 1981], 107).

14. Wheeler sees the simultaneously castrated and castrating Gorgon-like body of Duncan as the emblem of the world Macbeth brings into being (*Shakespeare's Development*, 145); I see it as the emblem of a potentially castrating femaleness that Macbeth's act of violence reveals but does not create.

15. The witches' power to raise storms was conventional; see, for example, Reginald Scot, *The Discoverie of Witchcraft* (London 1584; reprint, with an introduction by Hugh Ross Williamson, Carbondale: Southern Illinois University Press, 1964), 31; King James's *Daemonologie* (London, 1603), 46; and the failure of the witches to raise a storm in Jonson's *Masque of Queens*. Jonson's learned note on their attempt to disturb nature gives his classical sources for their association with chaos: see *Masque*, 11.134–37, 209–20, and Jonson's note to l.134, in *Ben Jonson: The Complete Masques*, ed. Stephen Orgel (New Haven: Yale University Press, 1969), 531–32.

16. Many commentators, following Freud, find the murder of Duncan "little else than parricide" ("Those Wrecked by Success," in *The Standard Edition of the Complete Psychological Works of Sigmund Freud*, trans. and ed. James Strachey [London, Hogarth Press, 1957], 14: 321); see, for example, Rabkin, *Shakespeare and the Problem of Meaning*, 106–9, Kirsch, "Macbeth's Suicide," 276–80, 286, and Watson, *Shakespeare and the Hazards of Ambition*, esp. 85–88, 98–99 (the last two are particularly interesting in understanding parricide as an ambitious attempt to redefine the self as omnipotently free from limits). In standard Oedipal readings of the play, the mother is less the object of desire than "the 'demon-woman,' who creates the abyss between father and son" by inciting the son to parricide (Ludwig

Jekels, "The Riddle of Shakespeare's *Macbeth*," in *The Design Within*, 240). See also, for example, L. Veszy-Wagner, "*Macbeth*: 'Fair Is Foul and Foul Is Fair,'" *American Imago* 25 (1968): 242–57; Norman N. Holland, *Psychoanalysis and Shakespeare* (New York: Octagon Books, 1979), 229; and Patrick Colm Hogan's very suggestive account of the Oedipal narrative structure, "*Macbeth*: Authority and Progenitorship," *American Imago* 40 (1983): 385–95. My reading differs from these Oedipal readings mainly in suggesting that the play's mothers acquire their power because the father's protective masculine authority is already significantly absent; in my reading, female power over Macbeth becomes the sign (rather than the cause) of that absence.

17. For those recent commentators who follow Barron in seeing pre-Oedipal rather than Oedipal issues as central to the play, the images of disrupted nurturance define the primary area of disturbance; see, for example, Barron, "The Babe That Milks," 255; Schwartz, "Shakespeare through Psychoanalysis," 29; Berger, "The Early Scenes," 27–28; Joan M. Byles, "Macbeth: Imagery of Destruction," *American Imago* 39 (1982): 149–64; Wheeler, *Shakespeare's Development*, 147–48; and Kirsch, "Macbeth's Suicide," 291–92. Although Madelon Gohlke (now Sprengnether) does not specifically discuss the rupture of maternal nurturance in *Macbeth*, my understanding of the play is very much indebted to her classic essay, "'I wooed thee with my sword': Shakespeare's Tragic Paradigms," in which she establishes the extent to which masculinity in Shakespeare's heroes entails a defensive denial of the female (in *Representing Shakespeare*: 170–87); in an unfortunately unpublished essay, she discusses the traumatic failure of maternal protection imaged by Lady Macbeth here. In his brilliant essay "Phantasmagoric *Macbeth*" (forthcoming in *ELR*), David Willbern locates in Lady Macbeth's image the psychological point of origin for the failure of potential space that Macbeth enacts. Erickson, noting that patriarchal bounty in *Macbeth* has gone awry, suggestively locates the dependence of that bounty on the maternal nurturance that is here disturbed (*Patriarchal Structures*, 116–21). Several critics see in Macbeth's susceptibility to female influence evidence of his failure to differentiate from a maternal figure, a failure psychologically the consequence of the abrupt and bloody weaning imaged by Lady Macbeth; see for example, Susan Bachmann, "'Daggers in Men's Smiles'—The 'Truest Issue' in *Macbeth*," *International Review of Psycho-Analysis* 5 (1978): 97–104; and particularly the full and very suggestive accounts of Barron, "The Babe That Milks," 263–68, and Kahn, *Man's Estate*, 172–78. In the readings of all these critics, as in mine, Lady Macbeth and the witches variously embody the destructive maternal force that overwhelms Macbeth and in relation to whom he is imagined as an infant. Rosenberg notes intriguingly that *Macbeth* has twice been

performed with a mother and son in the chief roles (*Masks of Macbeth*, 196).

18. Despite some overliteral interpretation, Alice Fox and particularly Jenijoy La Belle usefully demonstrate the specifically gynecological references of "passage" and "visitings of nature," using contemporary gynecological treatises. (See Fox, "Obstetrics and Gynecology in *Macbeth*," *Shakespeare Studies* 12 [1979]: 129; and La Belle, "'A Strange Infirmity': Lady Macbeth's Amenorrhea," *Shakespeare Quarterly* 31 [1980]: 382, for the identification of *visitings of nature* as a term for menstruation; see La Belle, 383, for the identification of *passage* as a term for the neck of the womb. See also Barron, who associates Lady Macbeth's language here with contraception ["The Babe That Milks," 267].)

19. *For* is glossed as "in exchange for" in the following editions, for example; *The Complete Signet Classic Shakespeare*, ed. Sylvan Barnet (New York: Harcourt, Brace, Jovanovich, 1972); *The Complete Works of Shakespeare*, ed. Hardin Craig (Chicago: Scott, Foresman, 1951), rev. ed. edited by David Bevinton (Chicago: Scott, Foresman, 1973); *The Riverside Shakespeare*, ed. G. Blakemore Evans (Boston: Houghton Mifflin, 1974); *William Shakespeare: The Complete Works*, ed. Alfred Harbage (Baltimore: Penguin, 1969); *The Complete Works of Shakespeare*, ed. George Lyman Kittredge (Boston: Ginn, 1936), rev. ed. edited by Irving Ribner (Boston: Ginn, 1971). Muir demurs, preferring Keightley's understanding of *take* as "infect" (see the Arden edition, p. 30).

20. Insofar as syphilis was known to be transmitted through the nursing process, there was some reason to worry; see, for example, William Clowes's frightening account, "A brief and necessary Treatise touching the cure of the disease called Morbus Gallicus" (London, 1585, 1596), 151. But Leontes' words to Hermione as he removes Mamillius from her ("I am glad you did not nurse him./Though he does bear some signs of me, yet you/Have too much blood in him" [*The Winter's Tale*, 2.1.56–58]) suggest that the worry was not fundamentally about epidemiology. Worry that the nurse's milk determined morals was, of course, common; see, for example, Thomas Phaire, *The Boke of Chyldren* (1545; reprint, Edinburgh: E. & S. Livingstone, 1955), 18. The topic was of interest to King James, who claimed to have sucked his Protestantism from his nurse's milk; his drunkenness was also attributed to her. See Henry N. Paul, *The Royal Play of "Macbeth"* (New York: Macmillan Co., 1950), 387–88. For the identification of colostrum with witch's milk, see Samuel X. Radbill, "Pediatrics," in *Medicine in Seventeenth-Century England*, ed. Allen G. Debus (Berkeley & Los Angeles: University of California Press, 1974), 249. The fear of maternal functioning itself, not simply of its perversions, is central to most readings of the play in pre-Oedipal terms; see the critics cited in note 17 above.

21. Many commentators on English witchcraft note the unusual
prominence given to the presence of the witch's mark and the
nursing of familiars; see, for example, Barbara Rosen's introduction
to the collection of witchcraft documents she edited (*Witchcraft*
[London: Edward Arnold, 1969], 29–30). She cites contemporary
documents on the nursing of familiars, for example, pp. 187–88, 315;
the testimony of Joan Prentice, one of the convicted witches of
Chelmsford in 1589, is particularly suggestive: "at what time soever
she would have her ferret do anything for her, she used the words
'Bid, Bid, Bid, come Bid, come Bid, come Bid, come suck, come suck,
come suck" (p. 188). Katharine Mary Briggs quotes a contemporary
(1613) story about the finding of a witch's teat (*Pale Hecate's Team*
[New York: Arno Press, 1977], 250); see also Wallace Notestein, *A
History of Witchcraft in England from 1558 to 1718* (Washington: American
Historical Association, 1911), 36; and George Lyman Kittredge,
Witchcraft in Old and New England (New York: Russell & Russell,
1956), 179. Though he does not refer to the suckling of familiars,
King James believed in the significance of the witch's mark, at least
when he wrote the *Daemonologie* (see p. 33). M. C. Bradbrook notes
that Lady Macbeth's invitation to the spirits is "as much as any witch
could do by way of self-dedication" ("The Sources of *Macbeth*,"
Shakespeare Survey 4 [1951]: 43).

22. In a brilliant essay, Peter Stallybrass associates the move from the
cosmic to the secular realm with the ideological shoring up of a
patriarchal state founded on the model of the family ("*Macbeth* and
Witchcraft," in *Focus on "Macbeth,"* ed. John Russell Brown [London:
Routledge & Kegan Paul, 1982], esp. 196–98).

23. Wilbur Sanders notes the extent to which "terror is mediated
through absurdity" in the witches (*The Dramatist and the Received
Idea* [Cambridge: Cambridge University Press, 1968], 277); see also
Berger's fine account of the scapegoating reduction of the witches to
a comic and grotesque triviality ("Text Against Performance,"
67–68). Harold C. Goddard (*The Meaning of Shakespeare* [Chicago:
University of Chicago Press, 1951], 512–13), Robinson ("The
Witches and Macbeth," 100–103), and Stallybrass, ("*Macbeth* and
Witchcraft," 199) note the witches' change from potent and
mysterious to more diminished figures in act 4.

24. After years of trying fruitlessly to pin down a precise identity for the
witches, critics are increasingly finding their dramatic power precisely in their indefinability. The most powerful statements of this
relatively new critical topos are those by Sanders (*The Dramatist and
the Received Idea*, 277–79), Robert H. West (*Shakespeare and the Outer
Mystery* [Lexington: University of Kentucky Press, 1968], 78–79), and
Stephen Booth ("*King Lear*," "*Macbeth*," *Indefinition, and Tragedy* [New
Haven: Yale University Press, 1983], 101–3).

25. For their "Englishness", see Stallybrass, "*Macbeth* and Witchcraft," 195. Alan Macfarlane's important study of English witchcraft, *Witchcraft in Tudor and Stuart England* (New York: Harper & Row, 1970), frequently notes the absence of the Continental staples: if the witches of Essex are typical, English witches do not fly, do not hold Sabbaths, do not commit sexual perversions or attack male potency, do not kill babies (see pp. 6, 160, 180, for example).

26. Macfarlane finds the failure of neighborliness reflected in the retaliatory acts of the witch the key to the social function of witchcraft in England; see ibid., 168–76 for accounts of the failures of neighborliness–very similar to the refusal to share chestnuts–that provoked the witch to act. James Sprenger and Heinrich Kramer, *Malleus Maleficarum,* trans. Montague Summers (New York: Benjamin Blom, 1970), is the *locus classicus* for Continental witchcraft beliefs: for the murder and eating of infants, see pp. 21, 66, 99, 100–101; for attacks on the genitals, see pp. 47, 55–60, 117–19; for sexual relations with demons, see pp. 21, 112–14. Or see Scot's convenient summary of these beliefs (*Discoverie*, 31).

27. The relationship between cosmology and domestic psychology is similar in *King Lear*; even as Shakespeare casts doubt on the authenticity of demonic possession by his use of Harsnett's *Declaration of Egregious Popish Impostures*, Edgar/Poor Tom's identification of his father as "the foul Flibbertigibbet" (3.4.108) manifests the psychic reality and source of his demons. Characteristically in Shakespeare, the site of blessing and of cursedness is the family, their processes psychological.

28. Although *his* was a common form for the as yet unfamiliar possessive *its*, Lady Macbeth's move from "while it was smiling" to "his boneless gums" nonetheless seems to register the metamorphosis of an ungendered to a gendered infant exactly at the moment of vulnerability, making her attack specifically on a male child. That she uses the ungendered *the* a moment later ("the brains out") suggests one alternative open to Shakespeare had he wished to avoid the implication that the fantasied infant was male; Antony's crocodile, who "moves with it own organs" (*Antony and Cleopatra*, 2.7.42), suggests another. (*OED* notes that, although *its* occurs in the Folio, it does not occur in any work of Shakespeare published while he was alive; it also notes the various strategies by which authors attempted to avoid the inappropriate use of *his*.)

29. Lady Macbeth maintains her control over Macbeth through 3.4 by manipulating these categories: see 2.2.53–54 ("'tis the eye of childhood/That fears a painted devil") and 3.4.57–65 ("Are you a man? . . . these flaws and starts . . . would well become/A woman's story"). In his response to Banquo's ghost, Macbeth invokes the same categories and suggests their interchangeability: he dares what man

dares (3.4.98); if he feared Banquo alive, he could rightly be called "the baby of a girl" (l. 105).

30. In "Phantasmagoric *Macbeth*," David Willbern notes the extent to which the regicide is reimagined as a "symbolic infanticide" so that the image of Duncan fuses with the image of Lady Macbeth's child murdered in fantasy. Macbeth's earlier association of Duncan's power with the power of the "naked new-born babe,/Striding the blast" (1.7.21–22) prepares for this fusion. Despite their symbolic power, the literal babies of this play and those adults who sleep and trust like infants are hideously vulnerable.

31. See Kahn, *Man's Estate*, 173, for a very similar account of this passage.

32. Shakespeare's only other use of *man-child* is in a strikingly similar context: Volumnia, reporting her pleasure in Coriolanus' martial success, tells Virgilia, "I sprang not more in joy at first hearing he was a man-child than now in first seeing he had proved himself a man" (*Coriolanus*, 1.3.15–17).

33. De Quincy seems to have understood this process: "The murderers are taken out of the region of human things, human purposes, human desires. They are transfigured: Lady Macbeth is 'unsexed'; Macbeth has forgot that he was born of woman" ("On the Knocking at the Gate in 'Macbeth,'" in *Shakespeare Criticism: A Selection, 1623–1840*, ed. D. Nichol Smith [London: Oxford University Press, 1946], 335). Critics who consider gender relations central to this play generally note the importance of the witches' prophecy for the figure of Macduff; they do not usually note its application to Macbeth. But see Kahn's suggestion that the prophecy sets Macbeth "apart from women as well as from men" (*Man's Estate*, 187) and Gohlke's central perception that, "to be born of woman, as [Macbeth] reads the witches' prophecy, is to be mortal" ("I wooed thee," 176).

34. See Kahn's rich understanding of the function of the term *cow'd* (*Man's Estate*, 191).

35. Many comment on this contamination; see, for example, Berger, "The Early Scenes of *Macbeth*," 7–8; Hogan, "Macbeth," 387; Rosenberg, *The Masks of Macbeth*, 45; Biggins, "Sexuality, Witches, and Violence," 265.

36. Watson notes the suggestion of Caesarian section here, though not its aggression toward the female. Barron does not comment specifically on this passage but notes breaking and cutting imagery throughout and relates it to Macbeth's attempt to "cut his way out of the female environment which chokes and smothers him" ("The Babe That Milks," 269). I am indebted to Willbern's "Phantasmagoric *Macbeth*" specifically for the Caesarian implications of the unseaming from nave to chops.

37. The reference to Macbeth as "Bellona's bridegroom" anticipates his interaction with Lady Macbeth in 1.7: only the murderous man-child is fit mate for either of these unsexed, quasi-male figures.

38. To the extent that ferocious maleness is the creation of the male community, not of Lady Macbeth or the witches, the women are scapegoats who exist partly to obscure the failures of male community. For fuller accounts of this process, see Veszy-Wagner, "Macbeth," 244, Bamber, *Comic Women*, 19–20, and especially Berger, "Text Against Performance," 68–75. But whether or not the women are scapegoats insofar as they are (falsely) held responsible for Macbeth's murderous maleness, fear of the female power they represent remains primary (not secondary and obscurantist) insofar as the male community and, to some extent, the play itself define maleness as violent differentiation from the female.

39. A great many critics, following Waith ("Manhood and Valor," 266–67), find the play's embodiment of healthy masculinity in Macduff. They often register some uneasiness about his leaving his family, but they rarely allow this uneasiness to complicate their view of him as exemplary. But critics interested in the play's construction of masculinity as a defense against the fear of femaleness tend to see in Macduff's removal from family a replication of the central fear of women that is more fully played out in Macbeth. See, for example, Wheeler, *Shakespeare's Development*, 146; and Berger, "Text Against Performance," 70. For these critics, Macduff's flight is of a piece with his status as the man not born of woman.

40. Critics interested in gender issues almost invariably comment on the centrality of Macduff's fulfillment of this prophecy, finding his strength here in his freedom from contamination by or regressive dependency on women: see, for example, Harding, "Women's Fantasy," 250; Barron, "The Babe That Milks," 272; Berger, "The Early Scenes," 28; Bachmann, "Daggers," 101; Kirsch, "Macbeth's Suicide," 293; Kahn, *Man's Estate*, 172–73; Wheeler, *Shakespeare's Development*, 146; and Victor Calef, "Lady Macbeth and Infanticide or 'How Many Children Had Lady Macbeth Murdered?'" *Journal of the American Psychoanalytic Association* 17 (1969): 537. For Barron and Harding, Macduff's status as the bearer of this fantasy positively enhances his manhood; but for many of these critics, it qualifies his status as the exemplar of healthy manhood. Perhaps because ambivalence toward Macduff is built so deeply into the play, several very astute critics see the fantasy embedded in Macduff here and nonetheless continue to find in him an ideal manhood that includes the possibility of relatedness to the feminine. See, for example, Kahn, *Man's Estate*, 191; and Kirsch, "Macbeth's Suicide," 294.

41. The triumph of the natural order has of course been a commonplace of criticism since the classic essay by G. Wilson Knight, "The Milk of Concord: An Essay on Life-Themes in *Macbeth*," in his *Imperial Theme* (London: Methuen, 1965), esp. 140–53. The topos is so powerful that it can cause even critics interested in gender issues to

praise the triumph of nature and natural sexuality at the end without noting the exclusion of the female; see, for example, Greene, "Macbeth," 172. But Rosenberg, for example, notes the qualifying effect of this exclusion (*Masks of Macbeth*, 654).

42. See, for example, Goddard, *Meaning of Shakespeare*, 520–21; Jekels, "Riddle," 238; John Holloway, *The Story of the Night* (London: Routledge & Kegan Paul, 1961), 66; Rosenberg, *Masks of Macbeth*, 626; and Watson, *Shakespeare and the Hazards of Ambition*, 89, 106–16. Even without sensing the covert presence of a vegetation myth, critics often associate the coming of Birnam Wood with the restoration of spring and fertility; see, for example, Knight, "Milk of Concord," 144–45; and Greene, "Macbeth," 169. Only Bamber demurs: in her account Birnam Wood rises up in aid of a male alliance, not the Saturnalian disorder of the Maying rituals (*Comic Women*, 106). My view coincides with hers.

43. When Malcolm refers to planting (5.9.31) at the play's end, for example, his comment serves partly to reinforce our sense of his distance from his father's generative power.

44. Paul attributes Shakespeare's use of the imagery of the family tree here to his familiarity with the cut of the Banquo tree in Leslie's *De Origine, Moribus, et Rebus Gestis Scotorum* (*Royal Play*, 175). But the image is too familiar to call for such explanation; see, for example, the tree described in *Richard II* (1.2.12–21).

45. As Wheeler notes, the description of Malcolm's saintly mother makes him "symbolically the child of something approximating virgin birth" (*Shakespeare's Development*, 146)–in effect another version of the man not quite born of woman. Berger comments on the aspiration to be "a nation of bachelor Adams, of no woman born and unknown to women" ("Text Against Performance," 72) without noting the extent to which this fantasy is enacted in the play; Stallybrass calls attention to this configuration and describes the structure of antithesis through which "(virtuous) families of men" are distinguished from "antifamilies of women" ("*Macbeth* and Witchcraft," 198). The fantasy of escape from maternal birth and the creation of all-male lineage would probably have been of interest to King James, whose problematic derivation from Mary, Queen of Scots must occasionally have made him wish himself not born of (that particular) woman, no matter how much he was concerned publicly to rehabilitate her image. See Jonathan Goldberg's account of James's complex attitude toward Mary and especially his attempt to claim the Virgin Queen, Elizabeth, rather than Mary as his mother as he moved toward the English throne (*James I and the Politics of Literature* [Baltimore: Johns Hopkins University Press, 1983], 11–17, 25–26, 119); see also Goldberg's very suggestive discussions of James's poetic attacks on women (ibid., 24–25) and his imaging himself as a man taking

control of a woman in becoming king of England (ibid., 30–31, 46).
Stephen Orgel speculates brilliantly about the ways in which James's
concerns about his own lineage and hence about the derivation of his
royal authority are reflected in *The Tempest*: James "conceived himself
as the head of a single-parent family," as a paternal figure who has
"incorporated the maternal," in effect as a Prospero; the alternative
model is Caliban, who derives his authority from his mother
("Prospero's Wife," *Representations* 8 [1984]: 8–9). Perhaps *Macbeth*
indirectly serves a cultural need to free James from entanglement
with the problematic memory of his witch-mother (portrayed thus,
for example, by Spenser in book 5 of *The Faerie Queene*), tracing his
lineage instead from a safely distanced and safely male forefather,
Banquo.

46. Although neither Berger nor Stallybrass discusses the function of
Birnam Wood specifically, I am indebted here to their discussions of
the ideological function of the play's appeal to cosmology in the
service of patriarchy, Berger seeing it as "a collective project of
mystification" ("Text Against Performance," 64), Stallybrass as "a
returning of the disputed ground of politics to the undisputed
ground of Nature" ("*Macbeth* and Witchcraft," 205–6). If, as
Bradbrook suggests, witches were thought able to move trees
("Sources," 42), then we have in Malcolm's gesture a literal
appropriation of female power, an act of making the unnatural
natural by making it serve patriarchal needs.

47. See Erickson's fine discussion of this geographic distinction
(*Patriarchal Structures*, 121–22).

ENGLISH EPICURES AND SCOTTISH WITCHES

Mary Floyd-Wilson

Our modern conceptions of race and nation only partly match those of Renaissance England. Drawing on a rich array of historical sources, Mary Floyd-Wilson explains how Shakespeare's contemporaries understood themselves, as natives of England, in relation to their northern neighbors and the rest of the world. She speculates about why an English playwright would set this tragedy in the supernaturally-saturated climate of Scotland.

ORTIFIED BY the witches' prophecies in act 5, Macbeth scoffs at incoming reports that his own soldiers are defecting: "Then fly, false thanes," he proclaims, "And mingle with the English epicures" (*Macbeth*, 5.3.7–8).[1] Macbeth's fearlessness grabs our attention here, distracting us, perhaps, from his slightly odd characterization of the enemy. Why should Macbeth call the English "epicures"? Those familiar with Anglo-Scottish relations of the period may recognize that Macbeth employs a stereotype that the Scots were abstemious, compared to their more indulgent southern neighbors.[2] And yet the insult

I thank Michelle Dowd, Carol Thomas Neely, Gail Kern Paster, Garrett Sullivan, and Lanis Wilson for their indispensable advice. I am also indebted to my writing group at the University of North Carolina at Chapel Hill (UNC–CH), as well as to the editors and an anonymous reader at *Shakespeare Quarterly*, for their generous and helpful critiques. I presented earlier versions of this paper at the Center for Medieval and Renaissance Studies at Ohio State University and the Institute of Arts and Humanities at UNC–CH, and I am grateful for the incisive feedback offered by both audiences. **1.** Quotations from Shakespeare's plays follow *The Norton Shakespeare: Based on the Oxford Edition*, ed. Stephen Greenblatt et al. (New York: W.W. Norton, 1997). **2.** For a concise history of the stereotype, see David Allan's "Manners and Mustard: Ideas of Political Decline in Sixteenth-Century Scotland," *Comparative Studies in Society and History* 37 (1995): 242–63. At the same time, the Scots (like all northerners, including the English) were often characterized as great drinkers; see *Macbeth: Texts and Contexts*, ed. William C. Carroll (Boston: Bedford St. Martin's, 1999), 292. Further complicating the Scots' paradoxical reputation are the repeated references in the Scottish histories to Saint Jerome's anecdote that he witnessed cannibalism among the Scots; see Carroll, 277.

Mary Floyd-Wilson, "English Epicures and Scottish Witches." *Shakespeare Quarterly* 57:2 (Summer) 2006, 131–161. Reprinted with the permission of The Johns Hopkins University Press.

still seems unsuitable. Since Macbeth is anticipating battle, calling his opponents fearful or cowardly would not only be more appropriate but also ring true as genuine Scottish mockery of the English.[3] So why should Macbeth call them a nation of gourmands?

Macbeth, of course, abuses the term "epicure" itself. He does not mean to invoke Epicureanism in its complex form as a classical philosophical position, revived (and rehabilitated) by many early modern thinkers and identified with Stoicism in its privileging of moderation and self-restraint.[4] Macbeth depends, instead, on a popular conception of epicures as degenerately self-indulgent and directly opposed to the tempered and controlled stoic.[5] While the insult is predominantly a moral judgment, it also involves assumptions about the ecologically embedded nature of early modern selfhood and ethnicity. Macbeth may critique the English diet, but he implicitly aims to cast the Scots as more temperate than the English in other ways as well—in habits, behaviors, and humoral complexion.[6] To be English, in the sense that Macbeth intends, is to incorporate what is external, foreign, and corrupting and to do so in excess.

Macbeth's characterization of the English can be traced to one of the play's recognized primary sources, John Bellenden's introductory chapter on Scottish manners in his 1540 Scots translation of Hector

3. See, for example, Thomas Craig, De *Unione Regnorum Britannia Tractatus*, ed. C. Sanford Terry (Edinburgh: Scottish History Society, 1909), 207–27 passim. The English syndicate of historians represented by Raphael Holinshed laments that the Scots tended to take credit for all British victories; see Holinshed, "The Historie of England," in *The First and second volumes of Chronicles* (London, 1587), sigs. B6r and D3ʳ. **4.** On the complex influence of Epicurean philosophy in seventeenth-century England, see Reid Barbour, *English Epicures and Stoics: Ancient Legacies in Early Stuart Culture* (Amherst: U of Massachusetts P, 1998); and Joshua Scodel, *Excess and the Mean in Early Modern Literature* (Princeton: Princeton UP, 2002). **5.** For the rote use of "epicure" as gluttonous and intemperate, see Pierre de La Primaudaye, *The French Académie* (London, 1586), sig. N7ᵛ. On the commonplace (and simplified) opposition made between epicures and Stoics, see Barbour, 15 and 17; and William R. Elton, "*King Lear*" and the Gods (San Marino, CA: Huntington Library, 1968), 272–76. The deployment of stoicism in Shakespeare is far from static: *Othello*, for example, vilifies excessive emotional control; see Mary Floyd-Wilson, *English Ethnicity and Race in Early Modern Drama* (Cambridge: Cambridge UP, 2003), 136. On anti-Stoicism, see Richard Strier, "Against the Rule of Reason: Praise of Passion from Petrarch to Luther to Shakespeare to Herbert," in *Reading the Early Modern Passions: Essays in the Cultural History of Emotion*, ed. Gail Kern Paster, Katherine Rowe, and Mary Floyd-Wilson (Philadelphia: U of Pennsylvania P, 2004), 23–42. **6.** Michael C. Schoenfeldt has argued that the control of diet played a significant role in producing the "parameters of individual subjectivity." See *Bodies and Selves in Early Modern England: Physiology and Inwardness in Spenser, Shakespeare, Herbert, and Milton* (Cambridge: Cambridge UP, 1999), 15. Most useful for my purposes, Schoenfeldt establishes a correspondence between Galenic regimens of diet and a Neostoic discipline of emotion (17–19).

Boece's *History and Chronicles of Scotland*,[7] Bellenden's introduction frames Boece's history as nostalgic and anti-English in its short description of ancient Scottish virtues. Some forty years later, English historian William Harrison included a fairly accurate translation of Bellenden's preface as the thirteenth chapter in his "Description of Scotland," published in Raphael Holinshed's *The Chronicles of England, Scotland, and Ireland.*[8] Harrison adheres to Bellenden's main thesis: before the Scots interacted regularly with their English neighbors, they lived in perfect harmony with their environment and possessed a natural temperance. But when Malcolm Canmore took the throne, Scotland suffered a huge influx of English immigrants, whose epicurean customs and practices corrupted the "auld" and rugged Scots, altering them in body and mind:

> [W]e began to haue aliance . . . with Englishmen, . . . and through our dailie trades and conuersation with them, to learne also their maners, . . . Heereby shortlie after it came also to passe, that the temperance and vertue of our ancestors grew to be iudged worthie of small estimation amongst vs.[9]

Not all of the Scots were equally affected by English degeneracy, however. The more removed and less civilized Highland Scots "reteine still their ancient spéech and letters, and almost all their old rites, whervnto in time past their forefathers haue béene accustomed."[10] In contrast, Bellenden aims his criticism at the Lowland Scots, who

7. "Ane prudent doctrine maid be the Auctore concerning baith the new Maneris and the auld of Scottis," in John Bellenden, trans., *The History and Chronicles of Scotland: Written in Latin by Hector Boece*, 2 vols. (Edinburgh: W. and C. Tait, 1821), l:liv–lxii. 8. It is well established that Shakespeare knew Harrison's translation. On his possible familiarity with Boece's Latin history or Bellenden's Scots translation, see A. R. Braunmuller's introduction to *Macbeth*, New Cambridge Shakespeare (Cambridge: Cambridge UP, 1997), 38. For brief references to English epicures, see Geoffrey Bullough, *Narrative and Dramatic Sources of Shakespeare*, 8 vols. (London: Routledge and Kegan Paul, 1957–75), 7:507; Kenneth Muir, *Macbeth*, Arden Shakespeare (Cambridge: Harvard UP, 1957), 150n; Henry N. Paul, *The Royal Play of "Macbeth": When, Why, and How It Was Written by Shakespeare* (1950; repr. New York: Octagon Books, 1978), 158; and David Norbrook, "*Macbeth* and the Politics of Historiography," in *Politics of Discourse: The Literature and History of Seventeenth-Century England*, ed. Kevin Sharpe and Steven N. Zwicker (Berkeley: U of California P, 1987), 78–116, esp. 107. Scottish historian (and King James's tutor) George Buchanan reiterates Bellenden's argument that the English influences after Macbeth's reign brought about deterioration. See *Rerum Scoticarum historia* (1582), exerpted in Carroll as "History of Scotland," 134. 9. William Harrison, "The description of Scotland," in Raphael Holinshed, *The Second volume of Chronicles* (London, 1586), sig. B5^V. I will quote from Harrison's English translation throughout, noting discrepancies in Bellenden where relevant. 10. Harrison, sig. B5^V.

have lost their ancestors' virtues by adopting English manners.[11] To reestablish the balanced, ideal ecology they once maintained, these Lowlanders are urged to resurrect their ancestors' virtues—a reformation that demands that they regulate their boundaries more closely—by observing what they ingest and whom they imitate.

As Timothy J. Reiss has demonstrated, "passibility" was the hallmark of early modern personhood. People were embedded in extended circles of shaping forces that included one's diet, one's family, the state, the natural environment, and the cosmological spheres.[12] Emphasizing the embodied mind's continual transaction with the world, Gail Kern Paster reminds us "to recognize how the porous and volatile humoral body, with its faulty borders and penetrable stuff, interacts differently with the world than the 'static, solid' modern bodily container."[13] In its Renaissance usage, passibility means the vulnerability inherent in being human. As John Donne observes in a sermon, "man was passible before [the Fall]: Every *alteration* is in a degree a *passion*, a *suffering*; and so, in those things which conduced to his *well-being, eating,* and *sleeping,* and other such, man was *passible*: that is, subject to *alteration*."[14] Although passibility entails subjection to the inconstancy of one's surroundings, it does not preclude the dynamic direction of one's will, particularly in monitoring those "things which conduced to . . . well-being," things otherwise known as the six Galenic "non-naturals." As the health manuals and medical treatises of the period repeatedly state, temperance was achieved by properly managing the non-naturals: air, diet, sleep and waking, rest and activity, excretion and retention, and the passions.[15] Whether instructed to carry a sweet bag of herbs for the nose, eat more fowl than meat, purge regularly, or moderate one's anger, early moderns were admonished to regulate the non-naturals

---

11. Bellenden's preface doubles as a behavioral handbook, "proffitable to the rederis; speciallie to sik men, that ar nocht gevin ouir immoderatlie to thair awin affectioun" (1:liv). 12. According to Reiss, "Passibility names experiences of being whose common denominator was a sense of being *embedded in and acted on by* these circles—including the material world and immediate biological, familial and social ambiences. . . . [T]hese circles *preceded* the person, which acted as *subjected to* forces working in complicated ways from 'outside.' But because of the embedding, that 'outside' was manifest in all aspects and elements of 'inside'—of *being* a person." See Timothy J. Reiss, *Mirages of the Selfe: Patterns of Personhood in Ancient and Early Modern Europe* (Stanford: Stanford UP, 2003), 2. 13. Gail Kern Paster, *Humoring the Body: Emotions and the Shakespearean Stage* (Chicago: U of Chicago P, 2004), 23. 14. John Donne, "Sermon XX," *Fifty Sermons* (London, 1649), sig. P6ʳ. 15. See Andrew Wear, *Knowledge and Practice in English Medicine, 1550–1680* (Cambridge: Cambridge UP, 2000), 154–209, esp. 156–57; and Louise Hill Curth, "The Medical Content of English Almanacs 1640–1700," *Journal of the History of Medicine and Allied Sciences* 60 (2005): 255–82.

for their physical and spiritual health. Moreover, the non-naturals functioned interdependently; for example, the season and the region affected when people bathed, what they ate, or how much they slept. Ideally, one sought the right measure of passibility—a temperate balance between ingestion and elimination or between openness and resistance. But some environmental forces—such as cold or corrupted air—could make it more difficult for a person to exercise his or her will in the management or redirection of external influences.

In the early modern period, a people's degree of passibility was a popular basis for establishing ethnic or national characteristics. Before the emergence of racialism, ethnic distinctions were drawn primarily from a geohumoral discourse. Organized along northern and southern regional divisions and authorized by a revered line of classical texts, geohumoralism held that variations in topography and climate produced variations in national characteristics. Northerners, including the English, were understood to possess barbaric, unruly humors that gave them bodily strength, hearty appetites, and slow wits. In describing the isolated Highlanders, for example, William Harrison observes that since they were not yet "corrupted with strange bloud and alliance," they flourished in the tough elements, proving "more hard of constitution of bodie, [able] to beare off the cold blasts, to watch better, and absteine long."[16] But once exposed to foreign influences, northerners' subjection to external elements habitually cast them as more vulnerable than southerners. In other words, geohumoral valuations prove anything but stable: indeed, the suppleness of the discourse allows for endless variations on how nationalistic writers appropriated and deployed humoralism to their own advantage. When idealized, the passibility of the English and Scots ensured a healthy ecology in the ebb and flow of their passions. From an English perspective, then, evil impassibility (epitomized in Shakespeare's works by the monstrous Iago) was often a characteristic of the hardened and hyper-civilized southerner, whose excessive self-control disconnected him emotionally from the external world.[17] As Reiss observes, "The evil of yielding to instability was the pole opposite the evil of absolute impassibility."[18] Among northerners, however, the fear remained that their openness could morph into a loss of any potential autonomy. In this vein, Macbeth's

16. Harrison, sig. A4^V. 17. Floyd-Wilson, *English Ethnicity and Race*, 132–60. In geohumoral discourse, southerners were thought to be less easily moved or persuaded; however, when these southerners were penetrated or affected, their passions could prove more volatile. Hence, Othello's statement, "Of one not easily jealous but, being wrought,/Perplexed in the extreme" (5.2.354–55). On the question of ethnological "hardness" and "softness," see Floyd-Wilson, *English Ethnicity and Race*, 102. 18. Reiss, 152.

insult implies that, unlike the unrestrained and decadent English, the Scots still possess a natural capacity to exercise temperance in their transactions with the world.

In calling the English epicures, Macbeth anticipates the ethnic transformations that Bellenden describes; thus, we may say that *Macbeth* portrays the last moment in Scottish history when the Scots possessed the "auld" temperance of their ancestors. If so, Shakespeare's coda to Bellenden's narrative is that his ancient Scots, the Macbeths, are anything but temperate. Shakespeare's play, in some senses, inverts the ethnological claims of Bellenden's argument. Set in the period immediately preceding Malcolm's reign, *Macbeth* represents an already-degenerate Scotland desperately in need of anglicized civility and government. Scotland suffers, instead, under the barbaric rule of the Macbeths, whose home in Inverness establishes them as the play's only Highlanders.[19]

But Shakespeare's reversal of Bellenden's distinctly Scottish assertions also moves the question of Scottish temperance beyond the more typical geohumoral realm of Galenic non-naturals into an environment saturated with demonic spirits. Perhaps most unfamiliar to modern readers is how the play's supernatural ecology rests on analogous conceptions of passibility and influence that characterize the period's ethnological distinctions. As Highlanders, the Macbeths' extreme passibility makes them especially susceptible to the elements. It is no accident, I will suggest, that the witches and evil spirits in *Macbeth* are predominantly elemental—they command and sometimes even embody the weather. Moreover, as many early modern writers maintain, these elemental powers marked them as indigenous to the world's northernmost regions, including both Scotland and Denmark, the supposed origin of many of King James's ideas about witchcraft.[20] Rather than bolstering the moral virtue of its people, the Macbeths' native environment may predispose them to a corruption more dangerous than

19. On "racialized" distinctions made between Highlanders and Lowlanders, see Braunmuller, 11; Arthur H. Williamson, "Scots, Indians and Empire: The Scottish Politics of Civilization 1519–1609," *Past & Present* 150 (1996): 48–63, esp. 59–66; Carroll, 271–79; and Christopher Highley, "The Place of Scots in the Scottish Play: *Macbeth* and the Politics of Language," in *Shakespeare and Scotland*, ed. Willy Maley and Andrew Murphy (Manchester: Manchester UP, 2004), 53–66. **20.** Christina Larner has speculated that it was during James's visit to Denmark in 1590 that he first became acquainted with continental views of witchcraft, particularly the idea of a demonic pact. See "James VI and I and Witchcraft," in *The Reign of James VI and I*, ed. Alan G. R. Smith (New York: St. Martin's Press, 1973), 74–90. On the importance and complexities of regional comparisons, see Christina Larner's *Enemies of God: The Witch-Hunt in Scotland* (Baltimore: Johns Hopkins UP, 1981), 192–203; and James Sharpe, *Instruments of Darkness: Witchcraft in Early Modern England* (Philadelphia: U of Pennsylvania P, 1996), 12, 30, and 32.

English manners and foreign dishes. In an attempt to distance England from the horror of unrestrained passibility, Shakespeare's play demonizes the Scottish fantasy of an environmentally produced temperance.

I

For John Bellenden, the ancient Scots' natural temperance was the effect of a harmonious relationship between their demanding environment and their hardy natures. He describes a hard pastoral world in which men and women thrive on adversity. Their temperance is exemplified by austere habits in eating and drinking and by courage and ferocity on the battlefield. It is especially the mother's role to encourage heartiness in the children from birth: in Harrison's rendition, the families slept "either vpon the bare floore or pallets of straw, teaching their children euen from their infancie to eschew ease, and practise the like hardnesse." Unless pregnant, Scottish women "marched as well in the field as did the men." Moreover, the mothers took "intollerable paines" to nurse their own young.[21] Further, according to Harrison's translation,

> They thought them furthermore not to be kindlie fostered, except they were so well nourished after their births with the milke of their brests, as they were before they were borne with the bloud of their owne bellies, nay they feared least they should degenerat and grow out of kind, except they gaue them sucke themselues, and eschewed strange milke.[22]

Nursing one's own child, in other words, ensures the ethnological purity of the Scots; they avoid the "strange milke" of wet-nurses because ingesting it may cause their offspring to degenerate from their nature and kind.[23] Breast milk transmitted more than nutrition to the child; it also carried character traits.[24] In particular, stories of

---

21. Harrison, sig. B5^r. **22.** Harrison, sig. B5^r. Bellenden writes, "thay held that thair barnis war degenerat *fra thair nature and kind,* gif thay war nurist with uncouth milk" (1:lvii; emphasis added), which more clearly indicates that "nature and kind" have an ethnological sense. Braunmuller notes this change in wording as an indication that wet-nursing in Bellenden can disrupt "genealogical or dynastic" inheritance (38). **23.** See Floyd-Wilson, *English Ethnicity and Race,* 57–60, for a discussion of this passage in relation to Edmund Spenser's description of the effect of Irish wet-nurses on the ethnicity of Old English offspring in *A View of the State of Ireland* (Dublin, 1633). **24.** On the transmission of "moral and ethical qualities" in milk, see Gail Kern Paster, *The Body Embarrassed: Drama and the Disciplines of Shame in Early Modern England* (Ithaca: Cornell UP, 1993), 200. Phyllis Rackin connects this idea to *Macbeth* in "Staging the Female Body: Maternal Breastfeeding and Lady Macbeth's 'Unsex me here,'" in *Corps/Décors: Femmes, Orgie, Parodie,* ed. Catherine Nesci, Gretchen Van Slyke, and Gerald Prince (Amsterdam: Rodopi, 1999), 17–29, esp. 23–25.

infants sucking martial valor from the breast were not uncommon.[25] Bellenden's assumptions about Scottish identity and breastfeeding are echoed by the seventeenth-century clergyman George Hakewill:

> The *High-landers* likewise in *Scotland*, and the wild *Irish* commonly liue longer then those of softer education, of nice and tender bringing vp, (which often fals out in the more civill times and countreyes) being no doubt a great enemy to *Longevity*, as also the first feeding and nourishing of the *Infant* with the milke of a strange dug.[26]

That both Hakewill and Harrison connect vitality and "eschew[ing] ease" with a mother nursing her own children implies that vigorous qualities were both communicated and preserved by these Scottish mothers. Civility, which is associated here with the introduction of strange milk from a strange dug, threatens the Scots' innate heartiness. In a sense, women are both the authors and the guardians of the old male Scottish temperance.

Given the brevity of Bellenden's preface, it is easy to see a correlation between the degeneration from "kind," which "strange milke" threatens, and the ethnic dilution wrought by the importation of foreign foodstuffs that accompanies Malcolm's accession. In particular, the English influence leads the Scots to ingest alien, imported substances, such as exotic wines, delicious meats, and "hot spices and drugs which are brought vnto vs from the hot countries."[27] These external influences engender dramatic changes in the habits, behavior, and temperament of the Lowland Scots, according to Harrison's version:

> whereas [our elders] gaue their minds to dowghtinesse, we applie our selues to droonkennes: they had plentie with sufficiencie, we haue inordinate excess with superfluitie: they were temperate, we effeminate: . . .
>
> Being thus drowned in our delicate gluttonie, it is a world to sée, how we stuffe our selues both daie and night, neuer ceasing to ingorge & powre in, till our bellies be so full that we must néeds depart.[28]

The Scots' degeneration is not simply a moral failing; it is also an internal physiological process brought about by the infection of

---

25. According to Kathryn Schwarz, "Stories of children who gain martial valor through being nursed by Spartan women" were not uncommon in the period, "recalling Volumnia's claim to Coriolanus: 'Thy valiantness was mine, thou suck'st it from me.'" See "Missing the Breast: Desire, Disease, and the Singular Effect of Amazons," in *The Body in Parts: Fantasies of Corporeality in Early Modern Europe*, ed, David Hillman and Carla Mazzio (New York: Routledge, 1997), 147–69, esp. 152–53. 26. George Hakewill, *An apologie of the povver and prouidence of God in the gouernment of the world* (Oxford, 1627), sig. V2ᵛ. 27. Harrison, sig. B5ʳ. 28. Harrison, sig. B5ʳ.

external elements. Dietary changes produce ineluctable consequences not just for the Scots' bodily health but also for their ethnic identity. They have become effeminate, corrupted with sloth, and drowned in avarice and lust. Increasingly vulnerable to the same environmental forces that once helped to sustain them, they find themselves unable to travel to colder climates without becoming inordinately heated with unnatural fevers. English corruption has disrupted the once-harmonious relationship between the Scots' bodies and their native environment. And the Scots' degeneration encompasses an internal physiological drama of obstruction and dysfunction brought about by external agents. Their minds are "clogged and overladen" with excess humors while their "vitall forces" are choked with "fatnesse."[29] The more deeply Bellenden anatomizes these physiological changes, the closer he comes to suggesting that corruption has seeped into their souls as well. Once the body's humoral fatness clouds the mind, "hir image of the diuinitie" will "be extinguished outright."[30]

Bellenden was not alone in his anxieties: other early moderns worried that the porous boundaries between environment, body, and mind also raised questions about the status of the soul. Technically speaking, at the intersection between the clogged humoral body and the potentially hampered soul were the animal spirits; within heavy or polluted flesh, the spirits could become "dulled, quenched, and damnifyed."[31] Once adversely affected by such variants as food, drink, passion, or air, these spirits could not, then, move with their natural alacrity through the body's passages or properly enact their liminal role as "bearers of information between natural and supernatural, visible and invisible, body and soul."[32] John Sutton explains

---

29. Harrison, sigs. B5ᵛ–B6ʳ.   **30.** Harrison, sig. B5ᵛ. Environment and ingestion were understood to have immediate effects on the vegetative and sensitive souls. For a historical discussion of the "close ties between body and soul," see Katherine Park, "The Organic Soul," *The Cambridge History of Renaissance Philosophy*, ed. Charles B. Schmitt, Quentin Skinner, and Eckhard Kessler (Cambridge: Cambridge UP, 1988), 464–84, esp. 468. As Park notes, most philosophers agreed that the rational soul remained unaffected by organic functions, yet at the same time "even they could be disrupted by physical illness or cerebral indisposition; . . . lunatics and idiots possessed a rational soul like other men, but it was prevented from functioning normally by physical abnormalities in the brain, which distorted . . . internal senses" (468). As La Primaudaye observes, intemperate drinking and eating hinders the operation of reason with rising "vapours" (sig. O3ᵛ).   **31.** Levinus Lemnius, *The Touchstone of Complexions*, trans. Thomas Newton (London, 1581), sig. A8ᵛ. On the animal spirits, see John Sutton, *Philosophy and Memory Traces: Descartes to Connectionism* (Cambridge: Cambridge UP, 1998), 23–49. According to Sutton, when philosophers argued that the animal "spirits were physical, the way was open for medical materialists to . . . heretically identify the soul itself with corporeal spirits" (34).   **32.** Sutton, 37. The variants that affected the spirits were primarily the Galenic non-naturals.

that the character and quality of the animal spirits "depended directly on influences picked up, usually through the blood but also directly through the skin, from climate, environment, nutrition, and emotion."[33] As physician Leonardus Lessius argues, it was by way of the animal spirits that a disordered vegetative soul could affect the sensitive and rational souls:

> ill humours do cloy up the muscles and the nerves through which the spirits have their course and passage: whereby it comes to passe, that the animall spirits (from which, as from the most generall and immediate instrument of the soul, all the vigour of the bodie in sense and motion is derived) cannot freely take their course, nor govern and order the bodie as they ought.[34]

Lessius's phrasing indicates that healthy animal spirits appear to possess their own agency, apart from the individual's reason or will, which helps to "govern and order" the body. Meanwhile, cloyed or clogged animal spirits lose the freedom of their "course and passage," as well as their communication with the sensitive and rational souls. Thus, the condition of the animal spirits can affect how quickly or sluggishly one feels emotion, how fixedly one holds a belief, or whether one senses the pangs of conscience.[35] If the spirits' movement is obstructed, impeding communication between mind, body, and soul, then individuals become not only internally fragmented (leading to the malfunctioning of individual parts) but also increasingly vulnerable to external influences.[36]

Within geohumoral discourse, many writers argued that a northern climate naturally debilitated the animal spirits. According to Levinus Lemnius, "they that dwell Northward and in cold regions" necessarily possess "thick Spirites." And when the spirits are "grosse" and "thicke," the mind is "ouerclowded."[37] Jean Bodin writes that the northern "Scythians" (those barbarians identified as ancient Scots and Picts)" are handicapped by thick humors as though by a weight, so that the

---

33. Sutton, 39. Lemnius, *The Touchstone of Complexions*, explains that animal spirits are diversely produced by "condition and nature of the Place, Ayre, Countrey and nourishment" (sig. C3ʳ). **34.** Leonardus Lessius, *Hygiasticon: Or, The right course of preserving Life and Health unto extream old Age: Together with soundnesse and integritie of the Senses, Judgement, and Memorie* (Cambridge, 1634), sig. C4ᵛ. **35.** Paster argues that the animal spirits "revolved around a social hierarchy . . . with low spirits belonging properly to those lower down on the social scale"; see *Humoring the Body*, 244. On the emotional and social tropes that comprise the discourse of "spirits," see also Gail Kern Paster, "Nervous Tension: Networks of Blood and Spirit in the Early Modern Body," in The *Body in Parts* (see n. 25), 107–25. **36.** Sutton, 47. **37.** Lemnius, *The Touchstone of Complexions*, sigs. B5ʳ and B8ʳ.

force of the intellect does not shine through."[38] Thomas Walkington, author of *The Optick Glasse of Humours*, insists that it is the cold northern air that causes the humoral "passages" of the northern Scythians to be "dammed up," which, in turn, "inflame[s]" and impedes their animal spirits.[39] Thomas Cogan, who devotes *The Haven of Health* to delineating a diet best suited for English bodies, claims that cold, moist air generates "repletion," which "breedeth cruditie," making the people prone to "inumerable maladies."[40] What these writers suggest is that the northern environment contributes to the sort of humoral imbalance that Bellenden blamed on English immigration.

Three years before Shakespeare wrote *Macbeth*, the accession of King James brought a flood of Scottish citizens to London. This flood, together with the king's proposal to unite England and Scotland, put new pressures on the question of whether the English and Scots were humorally indistinguishable.[41] Certainly, many English writers insisted on significant climatic differences between northern and southern Britain. But when it was politically advantageous, neither the English nor the Scots hesitated to stress their apparent similarities. Francis Bacon attempted to diffuse the xenophobia behind Parliament's resistance to union by praising the Scots' familiar qualities of mind and body:

> [T]hat for the Goods of the Mind and Body, they are *Alteri Nos, Other our selves*. For, to do them but right, we know in their capacity and understanding, they are a People ingenious; in Labour industrious; in Courage valiant; in Body hard, active and comely.[42]

For many early moderns, the ancient virtues that Bellenden ascribes to his Scottish ancestors are the same virtues that the English sought to preserve from their own barbaric past.[43] Yet this did not change

---

38. Jean Bodin, *Method for the Easy Comprehension of History*, trans. Beatrice Reynolds (New York: Columbia UP, 1945), 124. William Harrison acknowledges the Scottish-Scythian link explicitly in "The description of Britaine" in Holinshed, *The First and second volumes of Chronicles* (quoted by Braunmuller, 11). On the geohumoral significance of Scythians to English conceptions of ethnicity, see Floyd-Wilson, *English Ethnicity and Race*, 23–42. **39.** Thomas Walkington, *The Optick Glasse of Humors* (1631; repr., Delmar, NY: Scholars' Facsimiles & Reprints, 1981), 24–25. **40.** Thomas Cogan, *The Haven of Health* (London, 1596), sig. M6ᵛ. **41.** In *Method for the Easy Comprehension of History* (124), Jean Bodin lumps the English and the Scots together as typically northern in their humoral imbalances. While discerning subtle differences between the Germans and Hollanders, Lemnius suggests that the English resemble the Scots: both have "great stomacks & [are] angry" (*The Touchstone of Complexions*, sig. C2ʳ). **42.** Francis Bacon, *The Union of the Two Kingdomes* (Edinburgh, 1670), sig. C1ᵛ. **43.** Floyd-Wilson, "English Mettle," in *Reading the Early Modern Passions* (see n. 5), 130–46, and *English Ethnicity*, 48–66 and 161–83.

the fact that the more chauvinistic English writers characterized the Scots—particularly the Highlanders—as stubbornly uncivilized. Moreover, as David Armitage has recognized, the "regal union between England and Scotland after 1603 sharpened" King James's efforts to launch a strategy of internal colonization in Scotland by which Lowlanders sought to suppress and civilize the wild and savage Highlanders. Indeed, such efforts at colonization provided a "middle ground," an opportunity for the English and Lowland Scots to come together as "Britons."[44] King James himself viewed the Highlanders as intemperate barbarians, known for their detestable, godless, and possibly cannibalistic ways. As he saw it, rooting out the barbarism in the Highlands would succeed in removing "the reproach of the haill natioun' of Scotland."[45] Scots who valued their natural complexion, however, questioned whether they would retain their ethnic identity if the union came about.[46] From England's perspective, any civility that the Scots attained was attributed to anglicization.

The distinction between Scottish claims of temperance (rather than barbarism) and English claims of civility (rather than corruption) derives in part from the elasticity of geohumoral discourse, which allows for contradictory interpretations of temperance. In some geohumoral texts, there is an untroubled correlation between environment and complexion, so that "a barren countrey makes men temperat by necessitie."[47] And while temperance by necessity involves endurance and deprivation, it does not require self-discipline or self-restraint.[48] In contrast, Neostoic temperance is an actively cultivated virtue, achieved by breaking free of external influences through conscious and willful control. In outlining his Neostoic doctrine in *Tvvo Bookes Of Constancie*, Justus Lipsius acknowledges that the soil and air of one's country appear to be "strong fetters of nature" but insists that man must recognize these ties as tricks of custom. Place matters less than the inward

---

44. David Armitage, "Making the Empire British: Scotland in the Atlantic World 1542–1707," *Past & Present* 155 (1997): 34–63, esp. 43–45. **45.** Arthur H. Williamson, *Scottish National Consciousness in the Age of James VI: The Apocalypse, the Union and the Shaping of Scotland's Public Culture* (Edinburgh: John Donald Publishers, 1979), 132. On King James's prejudices against Highlanders, see Williamson, "Scots, Indians and Empire," 64; and Neil Rhodes, "Wrapped in the Strong Arms of the Union: Shakespeare and King James," in *Shakespeare and Scotland* (see n. 19), 37–52. **46.** See Craig, *De Unione Regnorum Britanniæ Tractatus*. See also John Russell, *A Treatise of the Happie and Blissed Unioun* (dated by its editors to ca. 1604/5), in *The Jacobean Union: Six Tracts of 1604*, ed. Bruce R. Galloway and Brian P. Levack (Edinburgh: Scottish History Society, 1985), 75–142, esp. 84. **47.** Jean Bodin, *The Six Bookes of a Common-weale*, trans. Richard Knolles (London, 1606), sig. Ccc1ʳ. **48.** Scodel defines "'necessitated' temperance" as "the involuntary and thus non-Aristotelian self-restraint of those too poor to indulge themselves" (168).

qualities of the mind.[49] In this view, the Scots' natural temperance, as described by Bellenden, would not be temperance at all. If it were, the Scots would not have yielded so easily to the influx of English vice.

II

There should be little question that in *Macbeth* Shakespeare draws on the complexities of geohumoralism and Neostoicism to interrogate the nature of Scottish temperance. Most plainly, the anglicization that Bellenden and Macbeth identify as epicurean contamination is represented as a medicinal purge for Scotland's "sickly weal" (5.2.27). In this light, Macbeth's defeat begins a civilizing process that the English intend to extend in the Jacobean union project, epitomized in the play's final scene when Malcolm converts the Scottish "thanes" to English "earls" (5.11.28–29). But unlike Bellenden or the geohumoral writers mentioned above, Shakespeare situates the question of Scottish temperance in an environment alive with supernatural forces that challenge our standard measures of how the self might interact with the world.

Shakespeare depicts Scotland's environment as paradoxically fair and foul—climatologically temperate and authentically demonic. Upon arriving at Inverness, Duncan observes, "This castle hath a pleasant seat. The air/Nimbly and sweetly recommends itself/Unto our gentle senses" (1.6.1–3). The line teases us with the possibility that the conditions in the Highlands may be, at least superficially, as pleasant as any other. Strangely, Banquo (who fails to mention his encounter with the evaporating witches on the nearby heath) affirms Duncan's appraisal, noting that since the "heavens' breath/Smells wooingly here," the martlet (or martin) has made the castle its home. These birds, he explains, "breed and haunt" only where the "air is delicate" (ll. 9–10).[50] The conversation underlines the ecological significance of well-being in the play; more startlingly, it also highlights Duncan's naiveté—his inability to detect "the mind's construction in the face" (1.4.12) or intuit the evil that awaits him. This dramatic irony may have affected *Macbeth*'s original audience on a visceral level, for foul odors from stage squibs (used to generate thunder and lightning in 1.1 and 1.3) could still have been lingering in the air.[51] And where Banquo and

---

49. Justus Lipsius, *Two Bookes Of Constancie*, trans. John Stradling (London, 1595), sigs. D4^r–E1^v. See also Guillaume DuVair, *The Moral Philosophic of the Stoicks* (London, 1598), sigs. C7^r–C8^r. The Neostoic argument directly counters the geohumoral view that barren countries naturally produce men who are restrained, vigilant, and disciplined; see, for example, La Primaudaye, sig. O5^r. **50.** Braunmuller observes that martlets "were common emblems of 'prudent trust' and 'harmony in the realm'" (128n). **51.** My thanks to Jonathan Gil Harris for bringing this possibility to my attention.

Duncan see evidence of martlets, Lady Macbeth hears the ominous raven croaking itself hoarse (1.5.36–37). Three years after *Macbeth*, Ben Jonson would employ the martlet in his *Masque of Queens* as a witch's familiar; the martlet's duty was to call the coven to its meetings (before turning into a goat for the witches to ride!).[52] As it turns out, it is the haunting and breeding presence of malevolent, supernatural forces that most dramatically differentiates Shakespeare's Scotland not only from Bellenden's Scotland but from Shakespeare's England as well.

Although it remains unanswerable whether the witches engender Scotland's "fog and filthy air" or that air breeds witches (1.1.11), *Macbeth* depends on a correspondence between witchcraft and weather.[53] The forces in the play that modern readers may deem "supernatural"—and make anachronistic assumptions in doing so—are predominantly meteorological in nature.[54] From the very first lines of the play, "When shall we three meet again?/In thunder, lightning, or in rain?" (ll. 1–2), the witches are identified with the elements. And while such associations between witches and weather are not unusual for the period, I will suggest that Shakespeare presents their powers as indigenous to Scotland in particular.

In the continental witchcraft texts that influenced Scottish notions of the supernatural, witches (and the devils who spurred them on) were widely understood to have powers to control the environment. As King James writes in *Daemonologie*, witches "can raise storms and tempests in the air either upon sea or land, although not universally, but in such a particular place and prescribed bounds as God will permit them so to trouble."[55] Witches purportedly directed winds and manipulated air for the very reason that disturbed winds or infected

---

52. Ben Jonson, The *Masque of Queenes* in *The Workes of Beniamin Jonson* (London, 1616), sigs. Kkkk6ʳ–Kkkk6ᵛ. Jonson cites Jean Bodin's *De la Démonomanie des Sorciers* (Paris, 1580) as one source of the martin's eerie associations. See also Thomas Lodge's *VVits miserie, and the VVorlds Madnesse: Discouering the Deuils Incarnat of this Age* (London, 1596): "This Diuell if he fall acquainted with you (as he did with the Arians) he ties you to *Martinet* their familiar, maketh you honour Sathan in forme of a Bull" (sig. C2ᵛ). **53.** The common association between foul air and witches renders Macbeth's curse redundant: "Infected be the air whereon they ride" (4.1.154). In glossing this line, Braunmuller observes that it was a "common belief" that witches rode infected air (198n). **54.** On "demonism [as] an aspect of the natural world," see Stuart Clark, *Thinking with Demons: The Idea of Witchcraft in Early Modern Europe* (Oxford: Clarendon Press, 1997), 168. Clark maintains that discussions of demonology and witchcraft in the period were often explorations of where to separate the natural from the supernatural. See Kristen Poole's discussion of the devil as part of nature with regard to Marlowe's *Doctor Faustus*, "The Devil's in the Archive: *Doctor Faustus* and Ovidian Physics," forthcoming in *Renaissance Drama* 35 (2006). **55.** Quoted in *Witchcraft in Early Modern Scotland: James VI's "Demonology" and the North Berwick Witches*, ed. Lawrence Normand and Gareth Roberts (Exeter: U of Exeter P, 2000), 395.

air could, in turn, stir or dull the body's spirits. In *The Secret Miracles of Nature*, Levinus Lemnius maintains that "evil spirits" have the power to "mingle themselves with our food, humours, spirits, with the ayre and breath, that we draw in and breathe out."[56] We must worry in particular about the effects of "outward winds," which are "commonly offensive to us, and by their penetrating force do us much hurt." And "if the Ayre be pestilent and contagious, it is more hurtfull than venemous and faulty meats . . . for it presently infects the heart and vitall spirits."[57] It was widely noted that people fall prey to witches, most often because of their complexion—they are humorally susceptible.[58]

Skeptical writers who dismissed the possibility of demonic possession still maintained that evil spirits could influence the behavior of those most vulnerable by manipulating the non-naturals, especially the passions: for "*spirites* and *diuels* they are able by *external obiects*, to stirre vp *affections* and *passions* in the *sensitiue appetite*" of the weak.[59] As Stuart Clark maintains, even by the end of the seventeenth century demonologists held that the devil and witchcraft "acted on the 'animal spirits' in the human body, thus interfering with the imagination, other mental functions, and the motor activities."[60] The first witch in *Macbeth*, for example, suggests a correspondence between blowing winds and draining the sailor "dry as hay" (1.3.17), supernatural actions that produce disruptions within the body's natural functions. They deprive a man of sleep until he "[s]hall . . . dwindle, peak, and pine" (22).[61] The witch's assertion anticipates the troubled sleep of Macbeth, Lady Macbeth, and to a lesser extent the entire realm of Scotland. Clark has also observed that "[v]arious internal physiological factors, together with differences of sex, age, and diet[,] made some people more prone" than others to such occult interferences.[62] As I suggested above, this vulnerability, or degree of passibility, was also a measure of ethnicity in the period.

Bellenden celebrates the Highland Scots' temperance as a natural fit between their bodies and the harsh environment. But as we saw, other writers of the period cast such temperance as "necessitated"—

---

56. Levinus Lemnius, *The Secret Miracles of Nature* (London, 1658), sig. Fff1ʳ.
57. Lemnius, *Secret Miracles*, sigs. Dd2ʳ–Dd2ᵛ. 58. Recall Hamlet's concern that his melancholy may have made him easy prey for the devil. See Robert Burton, *The Anatomy of Melancholy*, ed. Thomas C. Faulkner, Nicolas K. Kiessling, and Rhonda L. Blair, 4 vols. (Oxford: Clarendon Press, 1989–98), 1:193. The skeptic Reginald Scot surmises that it is humoral susceptibility that persuades poor old women to believe that they possess the powers of witchcraft; see *The discouerie of witchcraft* (London, 1584), sigs. F2ᵛ–F3ᵛ. 59. John Deacon, *Dialogicall Discourses of Sprits and Divels* (London, 1601), sig. E7ᵛ. Reginald Scot is almost entirely alone in reducing "demonic agents to a non-corporeal condition" (Clark, 212). 60. Clark, 188.
61. Acknowledging the sexual implications of "drain him" (1.3.17), Braunmuller notes the witch may "[intend] to be a succubus" (110n). 62. Clark, 188.

an enfeebling interdependence that compromised the exercise of the will. In a perverse sense, then, if Macbeth embodies the "auld" Scottish temperance, he is exceedingly vulnerable to environmental forces, from the persuasiveness of false rhetoric to the witches' supernatural soliciting. By inverting Bellenden's thesis, Shakespeare implies that the Macbeths' weakened ability to regulate their bodies' borders may be what identifies them as Highland Scots. Their efforts at regulation, notably framed in Neostoic terms, prove progressively more difficult in an environment where external spirits threaten to usurp the function of the internal spirits with every breath.[63] Ironically, their degeneration mirrors the effects of English Epicureanism, as Bellenden describes it.

Certainly, the play invites us at crucial moments to imagine how it might look and feel to experience thoughts and passions as disturbingly elemental or environmental—an occurrence that may have been familiar, although not wholly desirable, to the early modern English. Since supernatural forces violate psychophysiological boundaries, we are also left to wonder whether the thoughts and passions that the Macbeth's experience as proprietary—as dreadfully and inescapably their own—are not also affected. In presenting us with central characters remarkably vulnerable to the wicked forces in their world, *Macbeth* inevitably poses questions of culpability. Directed, shaped, and redirected by a potent environment, Macbeth frequently appears to have little control over his passions, desires, or thoughts—a lack of control that raises critical questions about his free will.[64] As the play progresses, Macbeth's prior fantasy of possessing a "single state of man" (1.3.139) increasingly gives way to internal fragmentation and the competing agencies of those internal parts.

---

63. On the play's interest in stoic emotional control, see Katherine Rowe, "Humoral Knowledge and Liberal Cognition in Davenant's *Macbeth*," in *Reading the Early Modern Passions* (see n. 5), 169–91; and "Minds in Company: Shakespearean Tragic Emotions," in *A Companion to Shakespeare's Works: The Tragedies*, ed. Richard Dutton and Jean E. Howard, 4 vols. (Oxford: Blackwell Publishing, 2003), 1:47–72.
64. For a succinct survey of varied forms of subjectivity represented in the witchcraft debate, see Katharine Eisaman Maus, "Sorcery and Subjectivity in Early Modern Discourses of Witchcraft," in *Historicism, Psychoanalysis, and Early Modern Culture*, ed. Carla Mazzio and Douglas Trevor (New York: Routledge, 2000), 325–48. On the complex question of Macbeth's free will, I cite only representative work: Walter Clyde Curry, *Shakespeare's Philosophical Patterns* (Baton Rouge: Louisiana State UP, 1937), 53–137; Willard Farnham, *Shakespeare's Tragic Frontier: The World of His Final Tragedies* (Berkeley: U of California P, 1950), 79–137; Wilbur Sanders, *The Dramatist and the Received Idea: Studies in the Plays of Marlowe and Shakespeare* (Cambridge: Cambridge UP, 1968), 253–316; Richard Waswo, "Damnation, Protestant Style: Macbeth, Faustus, and Christian Tragedy," *Journal of Medieval and Renaissance Studies* 4 (1974): 63–99; and Robert G. Hunter, *Shakespeare and the Mystery of God's Judgments* (Athens: U of Georgia P, 1976), 159–82.

Critics who focus on Macbeth's incapacities find it worrisome that he may be dismissible as an "automaton." As A. R. Braunmuller puts it, "If Macbeth could never act otherwise ... where is the tragedy...?"[65] Lady Macbeth recognizes that her husband could act otherwise when she worries that his nature "is too full o' th' milk of human kindness" (1.5.15); she anticipates that he may be easily swayed by feelings of kinship or pity, which are the very emotions that cause him to waver in 1.7. Despite his status as a warrior, which might suggest a resilient or hardened nature, Macbeth initially proves exceedingly passible—receptive to the witches' temptations, to Duncan's virtues, and to his wife's spirited rhetoric. "[R]ude" northerners, "not yet trayned to any disciplyne and learning" were, according to Lemnius, "like softe waxe, or as tractable and moyst claye."[66] There is little question that Macbeth allows himself to be influenced by evil rather than good—he exercises his will to achieve his "black and deep desires" (1.4.51)—but the brunt of his tragedy comes with the dawning recognition that once he has yielded, he is temperamentally and physiologically unable to reclaim his "single state of man."

If we take seriously some of the widespread beliefs in the period—beliefs in witches and evil spirits and the effects of extreme environments, as well as prejudices against Scottish Highlanders—we might also consider whether English chauvinism underlies Shakespeare's representation of Macbeth's interaction with his world.[67] My reading emphasizes the possibility that Shakespeare's *Macbeth* represents its protagonists' troubling susceptibility—and the diminished will it can imply—as barbarically Scottish. Rather than differentiating the Highland Scot from his fellow Britons by his appearance or customs, the tragedy indicates that ethnological differences may lie in how the unreformed Scottish body, mind, and soul interact with a dangerously animated world.

III

Scholars have long acknowledged that the circumstances that prompted King James's deep interest in witchcraft probably influenced Shakespeare's depiction of the supernatural in *Macbeth*.[68] The witch's

65. Braunmuller, 40. See also Bertrand Evans, *Shakespeare's Tragic Practice* (Oxford: Clarendon Press, 1979), 181–222, esp. 221. **66.** Lemnius, *The Touchstone of Complexions*, sig. A4[r]. **67.** As James Sharpe observes, there were both early modern skeptics and fanatics, with regard to supernatural beliefs. Most people, however, "were somewhere in between: willing to accept witchcraft as a possibility" (57). **68.** Anthony Harris, *Night's Black Agents: Witchcraft and Magic in Seventeenth-Century English Drama* (Manchester: Manchester UP, 1980), 40–43; and Carroll, 305–6. For a comprehensive study of King James and the witches, see Normand and Roberts and Stuart Clark, "King James's *Daemonologie*: Witchcraft and Kingship," in *The Damned Art: Essays in the Literature of Witchcraft*, ed. Sydney Anglo (London: Routledge and Kegan Paul, 1977), 156–81.

boasting that she causes the sailor's ship to be "tempest-tossed" (1.3.24) most likely alludes to the witch hunts of the 1590s, when witches in Denmark and Scotland were accused of raising storms and contrary winds in their attempts to sink the royal ships carrying King James and Anne of Denmark.[69] A pamphlet about the events, *News from Scotland* (1591), includes Agnes Thompson's confession that she and others helped bring about a tempest by tying the joints of a dead man to a cat, before traveling in "sieves" to the "midst of the sea," where they left the cat to work its peculiar magic.[70] What may have been equally fascinating to English readers, however, were the regional associations of specific kinds of witchcraft. Early modern writers assumed that northern climates fostered wickedness and sorcery. When King James in his *Dae-monologie* maintains that witchcraft flourishes in "Lap-land & Fin-land, or in our North Isles of Orknay and Schetland," he is repeating a commonplace of the period.[71] More precisely, it was understood that these northern witches, unlike those in England, were especially adept at controlling the climate. Keith Thomas has speculated that in England witches were rarely "suspected of interfering with the weather."[72]

Specifically, it was believed that witches in cold climates customarily sold winds to mariners. In describing the Isle of Man in "The description of Britaine," for example, William Harrison traces the origin of this business to the Scots:

that the people of the said Ile were much giuen to witchcraft and sorcerie (which they learned of the Scots a nation greatlie bent to that horible practise) in somuch that their women would

69. Harris, 40. The first witches charged with creating the tempests were located in Copenhagen; later, the accusations spread to Scotland (Larner, "James VI and I and Witchcraft," 80). **70.** Quoted in Carroll, 319. **71.** Quoted in Williamson, "Scots, Indians and Empire," 48. Olaus Magnus's 1555 *Description of the Northern Peoples*, trans. Peter Fisher and Humphrey Higgens (London: Hakluyt Society, 1996), is a primary source for the widespread notion that cold regions generated evil spirits and witchcraft. A sampling of early modern texts that assume a correlation between northern climates and sorcery include Jean Bodin, *De la Démonomanie des Sorciers*; Thomas Nashe, *Terrors of the night* (London, 1594); Alexander Roberts, *A Treatise of Witchcraft* (London, 1616); Thomas Heywood, *Gynaikeion: or, Nine Bookes of Various History* (London, 1624); and John Webster, *The Displaying of Supposed Witchcraft* (London, 1677). As Antonio de Torquemada (*The Spanish Mandeuile of Miracles* [London, 1600]) states, "there is in these Northerne parts, an infinite number of Sorcerers, Witches, Enchaunters, and Negromancers" (fol. 138ʳ). **72.** Keith Thomas, *Religion and the Decline of Magic* (New York: Charles Scribner's Sons, 1971), 437. There were exceptions, of course; a German visitor to England in 1592 noted, "Many witches are found there who frequently do much mischief by means of hail and tempests"; quoted in Stephen Greenblatt, *Will in the World: How Shakespeare Became Shakespeare* (New York: W W Norton, 2004), 343–44. George Gifford, in *A Dialogve concerning Witches and Witchcraftes* (London, 1593) explicitly notes that ill effects of witchcraft do not derive from the air in England but from "naughty people" (sig. A4ᵛ).

oftentimes sell wind to the mariners, inclosed vnder certeine knots of thred, with this iniunction, that they which bought the same, should for a great gale vndoo manie, and for the lesse a fewer or smaller number.[73]

Thomas Heywood reiterates accepted knowledge when he states that the "Witches in Lap-land; Fin-land, and these miserable and wretched cold countries . . . buy and sell winds betwixt them and the merchants" as frequently and "familiarly . . . as eating and sleeping."[74] In *A Treatise of Witchcraft* (1616), Alexander Roberts explains the process in detail:

[B]y the experience of our owne Nauigators, who trade in *Finland, Denmarke, Lapland, Ward-house, Norway,* and other Countries of that Climate, and haue obtained of the [witches] thereof, a certaine winde for twenty dayes together, or the like fixed period of time, according to the distance of place and strings tied with three knots, so that if one were loosed, they should haue a pleasant gale: if the second, a more vehement blast: if the third, such hideous & raging tempests that the Mariners were not able once to looke out, to stand vpon the hatches, to handle their tackle, or to guide the helme with all their strength; and are somtimes violently carried back to the place from whence they first loosed to sea; and many (more hardy then wise) haue bought their triall full deere, opening those knots, and neglecting admonition giuen to the contrary.[75]

When the witches in *Macbeth* give each other winds in order to produce tempests in the seaports (1.3.10–13), Shakespeare has marked them as notably more northern than the typical English witch.[76] In his invocation in Act 4, Macbeth praises the witches' meteorological

---

73. Harrison, "The description of Britaine," in *The First and second volumes of Chronicles*, sigs. D6ʳ–D6ᵛ. **74.** Heywood, *Gynaikeion*, sig. Nn5ʳ. **75.** Roberts, sig. D3ʳ. For another detailed description of the practice, see Magnus, 173. Ethel Seaton writes, "Of the many superstitions located in the north, the belief in the sale of winds and tempests was the most widespread"; see *Literary Relations of England and Scandinavia in the Seventeenth Century* (Oxford: Clarendon Press, 1935), 282. She cites Ranulf Higden, Thomas Nashe, John Fletcher, and Robert Burton, among others (282–87). In *The Hierarchie of the blessed Angells* (London, 1635), Thomas Heywood states that the winds were sold in knotted handkerchiefs (rather than ropes) for the merchants to "untye" (sig. Vulᵛ). Intriguingly, a napkin "with many knots" was one of the suspicious pieces of evidence passed between the accused witches of the Scottish trials (Normand and Roberts, 179). **76.** Muir glosses these lines with references in the period to witches selling winds in Ireland, Denmark, and the Laplands (12–13n).

powers almost exclusively. And the devastation they cause on both sea and land originates in the winds they have untied:

> Though you untie the winds and let them fight
> Against the churches, though the yeasty waves
> Confound and swallow navigation up,
> Though bladed corn be lodged and trees blown down,
> Though castles topple on their warders' heads,
> Though palaces and pyramids do slope
> Their heads to their foundations, though the treasure
> Of nature's germens tumble all together
> Even till destruction sicken....
>
> (4.1.68–76)

As far as I am aware, scholars have not glossed the line "untie the winds" as a reference to the alleged practice of northern witches selling winds in "knots."[77] More than a powerful metaphor, however, the phrase imbues witchcraft in *Macbeth* with an identifiably northern dominance over the environment and the bodies that inhabit that environment. That their chaotic interventions can tumble "nature's germens," or seeds, underscores the extent of their power. In an important gloss on this line, Walter Clyde Curry explains how most Renaissance writers believed that demons and witches worked within the "regular processes of nature," effecting what looked to be marvelous by manipulating unseen energies—nature's germens—present in all the elements.[78] The tumbling of nature's germens is what produces cosmological ruptures of "dire combustion," blowing chimneys down, turning animals wild, and shaking the earth (2.3.51–57).

Although critics have often noted the witches' capacity to control the atmosphere, they tend to characterize this ability as a limitation rather than a potent force. As Arthur F. Kinney and others have observed, the witch can subject the sailor "to storms, but she cannot kill him."[79] But we may be underestimating the shaping influence of the weather. Raising storms is not only a matter of causing bodily harm to seafaring men. To control the macrocosmic winds is to effect change (however haphazardly) in the microcosmic winds of passion. The literal relationship between the external world and one's internal weather—what Paster has identified as an "ecology of the passions"—is central to early modern

---

77. Henry N. Paul speculates that this line alludes to witches carrying winds in "bags which when untied release their contents" (248n and 297). Paul may be thinking of *The Odyssey*, where Aeolus gives Ulysses a bag of winds for his voyage. 78. Curry, 44, 40. 79. Arthur F. Kinney, *Lies Like Truth: Shakespeare, "Macbeth," and the Cultural Moment* (Detroit: Wayne State UP, 2001), 258.

conceptions of personhood.[80] What these Scottish witches stir is not simply the winds, but also the subtle elemental "spirits" of both air and water.[81] With their ability to vanish "[i]nto the air" so that "what seemed corporal/Melt[s] as breath into the wind" (1.3.79–80), it is impossible to mark a clear distinction between the witches and the elements they direct. Banquo tellingly notes that the "earth hath bubbles, as the water has," and these witches "are of them" (77–78). As Lemnius explains in *The Secret Miracles of Nature*, "evill spirits and Devills do sometimes joyn with the tempests, and administer fuell, secretly thrusting themselves into the mind of man … [to] vex and tear and torment it."[82]

In *The Hierarchie of the blessed Angells*, Thomas Heywood calls the witches who haunted Boece's Macbeth water "spirits," stressing that they were environmental in both their influence and constitution:

> Spirits that haue o're Water gouernment,
> Are to Mankinde alike maleuolent:
> They trouble Seas, Flouds, Riuers, Brookes, and Wels,
> Meeres, Lakes, and loue t' enhabit watry Cels;
> Thence noisome and pestiferous vapors raise.
> Besides, they Man encounter diuers wayes; . . .
>   And of this sort
> (Namely White Nymphs) *Boëthius* makes report,
> In his Scotch Historie: Two Noblemen,
> *Mackbeth* and *Banco-Stuart,* passing then
> Vnto the Pallace where King *Duncan* lay;
> Riding alone, encountred on the way
> (In a darke Groue) three Virgins wondrous faire,
> As well in habit as in feature rare.[83]

---

80. Paster, *Humoring the Body*, 9. For a provocative consideration of the ancient roots of wind's relationship to the history of selfhood, see Shigehisa Kuriyama, *The Expressiveness of the Body and the Divergence of Greek and Chinese Medicine* (New York: Zone Books, 2002), 233–70. Kuriyama writes, "Anchored in neither reason nor will, [the pneumatic self] is a self without essence, the site of moods and impulses whose origins are beyond reckoning, a self in which thoughts and feelings arise spontaneously, of themselves, like the winds whistling through the earth's hollows" (245). **81.** As Heywood writes, "The Finnes and Laplands are acquainted well/With such like Sp'rits, and Windes" (*Hierarchie of the blessed Angells*, sig. Vul^v). **82.** Lemnius, *Secret Miracles,* sig. Dd4^v. **83.** Heywood, *Hierarchie of the blessed Angells*, sigs. Vu2^r–Vu2^v. Heywood may have drawn his information from Robert Burton, who in describing various classes of devils also identifies the witches from Hector Boece's tale of Macbeth as "water Nymphs" or "Water Divells" in *The Anatomy of Melancholy*, 1:185. K. M. Briggs finds it surprising that Burton classifies "Macbeth's Fatae" as water spirits and not aerial ones; see *Pale Hecate's Team: An Examination of the Beliefs on Witchcraft and Magic among Shakespeare's Contemporaries and His Immediate Successors* (London: Routledge and Kegan Paul, 1962), 53.

Heywood's "White Nymphs" are atmospheric agents that generate "noisome and pestiferous vapors" to infect the minds and hearts of the most vulnerable. As "Virgins wondrous faire," they appear to have little in common with Shakespeare's wrinkled and bearded women. And although Heywood cites Boece as his source, Boece offers no physical description of the sisters. Perhaps they recall the three sibyls of Matthew Gwinn's 1605 Oxford play *Vertumnus sive Annus Recurrens*, who hailed King James as Banquo's successor.[84] But like Heywood's nymphs, the witches of *Macbeth* govern Scotland's water and air. Given their elemental nature, once Shakespeare's witches disturb the Highlanders' atmosphere, it becomes impossible to distinguish between internal and external provocations.

IV

That Macbeth is not just predisposed to the witches' promptings but somehow already embedded in the ecological fabric that produces them is hinted at in his first line, "So foul and fair a day I have not seen" (1.3.36). Notoriously, he echoes the Weird Sisters even before they meet. Soon after, the witches vanish "[i]nto the air . . . as breath into the wind" (79–80), leaving King James' mythical ancestor, Banquo, relatively unaffected, and Macbeth conspicuously conflates the witches' external influence with his own receptive nature:

> This supernatural soliciting
> Cannot be ill, cannot be good. If ill,
> Why hath it given me earnest of success,
> Commencing in a truth? I am Thane of Cawdor.
> If good, why do I yield to that suggestion
> Whose horrid image doth unfix my hair
> And make my seated heart knock at my ribs,
> Against the use of nature? Present fears
> Are less than horrible imaginings:
> My thought, whose murder yet is but fantastical,
> Shakes so my single state of man that function
> Is smothered in surmise, and nothing is
> But what is not.
>
> (1.3.130–42)

He starts with the premise that the prophecy's moral nature determines his physiological response to it; the inner workings of his

---

84. Quoted in Carroll, 333–34.

body and mind operate as evidence of external evil: "If good, why do I yield to that suggestion/Whose horrid image doth unfix my hair. . . ." Macbeth recognizes, in other words, that his passions are ecological. And yet, what begins as an external impression quickly becomes proprietary: the "horrid image" in his mind's eye, seemingly spawned by the witches' suggestion, is recast as his own "horrible imaginings"—a fantastical and murderous thought that stirs the passions and breaks up the unified self, whose parts acquire their own agency, distinct from Macbeth's individual will. "Function," however we may define it (as activity of the will, the mind, a physical organ, or the whole body), is smothered, passively and unintentionally, by thought. Taken literally, the internal smothering of Macbeth's "function" resembles descriptions of those clogged Scottish bodies, their animal spirits dammed up by an imbalance in the non-naturals that is variously attributed to the cold air they breathe and the foreign foods they eat.

Even when he wavers in his resolve to kill Duncan, Macbeth still understands his emotions in environmental terms. Once he commits regicide, Macbeth imagines, "pity" will stride a "blast" or tempest, and

> . . . heaven's cherubin, horsed
> Upon the sightless couriers of the air,
> Shall blow the horrid deed in every eye
> That tears shall drown the wind.
>   (1.7.22–25)

Temporarily distanced from the witches' "fog and filthy air" (1.1.11), Macbeth perceives a moral ecology in which the air, directed by a higher power than demons and witches, generates Christian sympathy. Environmental forces appear to shape his vacillation as much as they do his ambition. It is, of course, Lady Macbeth who revives her husband's resolution by nurturing and toughening his temperament in ways that evoke the ancient Scots' matriarchal structure. But where Bellenden represents the ancient Scots as strengthened by their mothers and corrupted by the English, Lady Macbeth's "mothering" implies that the Scots were already tainted before the English arrived.

What radically distinguishes Lady Macbeth from her kinswomen is that she interacts with an environment alive with evil spirits. To achieve the bold and bloody disposition associated with the ancient Scots, she calls on these malevolent "spirits" to transform her body. For Bellenden's warrior women, the harsh Scottish environment toughens them naturally and virtuously, but for Shakespeare's Lady Macbeth, it is her apparent interaction with supernatural forces that makes her a

Scottish Highlander.[85] Significantly, though, her transformation does not replicate the ancient Scots' temperament but instead anticipates the internal dysfunction Bellenden attributes to English contamination. Whether infected or not by demonic spirits, Lady Macbeth imagines a physiological interior that denotes corruption. She asks quite specifically that her internal fluids be thickened and her humoral passages clogged:[86]

> Come, you spirits
> That tend on mortal thoughts, unsex me here,
> And fill me from the crown to the toe top-full
> Of direst cruelty! Make thick my blood,
> Stop up th'access and passage to remorse,
> That no compunctious visitings of nature
> Shake my fell purpose, nor keep peace between
> Th'effect and [it]! Come to my woman's breasts,
> And take my milk for gall, you murd'ring ministers. . . .
>
> (1.5.40–48)

Lady Macbeth's incantation would verbally unite the elementally demonic agents that travel through the air and her own circulating animal spirits, which might "tend on mortal thoughts," reminding us how witches and devils were thought to affect and inhibit the proper functions of a vulnerable individual's body and mind.[87] The duality of Lady Macbeth's "spirits" blurs any distinction we might make between the internal will and external forces or, for that matter, between natural causes and the supernatural realm. Critics have identified Lady Macbeth as deliberate, controlled, and even stoic in this speech, perhaps underestimating her innate susceptibility.[88] Her request to "stop up th'access and passage to remorse" does implicitly critique the passionless stoic, who was regularly censured for lacking pity. But unlike the stoic, she is determined by her environment. In her resolve to "unsex" herself and to transform her milk to gall, Lady Macbeth perversely mirrors Bellenden's mothers, who labored to protect the purity

---

85. According to Rackin, while "Lady Macbeth seems to have inherited some of the fierceness of her ancient predecessors, she lacks their taste for blood" (19–20). See also M. C. Bradbrook, "The Sources of *Macbeth*," *Shakespeare Survey* 4 (1951): 35–48.
86. See Jenijoy La Belle, "'A Strange Infirmity': Lady Macbeth's Amenorrhea," *Shakespeare Quarterly* 31 (1980): 381–86.   87. Many scholars read the spirits Lady Macbeth invokes as demonic only; a significant exception is Paul H. Kocher, "Lady Macbeth and the Doctor," *SQ* 5 (1954): 341–49, who identifies them exclusively as her "animal spirits" (347). See, too, Rowe's discussion of the scene's material psychology in "Minds in Company," 49–50.   88. On the vexed nature of this "stoicism," see Rowe, "Minds in Company," 62–63.

of their tribe, even when their milk failed. As we noted, their labors proved futile in the face of corrupting English influences. Such necessitated temperance may look like stoicism, but it is shaped by externals, not the will. Lady Macbeth, likewise, appears autonomous when her body and mind are controlled by atmospheric agents.

Implicitly reworking Bellenden's thesis that breast-feeding ensured the Scots' masculine identity, Shakespeare presents Lady Macbeth as her husband's depraved nurturer, metaphorically exchanging his "milk of human kindness" (1.5.15) for the gall she now possesses.[89] Lady Macbeth makes her husband a man of "mettle" (1.7.73) by pouring her "spirits" in his ear (1.5.24)—spirits that ambiguously give her rhetoric both natural and supernatural effects. Fittingly, her words encourage him to imagine her breast-feeding:

> I have given suck, and know
> How tender 'tis to love the babe that milks me.
> I would, while it was smiling in my face,
> Have plucked my nipple from his boneless gums
> And dashed the brains out, had I so sworn
> As you have done to this.
>
> (1.7.54–59)

As Adelman has argued, Lady Macbeth's violent oath is intended to stir in Macbeth mingled feelings of fear and maternal longing, making him vulnerable to her perverse nourishment.[90] Not unlike the warrior women who transmitted their valor through milk, Lady Macbeth would draw on the gall in her breasts and the spirits in her body to convey boldness to her husband. She is Macbeth's nurse and mother, remaking his manliness and refashioning his complexion. Corrupted by his monstrous mother, Macbeth is a parody of Bellenden's celebrated Scottish temperance.

Despite the self-command she seems to display in this scene, her decline into somnambulism reveals just how completely Lady Macbeth lacks control. With a doctor present, Lady Macbeth's final scene invites the audience's diagnosis, inducing us to determine whether her sleep-

---

89. In Janet Adelman's brilliant analysis, "Macbeth imagines Lady Macbeth the mother to infants sharing her hardness, born in effect without vulnerability . . . and then reconstitutes himself as the invulnerable male child of such a mother"; see *Suffocating Mothers: Fantasies of Maternal Origin in Shakespeare's Plays, "Hamlet" to "The Tempest"* (New York: Routledge, 1992), 139. **90.** Adelman, 139. In Joanna Levin's reading, Macbeth is the "offspring" of Lady Macbeth's "maternal imagination"—a disorderly power in which the mother's perceptions and thoughts at conception or during pregnancy produced birthmarks or deformed the fetus in monstrous ways; see "Lady Macbeth and the Daemonologie of Hysteria," *ELH* 69.2 (2002): 21–55, esp. 42.

walking and inadvertent confessions point to a spiritual, psychological, or physiological disease.[91] Although Macbeth believes his wife suffers from a natural ailment, demanding that the doctor purge her of the "perilous stuff/Which weighs upon the heart" and troubles her brain (5.3.46–47), the doctor insists that all physic will fail. Her "disease," he explains, "is beyond my practice" (5.1.49). He is persuaded by Lady Macbeth's guilty behavior that his medicinal remedies will be fruitless: "More needs she the divine than the physician" (l. 64). But as Carol Thomas Neely has observed, contemporary discussions of physiological melancholy and spiritual despair suggest that the "doctor's confident distinction between diseases requiring divines and those requiring doctors may be too simple."[92] The doctor, of course, did not witness Lady Macbeth's attempt to conjure malevolent spirits. But if her summoning has produced material results, such an infection could stir the passions, clog the animal spirits, and produce the very perturbations of the mind that Lady Macbeth displays.

Even those physicians skeptical of the occult's power were likely to concede that natural symptoms could have a supernatural cause. In Edward Jorden's treatise, *A Briefe Discovrse of a Disease Called the Suffocation of the Mother*, for example, the physician aims to prove that a young girl's apparent signs of possession are the natural signs of an internal disease. He is confident that a learned physician can make distinctions among maladies, discerning "what is naturall, what preternaturall, and what supernaturall."[93] What proves trickier for Jorden, however, is determining the original *cause* of a disease, for supernatural powers can produce natural ailments:

> If the deuil as an externall cause, may inflict a disease by stirring vp or kindling the humors of our bodies, and then depart without supplying continuall supernaturall power vnto it; then the disease is but naturall, and will submit it selfe vnto Physicall cure. For externall causes when they are already remoted, giue no indication of any remedy.[94]

External causes, for Jorden, include not only the devil but also distempered air (especially the cold, which makes the humors "grose" and

---

91. See Carol Thomas Neely on the complex ways the public stage theatricalized forms of madness to elicit distinct diagnoses from the audience in *Distracted Subjects: Madness and Gender in Shakespeare and Early Modern Culture* (Ithaca: Cornell UP, 2004). **92.** In Neely's analysis, the "doctor explicitly reads Lady Macbeth's state as religious despair that is the result of guilt" (57). **93.** Edward Jorden, *A Brief Discovrse of a Disease Called the Suffocation of the Mother* (London, 1603), sig. C1ʳ; quoted in Neely, 48. For a full discussion of the circumstances behind Jorden's pamphlet, see Michael MacDonald, *Witchcraft and Hysteria in Elizabethan London: Edward Jorden and the Mary Glover Case* (London: Tavistock-Routledge, 1991), vii–lxiv. **94.** Jorden, sig. B3ʳ.

"crude") and excessive meat and drink.[95] In other words, the symptoms generated by the devil's influence may prove indistinguishable from those caused by epicurean indulgences or extreme climates. Although they admit that supernatural forces may produce natural diseases, both Jorden and Shakespeare's doctor attempt to draw lines between the natural and the supernatural that may not exist in *Macbeth*. This is a play, after all, that celebrates King Edward I's miraculous cure of the "evil"—a phenomenon that blurs distinctions between spiritual, physical, and symbolic realms. Some physicians suggested that adherence to such strict categories might even impede treatment. According to Lemnius, it is

> a laborious and very difficult matter to restore the body that is fallen sick, where the conscience is polluted with the spots of sinns, where the Organs of the senses, and the Spirits vitall and animall are vitiated. And it is no lesse troublesome, for a Church-man to give comfort to the soul, when the body is full of vitious humours; for by reason of the narrow consent and union of both parts, the vices of the mind fly upon the body, and the diseases of the body, are carried to the Soul.[96]

When Lady Macbeth's doctor insists "[m]ore needs she the divine than the physician," he makes plain that her sickness has outgrown the parameters of mere medicine. But we cannot be certain that the *cause* of her illness is intrinsically spiritual or mental. It may have extrinsic origins. As Jorden allowed, even if a patient is no longer subject to "continuall supernaturall power," she may suffer from corrupted humors. And active demonic possession is hardly necessary when the vital and animal spirits are "vitiated," and the diseases of the body "are carried to the Soul." Plagued by "thick-coming fancies" (5.3.40) that derive equally from within (her thick blood) and without (the thick night [1.5.48]), Lady Macbeth may suffer most because of her extreme passibility.[97] If Shakespeare aims to reverse Bellenden's portrait of ancient Scotland's strong female warriors, his representation

---

95. Jorden, sigs. Gl^v–G2^r, MacDonald acknowledges that both skeptics and demonologists could argue that natural symptoms may have supernatural causes (xxxii–xxxiii). *A Tryal of Witches, and the Assizes held at Bury St. Edmond's for the County of Suffolk; on the Tenth day of March, 1664* (London, 1682) claims that the devil working through witches afflicts people with "Distempers as their Bodies were most subject to . . . [the] swouning Fits were Natural, and nothing else but that they call the Mother, but only heightned to a great excess" (sig. D6^v).
96. Lemnius, *Secret Miracles*, sig. Rr4^v.   97. La Belle points to the parallels between "thick night," "thick-coming fancies/That keep her from her rest," and "thick blood," 383.

of Lady Macbeth's disintegration implies that Highland women are more susceptible to environmental forces than Highland men. Unlike Bellenden's matriarchs, whose ecological embeddedness supports the fostering of male temperance, Lady Macbeth's receptive nature has, ironically, brought about her psychological estrangement from both her husband and her surroundings.

It has become a critical commonplace to note that as Lady Macbeth declines, Macbeth seems to grow stronger and bolder. She has attempted to incorporate malevolent spirits to direct her husband's actions, bolstering herself to nurture him. Her role has been instrumental in shaping his environment. Macbeth, however, has direct and repeated contact with the witches, driving him to "do . . . and . . . do" (1.3.9) long after his wife has served her function. But to interpret Macbeth's actions as signs of strength is to miss how his borders, too, are irreversibly breached. Even before Macbeth does anything, Shakespeare confronts the audience with the question of where to locate his motivating impulses—in the air or in his head:

> Is this a dagger which I see before me,
> The handle toward my hand? Come, let me clutch thee.
> I have thee not, and yet I see thee still.
> Art thou not, fatal vision, sensible
> To feeling as to sight? Or art thou but
> A dagger of the mind, a false creation
> Proceeding from a heat-oppressèd brain?
>
> (2.1.33–39)

As Macbeth's analysis implies, the dagger could be a phantasmic vision of demonically stirred air. Or it could be a mirage projected by his imagination.[98] But attributing the dagger to his "heat-oppressèd brain" does not, in fact, discount the supernatural environment as a cause. Macbeth has already inhaled the witches' tainted air—air that could easily and unnaturally oppress the brain with heat. Either way, we are asked to see a man whose "mental interior" comprises "the world outside."[99]

The representation of Banquo's ghost, which only Macbeth can see, again puts pressure on where to draw the lines between inner and outer. As Stephen Greenblatt describes it, Banquo's ghost (as well as the

---

98. In a paper titled "Imagination and Self in Early Modern Europe," delivered at the conference "Inhabiting the Body/Inhabiting the World" in March 2004 at UNC–CH, Lorraine Daston discussed the early modern belief that strong imaginations could project visible images in the air. 99. The language is Gail Kern Paster's, in "Melancholy Cats, Lugged Bears, and Early Modern Cosmology: Reading Shakespeare's Psychological Materialism across the Species Barrier," in *Reading the Early Modern Passions* (see n. 5), 113–29, esp. 116.

witches in the play) seems to haunt "the border or membrane where the imagination and the corporeal world, figure and actuality, psychic disturbance and objective truth meet."[100] If the ghost is a delusion or a figment of Macbeth's overwrought imagination, then it derives from the Scot's thick and inhibited animal spirits. And if the ghost is a supernatural presence, it still suggests Macbeth's innate openness to his environment, where occult forces thrive and prey on those humorally most susceptible. Antonio de Torquemada in *The Spanish Mandeuik of Miracles* insists that in extreme northern climates, "euill Spirits doe there present themselues many times before the eyes of men, in bodies formed of ayre, with a fearefull and terrible aspect." He also observes, "There are amongst [northerners] often seene visions and Spirits, . . . appearing to them in likenes of some of theyr knowne friends, and suddainly vanishing away, so that the deuill seemeth to haue in those Septentrionall Countries, greater dominion & more libertie then in other parts."[101] And as Ludwig Lavater contends in *Of Ghostes and Spirites* (1596), "by a certaine peculiar operation of nature, some men behold that which others in no wise can perceive."[102] Macbeth's reaction to the ghost points up the lack of ecological balance that characterizes such extreme possibility. He describes a rupture in his identity ("strange/Even to the disposition that I owe" [3.4.111–12]) and an expansion outward—encompassing the unseen connections of a sentient cosmos:

> Stones have been known to move, and trees to speak,
> Augurs and understood relations have
> By maggot-pies and choughs and rooks brought forth
> The secret'st man of blood.
>
> (ll. 122–25)

Unwittingly, he anticipates how the environment, or the moving Birnam Wood, will defeat him.

Resolved to visit the Weird Sisters again, Macbeth confesses that his will is limited by the cumulatively numbing effects of his violent actions: "I am in blood/Stepped in so far that, should I wade no more,/Returning were as tedious as go o'er" (ll. 135–37). His doomed perception is attributable, in part, to the disconnections in his thought processes: "Strange things I have in head that will to hand,/Which must be acted ere they may be scanned" (ll. 138–39). Macbeth's anatomy

100. Stephen Greenblatt, *Hamlet in Purgatory* (Princeton: Princeton UP, 2001), 193. 101. De Torquemada, fols. 120ᵛ and 139ʳ. 102. Ludwig Lavater, *Of Ghostes and Sprites, VValking by Night, And of straunge Noyses, Crackes, and sundrie forewarnings* (London, 1596), sig. M1ᵛ.

of his own thinking suggests not only a failure in the communicative work of the animal spirits but also an external or "strange" origin to his thoughts. As David Norbrook observes, "More and more [Macbeth's] mind becomes dissociated from his body, his thoughts from his words; he becomes a mere machine for generating deeds."[103] His dissociation appears to be complete when the apparitions show him Scotland's future kings—Banquo's heirs stretching out to James I of England. He stands "amazedly," as music plays and the witches dance; in what appears to be a courtly masque, the witches infect and manipulate Macbeth's "spirits" yet again:

> Come, sisters, cheer we up his sprites,
> And show the best of our delights.
> I'll charm the air to give a sound
> While you perform your antic round. . . .
>
> (4.1.143–46)

With his spirits cheered, Macbeth articulates a disconnection between his will and his actions: "The very firstlings of my heart shall be/ The firstlings of my hand. And even now,/To crown my thoughts with acts, be it thought and done" (ll.163–65). As Rebecca Bushnell has noted, Macbeth's relatively calm demise differentiates him from traditional tyrants, who tend to grow increasingly passionate as their power slips.[104] It is in this state that Macbeth identifies the English as "epicures," perhaps implying that he—as a Scot—exercises a measure of stoic restraint.

What may look like stoicism, however, may be necessitated barrenness, produced by the unrestrained interaction between Macbeth's porous boundaries and the infected air. Near the close of the play, Macbeth's terror seems to have evaporated entirely: "I have almost forgot the taste of fears," he says (5.5.59).The sound of women shrieking fails to affect his senses, raise his hair, or startle him.When his wife dies, the Scot's lack of grief (which stands as the definitive stoic test for apathy) resembles, according to Benjamin Boyce, "the enviable Stoic condition of wise calm":[105]

> She should have died hereafter.
> There would have been a time for such a word. . . .
> Life's but a walking shadow, a poor player

<hr />

103. Norbrook, 102. **104.** Rebecca W. Bushnell, *Tragedies of Tyrants: Political Thought and Theater in the English Renaissance* (Ithaca: Cornell UP, 1990), 130.That most staged tyrants were southern rather than northern may help account for this distinction. On Macbeth's "stoicism," see Rowe, "Minds in Company," 62; and Benjamin Boyce, "The Stoic *Consolatio* and Shakespeare," *PMLA* 64 (1949): 771–80. **105.** Boyce, 779.

That struts and frets his hour upon the stage,
And then is heard no more. It is a tale
Told by an idiot, full of sound and fury,
Signifying nothing.

(5.5.16–17, 23–27)

Yet the perceived apathy of this speech stems not from emotional restraint but from an absence of borders. Macbeth imagines that his existence is identical with the walking shadows, spirits, and ghosts he has witnessed: insubstantial, unreliable, and indistinguishable from environmental noise. His language also recalls Harrison's translation of Bellenden's most damning characterization of the infected and anglicized Scots: "yet are they but dead people, reuiuing againe, leading the rest of their liues like shadows, and walking about as if they were buried alreadie."[106] In what appears to be an inversion of Bellenden's thesis, Macbeth's intemperate vision of life eerily anticipates the Scottish degeneration that is supposed to occur after Malcolm takes the throne.

IV

Most modern critics agree that *Macbeth* ends uneasily. For one thing, it is unclear whether Malcolm's reign will end the cycle of violence. For another, Macbeth's defeat depends heavily on the exclusion of women, which may strike us as a shaky foundation for rebuilding a society. And given that female spirits may still contaminate the Scottish air, the fantasy of exclusion relies entirely on male invulnerability. Scotland's health will be determined in particular, it seems, by Malcolm's capacities to govern and reform. On a superficial level, at least, there is little question that Malcolm represents an anglicizing force. In the sources, Malcolm has resided in England for fifteen years. By associating Malcolm loosely with Edward the Confessor's generous patronage and healing powers, Shakespeare underscores England's positive influence. Malcolm initiates the importation of English customs when he converts the Scottish thanes to earls in the play's final scene. For some in the English audience, this act would have been recognized as an extension of Malcolm's supposed homage to King Edward I, a significant precedent for relations during Jacobean union.[107] That is to say, in bringing English titles to Scotland, Malcolm places his country in its properly submissive role in relation to England. In order to counter

106. Harrison, sig. B5ᵛ. Bellenden writes, "thay ar bot ane deid pepill; levand, and buryit in sepulture, havand bot ane schadow of life" (1:lxi).   107. Norbrook, 95. Sir George Buc wrote a panegyric in 1605 that "presented the alliance between Malcolm and Edward as prefiguring the Union" (Norbrook, 96).

and even trump the troubling Scottish environment, the English aim to civilize the Scottish people—a process that depends, ironically, on their openness to external influences.

The long exchange between Macduff and Malcolm in 4.3 serves as an assessment of whether Scotland's future king is up to the task. It is a puzzling scene; it plants doubts as much as it reassures. In testing Macduff's loyalty, Malcolm claims to outstrip Macbeth in corruption, only to then "[u]nspeak" his "own detraction" (4.3.124). As many critics have noted, what Malcolm reveals most definitively is his ability to dissimulate, a characteristic Macbeth notably lacked. The Neostoic Lipsius admits that constancy depends, at times, on putting on a false front, a necessity that he recognized was akin to Machiavellianism.[108] Not coincidentally, Macbeth's susceptibility to the environment and his inability to adopt a political mask were stereotypically northern traits that the English actively sought to remedy in themselves.[109] Taking on the role of the Scots' reformer, Malcolm's first act is to teach Macduff to redirect his passions, advising him to quell his grief by translating it into usable anger.[110] In stark contrast to Macduff's mourning, however, is the emotional restraint of the Englishman Siward, who refuses to grieve for the son he loses in battle. From an English perspective, Siward may be the true hero of *Macbeth* for his untutored ability to rise above his grief and remain constant in an infectious environment. In Holinshed's chronicles of England for the period that corresponds with Macbeth's overthrow, Siward's stoicism is the most prominent detail the English historians report in their account of Scotland's troubles.[111]

But the exchange between Macduff and Malcolm is disturbing, in part, because it is haunted by what it omits from the Scottish sources. In Boece and Holinshed, Macduff is persuaded that Malcolm "is so replet with the inconstant behauiour and manifest vices of Englishmen, that he is nothing woorthie to inioy [the crown]."[112] And in

108. Justus Lipsius, *Sixe Bookes of Politickes or Civil Doctrine*, trans. William Jones (London, 1594), sig. Q3ʳ. On Malcolm's Machiavellianism, see Barbara Riebling, "Virtue's Sacrifice: A Machiavellian Reading of *Macbeth*," *SEL* 31 (1991): 273–86.
109. See, for example, the preface to Thomas Wright, *The passions of the minde in generall* (London, 1604), sigs. A3ᵛ–A6ʳ. 110. See Rowe, "Minds in Company," 64.
111. Admiration for Siward's stoicism is continued in the report of his death: "O stout harted man, not vnlike to that famous Romane remembred by *Tullie* in his *Tusculane questions*, who suffered the sawing of his leg from his bodie without shrinking, looking vpon the surgeon all the while, & hauing no part of his bodie bound for shrinking!" (Holinshed, "The Historie of England," sig. Q6ᵛ).
112. Holinshed, "The historie of Scotland," in *The Second volume of Chronicles*, sig. P4ʳ. The omission is discussed in Sally Mapstone, "Shakespeare and Scottish Kingship: A Case History," in *The Rose and the Thistle: Essays on the Culture of Late Medieval and Renaissance Scotland*, ed. Sally Mapstone and Juliette Wood (East Linton, East Lothian, Scotland: Tuckwell Press, 1998), 158–89, esp. 182.

George Buchanan's history, Malcolm's retitling of thanes as earls is censured as being no less barbarous than Scottish honors. In other words, Scottish versions of Macbeth's tale insistently remind us that the Scots traced their intemperance to anglicization. Some members of Shakespeare's audience would have known that Malcolm's "Englishness" was derived not only from his time in England but also, more directly, from the women in his family: his mother, who was the daughter of Siward, earl of Northumberland, and his future wife, Queen Margaret, the last of the Saxon line.[113] Indeed, several historians recognized that if the English civilized the Scots during Malcolm's reign, it was by way of Queen Margarets influence. Margaret was well known for having changed the customs, diet, and religious practices of the Scots.[114] Although success in *Macbeth* appears to depend on the excision of women, the *Chronicles* tell us that it was an English woman who transformed the Scots into civilized men—or epicures, depending on one's perspective. And if it was anglicization by a woman that made the Scots "epicures," the question of whether the English can exercise temperance in their interactions with the world remains open.

The dramatic thrust of *Macbeth* is its representation of a hero whose tragedy may be inseparable from overwhelming environmental forces, made tentatively Scottish by their supernatural element. Not unlike Bellenden, the English also heartily celebrated their own primitivism and made subtle claims to a natural temperance that they pitted against the excessive epicurean corruptions of more southern nations. But *Macbeth* positions England in the south, thus demanding a revised vision of what constitutes a healthy ecology in the British Isles. By demonizing the far north, Shakespeare's Jacobean play anxiously seeks to preserve a distinct English environment and disposition in the face of an influx of Scottish immigrants who stubbornly refused to equate Englishness with temperance.

---

113. Carroll, 142. **114.** See George Buchanan, *The History of Scotland* (London, 1690), sigs. Ee3ᵛ–Ee4ʳ; and Holinshed, "The historie of Scotland," sig. P5v. As Margaret's medieval biographer Bishop Turgot writes, "It was due to her that the merchants who came by land and sea from various countries brought along with them for sale different kinds of precious wares which until then were unknown in Scotland"; see *The Life of St. Margaret*, trans. William Forbes-Leith (Edinburgh: William Patterson, 1884), 40. By way of refutation, Thomas Craig acknowledges that the English held that the Scottish kings needed to be mollified by an English maternal line (*Scotland's Soveraignty Asserted* [London, 1695], sig. G2ʳ).

SHAKESPEARE THE ILLUSIONIST: FILMING THE SUPERNATURAL

Neil Forsyth

Successful films of Shakespeare's plays adapt not only the works themselves but also the cinematic conventions that suit their genres. As Neil Forsyth explains, Shakespeare's ghost plays—Macbeth in particular—pose a special challenge to filmmakers, who must navigate the dual histories of film as a realist recording medium and as an illusionist's art. Forsyth's essay is reprinted here in an abridged form with new illustrations from two films: by Orson Welles, and Roman Polanski. His insights may be applied to any film adaptation of the play.

REGINALD SCOT's 1584 treatise *The Discovery of Witchcraft* has a section entitled "To cut off one's head, and lay it in a platter, &c, which the jugglers call the decollation of John the Baptist". Scot explains how the Elizabethan playhouses worked this particular conjuring trick by means of a stage-device that looked like a pillory, and which showed one actor's head as if it belonged to another body. Other contemporary documents describe many similar illusions, which seem to have been common on the stage as well as on street-corners. Opinion was divided about their value: Ben Jonson despised their vulgarity in the Induction to *Bartholemew Fair*, some denounced them as witchcraft, others felt that

> if these things be done for recreation and mirth, and not to the hurt of our neighbour, nor to the profaning and abusing of God's holy name,

---

1. Samuel Rid, *The Art of Jugling or Legerdemaine*, London: 1612: B2v, quoted in Michael Mangan, "'. . . and so shall you seem to have cut your nose in sunder': Illusions of Power on the Elizabethan Stage and in the Elizabethan Marketplace", *On Illusion: Performance Research* I.3 (1996), p. 53. The text is reprinted with helpful notes in *Rogues, Vagabonds, & Sturdy Beggars: A New Gallery Of Tudor And Early Stuart Rogue Literature* ed. Arthur F. Kinney (Amherst: University of Massachusetts Press, 1990). See more generally Linda Woodbridge, *The Scythe of Saturn: Shakespeare and Magical Thinking* (Urbana; University of Illinois Press, 1994), pp. 1–11 and Edward Claflin and Jeff Sheridan (1977), *Street Magic—An Illustrated History of Wandering Magicians and Their Conjuring Arts* (New York: Dolphin Books, Doubleday and Co, 1977).

Neil Forsyth, "Shakespeare the Illusionist: Filming the Supernatural." *The Cambridge Companion to Shakespeare on Film.* Ed. Russel Jackson. Cambridge, UK: Cambridge UP, 2000. 274–284. Reprinted with the permission of Cambridge University Press.

then sure they are neither impious nor altogether unlawful, though herein or hereby a natural thing be made to seem supernatural.[1]

It would be a mistake therefore to assume that members of Shakespeare's audience automatically suspected that such "jugglers" were in league with the devil, even though several contemporary plays, from *Doctor Faustus* to *Friar Bungay* to *Volpone* exploit that idea—for fear, for laughs, for satire. The inherent theatricality of Shakespeare's plays (disbelief only partially suspended) means there is room for lots of stage-tricks in the midst of the ordinary pretences of his theatre (costumes, stage-voices, boys as women). Both depend on illusion, but there is also a complex relationship, often a necessary conflict, between the representation of the mundane and the marvelous.

From its beginnings, the art of film has also pulled in two different directions, towards realism and towards magic.[2] One tendency derives from the Lumière brothers, who came to film from photography, and who at first simply tried to reproduce time and event accurately—a train arriving at the station or the famous shot of workers leaving the Lumière factory. The other is the tradition of Georges Méliès, a stage magician turned cinéaste, many of whose films had the words *nightmare* or *dream* in their titles. The Lumières recorded reality; Méliès transformed it. What began with Méliès continued in the grand guignol ideas of Eisenstein and his "montage of attractions", in Cocteau's surrealism, in experiments like James Stewart's dream of falling in Hitchcock's *Vertigo* and the final sequences of Kubrick's *2001*; it is manifest in animation, in the Spielberg-style special effects which have so outdistanced what Méliès could manage, and it survives especially in the immensely popular horror-movie genre, where ghosts and witches and diabolical possession are six-a-penny.

These two contradictory traditions come together, as in Shakespeare's theatre, in the idea of illusion. Stage- or film-magic depends on visual illusion, but then so does the representation in still cinematic shots on celluloid of moving images in familiar, recognizable

---

2. A brief description of this common view of film aesthetics will be found in James Monaco, *How to Read a Film* (London: Oxford University Press, 1981), p. 236. It was popularized by André Bazin but David Bordwell, *On The History of Film Style* (Cambridge, Mass: Harvard University Press 1997, 44) regards it is too rigid a distinction. The most uncompromising theoretical discussion is by Noel Burch in, for example, *Life to These Shadows* (London, British Film Institute, 1990). There he argues that Méliès defined the dominant film practice from 1894 to 1914, which was largely anti-naturalist. It was 'the last great Western narrative art that was at once both popular and, to a large degree, *presentational*, that is, morphologically closer to the plebeian circus and the aristocratic ballet than to the theatre of the middle classes, that *representational* art par excellence' (p. 241).

settings—exploiting the tendency of the eye to perceive a sequence of still shots as moving when projected at the right speed. Indeed Méliès's reaction to the first Lumière showing brings the two explicitly together. He was at first dismissive to see merely a still photo of a street scene, but then it started to move, and he was enchanted. He writes:

a still shot of the Place Bellecour in Lyon was shown. Somewhat surprised, I just had time to say to my neighbour, 'They got us all here for projections like this? I've been doing them for over ten years', when a horse pulling a wagon began to walk towards us, followed by other vehicles and then pedestrians, in a word all the animation of the street. Before this spectacle we sat open-mouthed, stupefied, astonished beyond all expression.[3]

And almost immediately Méliès started to adapt stage magic to film.[4]

This kind of *trucage* (tricks or special effects) was part of a wider phenomenon in the days of the nascent cinema. Spiritualism and table-tapping were frequently practiced by stage-magicians turned charlatans as a more lucrative source of income. Hypnotism or Mesmerism was a common theatrical spectacle. And apart from the enormously popular stage-conjuring as practiced by Méliès at the Théâtre Robert Houdin, and by his English mentor John Neville Maskleyne at London's Egyptian Hall, another ingredient in the background of early film is that popular genre, Victorian fairy paintings, some of which were actually illustrations for Shakespeare plays such as *A Midsummer*

3. George Sadoul, *Histoire Général du Cinéma*, t. I, *L'Invention du cinéma 1832-1897* (Paris: Denoël, 1948), p. 279, my translation. On Méliès, see Madeleine Maltete-Méliès, ed., *Méliès et la naissance du spectacle cinématographique* (Paris: Klincksieck, 1984), pp. 53-58. For a review of some relevant films, see Maïté Vienne, *La Figure de l'Ange au Cinéma* (Paris: Cerf, 1995); see also Marina Warner, "The Uses of Enchantment", in *Cinema and the Realms of Enchantment*, ed. Duncan Petrie (London: British Film Institute, 1993), pp. 13-35. Regular attractions of the time were a magic-lantern show and a shadow projection. Since Antoine Lumière, father of the photographic brothers, rented a studio above the Robert Houdin theatre where Méliès performed, it is possible that he knew about the new invention before this famous viewing of the street scene in Lyon.   **4.** See Tom Gunning's argument for early cinema-goers as sensation-hungry and astonished by attractions in a series of articles: "Primitive Cinema: A Frame-Up? or The Trick's On Us", *Cinema Journal* 29 (Winter 1988-89), "The Cinema of Attraction[s]", in *Early Cinema: Space, Frame, Narrative*, eds. Thomas Elsaesser and Adam Barker (London: British Film Institute, 1990), pp. 56-62, and "An Aesthetic of Astonishment: Early Film and the (In)Credulous Spectator", in *Viewing Positions*, ed. Linda Williams (New Brunswick: Rutgers University Press, 1995), pp. 114-33.   **5.** For a fine set of illustrations, see Benjamin Darling, *Shakespeare on Fairies and Magic* (Saddle River, NJ: Prentice Hall Press, 2001).

Night's Dream or *The Tempest*.[5] Recall too those famous late Victorian photographs of fairies taken by children that Conan Doyle believed in, but which were admitted as fakes when the children had become old women (1983).[6] Méliès and his followers were adapting a powerful tradition to a new art form.

They were not, though, working only for an audience of credulous bumpkins. Their shows depend on a double sense of belief and incredulity, as Méliès's own theatre of magic depended on a decline in belief in the supernatural. We admire the magician's skill, and in film we admire the power of the apparatus itself. Successful illusion is still understood as illusion, even if we cannot see exactly how it is done. Furthermore the prevalence of images of machines such as the train directs our attention (or reflection) towards the mechanical power of the means of reproduction.[7]

The basic argument of this essay, then, is that Shakespeare films can be read according to how they exploit this informing doubleness of film, and in particular how they use the Méliès dimension, the magic and the *trucage*, to represent the Shakespearean supernatural—fiends, fairies, ghosts and witches. "Illusionist" thus retains its double meaning: film itself is illusionist, but within it there is the doubled illusionism of Méliès, illusion within illusion.

Three aspects of what Méliès did for film are important for this approach. First, more generally, *le septième art* (the seventh art) was permanently marked by his infusion of stage-magic into the screen tradition, to the point that it could never be simply a realist medium. Second, the point of view given to the film viewer is essentially that of the theatre audience out front, so that we look at the screen as we look at the stage through its proscenium arch, aware (more or less) that we are attending a show. This point of view is familiar to anyone who has seen one of those early Méliès films, and it was seriously modified as further techniques were invented. It remains, nonetheless, a key element of cinematic allusions to Méliès. Third, Méliès very early on liberated screen time from real time by simply stopping the camera while he made an adjustment to the staged show. The disappearing lady trick, one of his most popular, he effected on film simply by stopping the camera while the lady gets out from inside the frame that supports

6. The story of Elsie Wright and the Cottingley Fairies hoax is told at http://www. unmuseum.org/fairies.htm/. 7. cf. Gorky's account of a 1896 showing at an exhibition in Moscow: "It speeds right at you—watch out! It seems as though it will plunge into the darkness in which you sit, turning you into a ripped sack full of lacerated flesh and splintered bones.... but this too is but a train of shadows. Belief and terror are larded with awareness of illusion, even bleak disappointment of the ungraspable phantom of life itself", quoted by Gunning in *Viewing Positions*, p. 118.

the cloth covering her, such that when the camera starts up again, the cloth can be removed . . . and the lady has vanished. This simple trick (the stop-action method or 'substitution-splicing') is at the origin of all the ways filmmakers extend the possibilities of illusion.[8]

Nevertheless one soon notices a certain unease about spectacle and illusion in the style of Shakespeare films and in the discussion of them. There are several reasons for this. One is no doubt the long-standing suspicion of theatre itself in Anglo-Saxon, Puritan-based culture, connected with suspicions about dressing-up, pretending to be someone else, sexual license, and in its more extreme forms the denunciation of theatre as a tool of the devil. In the case of the Shakespearean tradition, there is a further ingredient: the late Victorian and Edwardian theatres had fully developed the tendency that began in the Restoration theatres toward pictorial representation within the frame of grandiose West End proscenium arches, but the influential William Poel had begun a counter-trend to get away from the splendid spectacles and to reconstruct a supposedly pure and unscenic theatre such as Shakespeare himself was imagined to have worked in.[9] Many modern Shakespeareans, still influenced by Poel and what he stood for, will have wanted anything but a return to complex stage "devices"[10] and the discredited elaboration of costume and spectacle, even in the new medium of film. This discomfort with pictorial illusion also has something to do with the fact that film-art grew up with Modernism, in which high and low art-forms were fiercely separated, so that "special effects" are for children or certain subgenres, horror and sci-fi, not the serious mainstream.

All this suspicion makes it especially difficult when what is being presented cannot but be supernatural, like the ghost of Hamlet senior. In Tony Richardson's 1969 film of *Hamlet*, Nicol Williamson has a strong light shining in his face whenever the ghost is "present". But we see nothing. Laurence Olivier (1948), who managed well the

---

8. These early shows have been widely copied and reproduced on video. See for example, *Georges Méliès: cinema magician*, a film by Patrick Montgomery and Luciano Martinengo, 1978/1994, or *Camera—Moving Pictures: no. 2, Georges Méliès*, Granada Television/Educational Film Services, 1981/1991. An example available on YouTube is http://www.youtube.com/watch?v=zs5BBaNJ6mg. See also Michael Brooke's blog at http://filmjournal.net/melies/.   **9.** Marion O'Connor, *William Poel and the Elizabethan Stage Society* (Cambridge: Chadwyck-Healey, 1987, with slides).   **10.** "Devices" translates literally the Greek word *mechane*, from which derives English "machine": the word occurs most famously in the phrase "deus ex machina", a common scene in Greek drama but one of which Aristotle is famously suspicious as a way to solve the complexities of the plot. Even the author of a book on Shakespearean magic like Linda Woodbridge can still write of "certain superficial and flashy theatrical effects like Joan of Arc's spooky demons or Margaret's flesh-creeping curses" (p. 11): she is more interested in the "deep structure of what happens in the plays".

midnight darkness for the battlement scenes that the afternoon Globe could not aspire to, was famously dissatisfied with his misty, dry-ice ghost, to the point that he dubbed in the voice himself. And he makes much of Horatio's rational scepticism. As the ghost leaves at the sudden cock-crow, we cut back to the watching soldiers in a long shot and way below, as if the camera is now where the ghost was, looking back down as it floats off up into the cloud. Then Horatio guarantees the truth of the experience by "the sensible and true avouch of my own eyes"—a line that in this context refers to the cinematic experience, to the magical vision. The motif of the sceptic convinced guarantees not simply the reality of the ghost but the authenticity of what might otherwise seem to the audience, and certainly to Olivier, like a hokey ghostie film, not high classic art. And Franco Zeffirelli too (1990) has trouble with the ghost, so that Paul Scofield seems merely to have dropped in for a serious talk with his son, but hardly to come from a different dimension.

•   •   •

Macbeth is a different case from *Hamlet*. There is less diffidence about filming the supernatural, which is obviously central to the play, and this encourages film directors to cross the divide between high and low culture. Banquo's ghost is usually fully represented and marvelously horrifying: both Orson Welles and Roman Polanski borrow directly from horror traditions, Polanski explicitly using its bloody violence as well, while Akira Kurosawa has his own clear cultural sense of how a ghost will appear, and how others will react. Indeed the artistic (though not commercial)[11] success of these *Macbeth* films is due partly to the eerie power of these supernatural visitations. Their very presence makes stage or screen *Macbeths* fun to watch. And as Nicholas Brooke argued in his 1990 Oxford edition, *Macbeth* is all about illusion. Thus the transfer to screen- from stage-illusion can heighten the focus of the play rather than distract us with too much dry ice or other chemical magic. Already in *Hamlet* the status of the ghost is problematic ("Be thou a spirit of health or goblin damned?"). Yet in *Macbeth* the question of the supernatural and its status is central: are these village women or supernatural, hellish visitants, devilish minions? is the dagger I see before me really there? is Banquo's ghost?

That illusion is central to *Macbeth* is announced by the non-naturalistic prologue suggesting reversals of what we see ("fair is foul and foul is fair", and later, that definitive "nothing is but what is not").

11. See Samuel Crowl on the deadening legacy of the Polanski film in *Shakespeare Observed* (Athens: Ohio University Press, 1992), pp. 19-34.

Illusions of various kinds then dot the play. The sleep-walking scene is representative of the role of delusion (caused by psychological disturbance, and recognized as such on stage by doctor and nurse, and so by the whole audience). But the Birnam wood scene is more ambiguous. Macbeth is tricked by the prophecy, and though the event itself is explained beforehand as a military tactic, it is not so understood by its first observers: the Messenger says he saw it but knows not how to say it, and finally admits that "Anon methought the wood began to move" (5.5.33). Thus the characters (or some of them), but not the audience, are deceived, and the scene is a good example of purely naturalistic illusion, supposedly at work in the ordinary world. The head of Macbeth, on the other hand, brought on at the end, is a characteristic stage illusion and obviously intended, at least momentarily, to horrify. But the main ingredients of this pattern of illusion are as follows:

1) *Weird sisters.* They are visible to all, but ambiguous. Are they village witches (a word only used once in dialogue, though regular in the stage-directions of the Folio) or supernatural beings (*weird* means "fate": its loose modern meaning begins only in the 19th century)? They can foresee, but what can they actually do? In their own words, "Though his bark cannot be lost/Yet it shall be tempest-tossed" (1.3.23-4), which suggests their power is limited. They vanish into air as Macbeth says, "as breath into wind"(1.3.79), and Banquo wonders if they were there or "have we eaten on the insane root/ That takes the reason prisoner?" (83-5).

2) *The dagger.* This is the opposite case. It has a definite form, but is seen only by Macbeth, and he seems to realize it is not there:

Art thou not, fatal vision, sensible
To feeling as to sight? Or art thou but
A dagger of the mind, a false creation
Proceeding from the heat-oppressèd brain? (2.1.37-40)

Macbeth confuses the matter further by drawing his actual dagger and then seeing the illusory one as more vivid, now with "gouts of blood/ Which was not so before" (47-8). Words create the dagger, plus the actor's gestures, which focus on the place where the dagger is not.

3) *Banquo's ghost* is again a different case: it is seen by Macbeth but not by others on stage. It was also seen by a witness (Simon Forman) at the 1610 Globe performance, yet Lady Macbeth says to her husband "You look but on a stool" (3.4.68). The Folio (1623) has an entrance for the ghost, yet the stage-history of the scene shows it can be done with or without: bring the ghost on stage and the spectator sees what Macbeth sees, but with an empty chair the reactions of the others predominate, we are outside the hallucination, and Macbeth has gone (temporarily)

mad.[12] The scene is similar to the last appearance of the ghost in the *Hamlet* closet-scene when he is seen by Hamlet (and usually the audience too), but not Gertrude. Was there in fact a convention, understood by the audience, in which at this structural slot in the play the ghost may appear only to the main character? Yet the scene is different from the parallel *Hamlet* scene in that the ghost neither speaks nor acts, nor requires action: Shakespeare's focus is on the reactions of Macbeth and the others present. The objective status of the ghost is unclear.

4) *Apparitions.* The climax of these scenes comes with the apparitions of 4.1, which is the fullest weird sister scene and the last. It does not mystify, but simply amazes, and it can be done with simple stage-devices: cauldron, smoke, trap, or less.

There is a clear distinction in each of these cases between realism and supernatural phenomena, but the relation between them is shifting, and neither the mundane nor the supernatural is uncomplicated. Brooke may be right (p. 23) to propose that no clear answer is possible to the question of the role of illusion in the play, but in that case the result of any given production may be merely confusing. Polanski's film is just that.

Polanski's 1971 *Macbeth* is an odd mixture: it gets some things right and a lot wrong. Essentially Polanski was working within the naturalistic conventions of Hollywood, which left him rather lost when it came to the supernatural bits. Rather like his Macbeth (Jon Finch), who tries and fails, with accompanying eery sounds, to grasp the floating image of a dagger (obvious enough to the eye of the audience, indeed sparkling with a Disney or washing-powder radiance, Figure 7), Polanski lacks any context, inherited or invented, within which to represent the sheer strangeness of the play.

Polanski sets the film in a pre-Christian Scotland given over to a demonic cult, yet visually his witches are no "secret, black and midnight hags". Though they are certainly not attractive, Polanski chooses to present these ambivalent creatures as rural women, not devilish spirits: they keep goats, they live in daylight (indeed much of the film, curiously, takes place in bright daylight), they are apparently worshippers of the earth-goddess, at least as such creatures might be imagined in California, and they function as a modern coven, living in caves (Figure 8) and eating raw food because it is good for you.

An illustration of this uncertainty is Polanski's treatment of 4.1, the last visit to the witches including the apparitions. At the beginning Macbeth and Lady Macbeth mount the stairs to bed, which indicates

---

12. Marvin Rosenberg, *The Masks of Macbeth* (Berkeley: University of California Press, 1978), pp. 441-450.

Fig. 7. Jon Finch pursues the ultra-bright dagger in Roman Polanski's *Macbeth*, 1971.

that this is to be partly a dream sequence. But it quickly escapes from dream status, and takes on a kind of hallucinogenic quality. While he lies in bed, Jon Finch recites his remarkable lines from 3.4 about going to the weird sisters again ("I am in blood/Stepped in so far, that should I wade no more,/Returning were as tedious as go o'er...*Strange things I have in head*, that will to hand/That must be acted ere they may be scanned" (my italics).[13] Francesca Annis sleeps beside him. But then suddenly we see her from below, standing outdoors, a commanding Hecate-like figure, as if she is the spur to his intent, and he is up and away on horseback to a strange powerful music in an eerie but bright light.

On the heath he meets the women and the scene's problems begin. The woman who greets him takes him literally by the sword and leads him down into the earth, underground, obviously into "Hell",

13. Polanski's notorious and gratuitous violence makes these lines, according to E. Pearlman, the film's "text". See "*Macbeth* on Film: Politics", *Shakespeare and the Moving Image*, p. 254. One may question, though, whether the violence of this Polanski film, at least, is "gratuitous" in any serious sense, in spite of its tangential relation to the clearly gratuitous Charles Manson murders of Polanski's wife, Sharon Tate, and friends (1969).

Fig. 8. "Secret black and midnight hags" as naked women of the earth. Roman Polanski's *Macbeth*, 1971.

or Avernus. In general the women are done up like Breughel peasants, not a bad idea in itself (all *cinéastes* need to find a visual reference of some kind in which to locate the world of the play), but here it jars with the supernatural implications of Hell and of these witches and their "masters". In order to prepare for the vision of these masters, Jon Finch drinks the liquid from the cauldron, for all the world as if he is anxiously determined to get high (in spite of various stage imitations, please note that this drinking of the witches' brew is not in Shakespeare's text). The visions that follow are rather bewildering (as perhaps they should be) in their styles and points of reference.

Yet the real problem, cinematically and thematically speaking, is when Finch draws his sword and violates the border of the vision world by beheading Macduff (who is himself, it seems, dressed as a reference to a knight in Eisenstein's famous *Alexander Nevsky* battle on the ice, and so to film ghosts in Polanski's head, but ghosts who have no business in *Macbeth*). When Malcolm and Donalbain appear as Polanski's version of the third apparition (in Shakespeare a child crowned with a tree branch), we are inevitably reminded of a

California LSD experience in magical daylight, and the parallel may have a certain period interest for sixties' reference to and discussion of the sources of the supernatural. But the real significance, within the film's own terms, of this use of the Duncan sons in the vision is to prepare us for Polanski's addition to the plot, the return of Donalbain at the end of the film, and to remind us of the actor's characteristic limp. (The last shot of the film shows him going back to visit these underground witches in this same dream/heath landscape: is the cycle of violence is to be renewed, this time by a civil war between the brothers?) At the end of this whole "masters" sequence, Jon Finch wakes up in the forest, or on the heath (the landscape is not clear), but certainly not in his bed (which would have been unforgiveable bathos). He then denounces the women who guided this bizarre acid trip as "infernal", using Macbeth's line from 4.1.155.

Undoubtedly Polanski is interested in making something horrific of the witches, but he is caught between conflicting ideologies. He wants to suggest, it seems, that the witches could be seen from a political and feminist perspective as earthy and rebellious, healthily disrespectful of masculine and royal authority, but he cannot go very far along those lines without overbalancing the meaning of the whole film, which remains a serious and tragic engagement with evil. And at the same time, he has an irremediably adolescent attitude to the supernatural and horror in cinema, as witness that tediously unfunny version of the Dracula plot, *The Fearless Vampire Killers* (dir. Polanski, 1967). So the last thing Macbeth sees as he dies is a confused, swirling vision of the surrounding soldiers, but we then realize we are being shown all this from inside the severed head: these are the terminal spasms after the beheading (Figure 9).[14]

It is Orson Welles, perhaps, who most fully exploited the magic tradition, but in characteristically original ways, for his own 1948 *Macbeth*. The film was withdrawn from the Venice Film Festival in favor of Olivier's *Hamlet* in that year, an event with which Wellesians and serious film-buffs (as opposed to Shakespeareans) have never really made their peace. Indeed Anthony Davies argues that, in spite of all its flaws, and they are many, it is the film which separates mere Shakespeareans from those who take cinema seriously as high art[15]. In the history of Shakespeare films, this is the one that, for many, authorizes the cinematic assertion of one's right to revise Shakespeare in the terms of cinema's own spatial and imaginative possibilities.

14. See Kenneth S. Rothwell. *A History of Shakespeare on Screen* (Cambridge University Press, 1999), p. 160. 15. Anthony Davies, *Filming Shakespeare's Plays* (Cambridge University Press, 1988), p. 83-4.

Fig. 9. The severed head. Roman Polanski's *Macbeth*, 1971.

In this high claim Welles' *Macbeth* is, I think, largely unsuccessful, partly because of the minuscule budget with which Welles had to work, and partly because the vision Welles imposes on the film as a whole (symbolized by that peculiar invention, the Holy Father) risks trivializing its politics and making a mere allegory out of the opposition between these dark primitive forces and the uncertain and tentative reaching of the film's world towards Christianity.[16] These allusions to a supposedly pre-Christian Scotland are everywhere in the visual images of the film, in the stark structures of the already ancient castles, the bizarre caves and spaces we enter through a combination of skilful camera-work and papier-maché, the spiky, deliberately un-Christian crosses on the long staffs like divining rods the witches carry (to contrast with the infrequent occasions where the Christian cross itself is represented), and also in the values of all the main characters, or such lines as they have left to them from the truncated script.

16. Welles imposed a similar but inverted allegory on Falstaff, who, he claimed in several interviews, stands for the "old England" being lost in the drive toward the mechanical modernity of Henry V.

And those lines, unpardonably, laughably, the actors speak in fake stage-Scots. (Although not if you have only seen the 1950 re-take ordered by the RKO studio when someone told them how bad the language sounded, and which mixed in often unsynched voices.[17]) The film is nonetheless filled with moments of genius, and some of them have to do with how Welles thought out the supernatural dimension.

A fine German-French-Swiss TV programme entitled "The Lost Films of Orson Welles" (1995) begins with a delicious clip which shows a youngish Welles marching imperiously onstage and performing a magic trick, for all the world as if he were a reborn Méliès, bringing out of a magician's bucket not a flock of doves but a lovely white duck. Merely by staring at it intently Welles subdues and even frightens this poor duck till its head draws back and its neck curves like a swan of Avon. Welles then discusses for his TV audience "The Illusionists, the Stage Illusionists, [whose] last great days came to end with the last great days of the stage and theatre magicians. There were giants in those days. That was when theatre was theatre, still beglamoured and bedazzled with theatricality" and he goes on about "those grand old wonder workers" and "illusion in the high old style". He is apparently talking partly about the late nineteenth-century and partly about his own childhood ("Magic has an innocence that appeals to me, it's a return to childhood, it's like playing with toys, it's pure play, and a little more than that, it can have a kind of second-rate poetry that I find attractive, when you suspend disbelief and it becomes a very good kind of theatre"). He is also partly imagining a mythical past ("giants in those days"), imbued with Poel's ideas of Shakespeare's stage. Welles was fascinated by stage-magic, and any study of Welles which does not begin from there, and from his parallel urge to hold an audience with his rhetoric at the expense of truth, risks serious misunderstanding.

Arguably it is this Welles who reveals the true Shakespearean possibilities in the art of film, the magic swan often hidden in the folds of Lumière realism. Like Shakespeare, Welles knew that the art he worked with needs often to present its own forms not only as the vehicle but as the tenor of its meanings. In Shakespeare this takes the form of those ubiquitous stagings of theatrical shows, from the straightforward plays-within-plays to the more complex scenes in which, say, a shrew is

17. In 1979 the film was restored by the UCLA film archive, and this version, including the Scots accents, is the one available commercially. The fullest account of these matters is in Michael Anderegg's *Orson Welles, Shakespeare and Popular Culture* (New York: Columbia University Press, 1999), pp. 90-97. Note especially Anderegg's argument that the visible cheapness of the film is turned by Welles to his advantage; this is a shabby Scotland where, in a word, "to be thus is nothing" rings true: it "points up the futility and barrenness of the tyrant's ambitious designs" (p. 85).

induced to play the obedient wife or a Malvolio is tricked into playing the kind of theatrical role he apparently despises. In Welles, we see it in those moments in which he shows film as being not simply representational but fundamentally about itself. At one point, for example, Welles allows the camera to stand in the place of Banquo's ghost in order to look back at Macbeth—which can be read as a reminder that film is itself merely a ghost, light passing through a strip of celluloid and projected onto our present from some past when the shooting took place.[18] In this complex scene with Banquo's ghost Welles shows himself fully in command of the art of cinema. On stage you have to choose whether you want a ghost or an empty chair, but Welles gives us both, cutting between the horrified Macbeth's deep-focus vision of the ghost sitting at an empty table, and the increasingly bewildered guests who see, like Lady Macbeth, only an empty chair.[19] Is Macbeth's vision hallucination or reality? Méliès or Lumière? There is no way to tell.

Long before he made the film, Welles had staged the play in 1936 at the Lafayette, a Harlem theatre, and he set it in "the rank and fever-stricken jungles of Haiti", using drums and voodoo references to produce "a witches' scene that is logical and stunning and a triumph of the theatre art . . . If it is witches you want, Harlem knows how to overwhelm you with their fury and phantom splendour".[20] The production risked trouble in view of the recent Harlem riots, about which Welles was pretty naive. Word got about that, in what was quickly known as "the voodoo Macbeth", black culture was being made fun of, "a campaign to burlesque negroes". Welles, or so he thought, was able to convince the angry crowds that it was not so, and that on the contrary he was making use of black actors and voodoo for important cultural statements.[21] And indeed he was doing something radically new and different—putting on Shakespeare with the Negro Theatre Unit, using Roosevelt's New Deal funds from the Federal Theatre Project.

---

18. Welles' Banquo banquet had been entirely different in the stage version, with dance music by Virgil Thompson forming part of a genuine melodrama (musical play). The film scene, by contrast, exploits candle light in darkness, depth of field, and bizarre devices like a close-up of Macbeth's pointing finger and shadow which lead the camera and the viewer inexorably towards our first view of the ghost. **19.** See Lorne Buchman's analysis of this scene in *Still in Movement* (Oxford: Oxford University Press, 1991), pp. 21-2. **20.** Brooks Atkinson, the *New York Times* reviewer, quoted in Simon Callow, *Orson Welles: the Road to Xanadu* (London: Vintage, 1996), p. 237-38. **21.** So at least he tells Professor Richard Marienstras, in an unpublished videotaped interview. But beware: what Simon Callow says of newspapers is just as true of interviews, that Welles "was unable to resist a fix of publicity; merely to see a reporter's notebook was to unleash his powers of invention" (Callow, p xii).

For his film, though, made more than ten years later, Welles abandoned Haiti and black actors, returned the imagined setting to Scotland, but retained the important idea of the voodoo doll. The image instantly makes the witches dominant, and this dominance Welles manages spatially in the first scene, even before the credits (Figure 10).

A small crowned effigy is seen at the level of the witches' feet, indeed we see the witches themselves constructing the clay form of the doll. It is the doll rather than the man himself that is decorated with Macbeth's sequence of honors, Glamis, Cawdor, king, and then finally beheaded at the end of the film. Thus, rather than use any *trucage* for Macbeth's own head, Welles invests this local Americanized black magic with most of the film's import.[22]

Fig. 10. The witches with their divining rods and the voodoo effigy of Macbeth at their feeet. Orson Welles' *Macbeth*, 1948.

REPUBLIC/THE KOBAL COLLECTION

22. Polanski's (1971) opening scene drew from Welles' (1948) in this as in other respects: his witches bury emblems of despair in the sand, a noose and a dagger in a severed hand, and immediately we hear the sounds of battle on the soundtrack as the credits roll: the witches, as powerful here as in Welles, have produced their first example of ordinary evil, war. See Norman Berlin, "*Macbeth*: Polanski and Shakespeare", *Literature/Film Quarterly I,* no. 4 (Fall 1973) and Lorne M. Buchman, *Still in Movement* (Oxford: Oxford University Press, 1991), p. 70.

The result is a strange, compelling but somehow constrained and even zombie-like Macbeth; Welles plays the role himself, with great fatigue at times, as if he is weary of the role he is being asked to play by these tyrannical directors. Perhaps in this respect the witches represent the role of Republic Pictures boss Herbert Yates, who had insisted on a low budget (less than $900,000) and a 3-week shooting schedule.

From another point of view the witches are a version of Welles's as the film's director, getting as much as he can out of his exhausted cast. These witches are their own "masters", not merely representative of that pre-Christian primitive world, but perhaps actually running it. So the play's 'masters' sequence of future visions is omitted: Macbeth himself sees the visions of 4.1, his body lit and centrally positioned on the screen as if at the bottom of a pit, but we don't. (Perhaps Tony Richardson thought of this Welles idea, forced on him by the minimal budget, as the solution for his own supernatural problem: how to render the Hamlet ghost, which he too does as a white light on the main character's face.) Yet through the power the witches thus acquire, the world of the film created by Welles resembles nothing so much as Dorian Gray's. The Macbeth world is taken over at the end by the strange voodoo double—so intense is Welles fascination with what makes the play, and the film, magical—as the beheaded doll comes to represent, but also to substitute for, the human world of murdered kings and bloody battle.

In various ways, Welles makes film and magic traditions overlap. His aim is to show the forces of darkness taking over, even in power already, and to do so he uses melodrama and horror movie techniques rather than more traditional theatre.

The original Lafayette Theatre production turned on what Richard France calls "stagey responses which make horror movies both ridiculous and yet exhilarating". This can be very wearying, he adds, as some of the film acting also shows, but it quite deliberately links Welles' picture with the techniques we associate with early, silent film. Spectacle predominates over dialogue, as in the nineteenth-century melodrama with which the stage-magic tradition is closely linked.[23]

Voodoo drums were present on stage in Harlem, and Welles retains them for the screen, as in the transition from the banquet to the witches scene of 4.1. And these drums produce a splendid instance of horror-melodrama by ceasing at the exact moment when the axe falls on Cawdor's neck. Each film episode is thus linked with the underlying theme of the dark powers which both prepare the way for,

23. Richard France, "The 'Voodoo', *Macbeth* of Orson Welles", *Yale Theatre*, 5 (1974), 66-78.

and then gradually entrap, Macbeth. Indeed the whole film is shot in a kind of recurrent and encircling gloom, occasionally lifted for the important light-dark and open-closed contrasts. This, together with the violently disjunctive editing, sharp vertiginous angles, and turbulent weather, make for an expressionist style, clearly developed from films like Murnau's 1926 *Faust*.

To all this Welles deliberately adds a sense of helpless desperation, of the kind we feel in nightmare, thus making the spectator personally conscious of his inability to intervene on the screen. And Welles' own acting of Macbeth, as if sleepwalking at times, underlines this experience of conscious helplessness: indeed he puts himself into his wife's sleepwalking scene as a silent but obvious spectator, much closer to the audience and larger on screen than the doctor or nurse, and like us as we watch Lady Macbeth rush away to her suicidal leap off the cliff onto the rocks and sea below. In Shakespeare, this death is simply reported to Macbeth. Welles's decision to link it to the sleepwalking scene and to include Macbeth as spectator is an attempt to render in cinematic terms the odd detachment of Macbeth's famous reaction, "She should have died hereafter./There would have been a time for such a word./Tomorrow and tomorrow. . ." (5.5.17-19).

For most of these points, the opening sequence of the film can serve as an example, in particular of how cinematic and thematic references overlap. Welles mixes several uses of dissolve with this (supposedly) Scotch mist as it swirls and then clears for the image of the Celtic cross, then obscures again and reveals the witches up on their precarious papier-maché rock, then closes and opens for the surface of their cauldron, then for the clay doll. The bubbling cauldron in fact takes over the whole screen, sucking us in, to the point that it becomes a self-referential image of the film itself, deliberately evoking the magical side of film tradition, and requiring the spectator to pass through that surface into the worlds of both the film and the witches. Thus both the witches and the ghost evoke in Welles specific techniques of the art of film and suggest with which tendency, Méliès or Lumière, he has most artistic sympathy. But these recurring representations of instability also evoke dream or nightmare and produce in some spectators the need to escape or awake. Indeed, when I have watched Welles' *Macbeth* in the cinema, I sense a pervasive restlessness around me, linked, I am sure, to his sense of the darkness of this pre-Christian, sinister nightmare as akin to the darkness of the cinema where we are required to sit patiently and watch.

Nightmare is important also for what is certainly the most original version of *Macbeth*. All critics who have reflected on Shakespeare films recognize that *Kumonosu-jō* (*Throne of Blood*, 1957) is a key film, acknowledged by many as the greatest. When he adapted *Macbeth* to Japanese traditions Akira Kurasawa had not only to choose an appropriate historical context which allowed the basic issues of fealty and treachery to have their starkest meanings, but also to find cinematic styles which could render the peculiar mixture of power and helplessness essential to Shakespeare's play, in particular to its use of the supernatural.

Of all the scenes in the film, the first forest scene is the one that has been most thoroughly analyzed, since it shows the peculiar qualities of the film so clearly. Commentators note the way the rain is picked up in the verticality of the trees, stress the symbolic use of the horses, praise the vigor of the tracking shots which move the two actors through and ever deeper into this forest as labyrinth, and pore over every detail of the encounter with the single spirit who substitutes for the Shakespearean witches. It is hard to add much to this mass of commentary, but the film will respond well to our basic premise about the importance of the double tradition within film language.

First we need to acknowledge that the two actors who play Washizu and Miki (the Macbeth and Banquo figures) are two of the finest in Japanese cinema, and in the case of Toshiro Mifune, of world renown. The vigour and anxious bravery with which he plays the role of a loyal, stolid, somewhat unreflective samurai gradually tempted by prophecy and wife to murder his lord is exemplary of a whole style of realistic cinema acting (though it may look stylized to Western eyes unfamiliar with Japanese conventions). The contrast between the powerful physical presence of these two warriors in their dark clothes and the slightness of the androgynous white spirit is one of the most striking aspects of the scene. And indeed the contrast embodies the opposing moods and styles that are here brought into contact: speed and stillness (both of actors and of camera), dialogue and solitary song, noise and quiet, dark and light, physical and spiritual power, life and death, nature and the supernatural.

The scene occurs relatively early in the film, though not so early as its equivalent in Shakespeare, since the whole historical and political setting has first been established—the troubled civil strife at the end of feudalism in the 16th century. Then, even as the two horsemen enter the forest they pause and comment on the strangeness of the terrible storm of lightning and rain, and allow the audience to notice the oddity of the lighting: already through backlighting and a mist effect whiteness is beginning to infect the screen. Initially the two riders canter about in this dark wet place, shot through the tangled branches of the undergrowth, alternately in still and then fast tracking shots. Gradually we realize from the reversals of direction and camera angle that they are in fact lost: they notice this by recognizing that they have doubled back over their own hoofprints, but obtusely and ironically they congratulate each other on knowing the terrain, unlike the enemy, who will certainly get lost in this Tangled Web Forest. Then Washizu (Macbeth) rather pointlessly fires an arrow up into the tall tops of the backlit trees and immediately we hear on the sound track an uncanny laugh, and the horses whinny: the sense of oddity, at the very least, is jolting, but the action of firing the arrow preserves the ambiguity about who causes what. The two men determine to cut their way out, but another sequence of fast horse riding brings them still deeper into the forest. A mist is slowly rising. In all the medium shots of fast horse-riding, instead of tracking the camera remains stationary, simply turning rapidly on its stand as the horsemen ride in a circle around, through the bushes and trees of the forest: the position of the camera locates and anticipates for us the focus of the scene which follows, the white spirit of the forest. Camera and supernatural are again one.

Now comes, suddenly, the strange sight of a white bamboo cage-like structure, behind a large tree. We perceive it from behind the two men on horseback, who have now stopped moving but whose horses still stir restlessly. Cut back to them for a powerful reaction shot. "My horse has never been so frightened", says Washizu, sure that an evil spirit is blocking their way. Courageously he controls his horse and forces it toward the camera, and so, in the narration, toward the spirit. The two men now say they see the spirit, and in one of several extraordinary film moments Washizu (Toshiro Mifune) makes to shoot the spirit (is it a him/her?) with his bow. But just at this moment on the soundtrack begins a strange song or chant, and so, unlike Polanski's Jon Finch, Washizu desists, allowing the spirit world to remain, at least for the present, separate, inviolate, not penetrated by a human weapon. Cut back to the two men whom we watch dismount, still looking towards the source of the sound, and they then move forwards, the camera following them till they stop, then continuing till it shows the spirit in medium shot, white, utterly other, spinning thread from one reel to another as it sings. Reaction shots show the two men transfixed, peering through the undergrowth and into the white-lit scene. Finally they move sideways and the camera comes in round behind them till it shows us the full scene framed by the two warriors, light framed within the dark forest, a film within a film.

The two warriors quickly become spectators of a magic show, frontally presented as in the Méliès films, rather than from a constantly shifting viewing position in what became the classical style, to absorb the spectator into the film-space. Indeed arguably the scene combines Lumière and Méliès traditions but keeps them distinct: the watching warriors framing the screen still belong to the outside or Lumière world of history—battle, horses, rushing messengers and feudal hierarchies—even though they are momentarily lost in this strange forest which is now revealing its secret soul. But the scene they look in at, the camera now still, is pure Méliès.

Japanese legends about androgynous seers make Kurosawa's witch-substitute exactly right for the world of the film, which is successful because of its total adaptation to "Shakespeare without the words".[24] There on screen is this unutterably strange spirit, chanting and spinning, mesmerising us as we watch the thread cross from reel to reel. Unmistakably this is destiny, and indeed the thread is near its end already. But even more clearly than in the case of the cauldron's surface in Welles, the spinning reels also refer to the magic art of film itself.[25]

The two warriors now step forward and open the door of the cage and ask the spirit what it is and whether it can speak. The scene is then framed again, a clear Méliès reference, as the two warriors look in from outside the frame while the spirit prophecies the equivalent of Macbeth's three promotions, including that Washizu will eventually be boss of Spider Castle (the French chose this more exact term for the title of the Film, *Le Chateau de l'Araignée*).[26] Miki too (Banquo) gets his own prophecy. At end of the sequence we suddenly and for the first time see the scene from the back, reversing the Méliès position, putting us backstage as the spirit answers Miki's questions. But the vision is still there, and no less mysterious. After one reaction shot, we see it from behind as it rises and with a sudden gust of wind disappears, blown away or simply taken back into the spirit world, magicked away like the disappearing lady of Méliès. As in Kozintsev's *Hamlet*, ghost and spirit and wind are aligned thematically, reinforcing a folk idea and one that in many languages also links them etymologically.

---

24. See Dennis Kennedy, "Shakespeare Without His Language", in *Shakespeare, Theory and Performance*, ed. James C. Bulman (London: Routledge, 1996), pp. 133-148, on performances of Shakespeare in translation.   **25.** Jack Jorgens, "Kurosawa's *Throne of Blood*: Washizu and Miki Meet the Forest Spirit", *Literature/Film Quarterly* 11 (1983), pp. 167-73, first suggested that the reels were a metaphor for the projector or the editing table. Peter S. Donaldson, *Shakespearean Films/ Shakespearean Directors* (Boston: Unwin Hyman, 1990), p. 76, adds other metacinematic references.   **26.** The Japanese title, *Kumonosu-jō*, means "The Castle of the Spider's Web". Kurosawa explained that the wood around the castle, in the civil-war times of Noh drama, was often designed like a maze to catch the invaders "as if in a web": see Roger Manvell, *Shakespeare and the Film* (New York: A.S. Barnes, 1979), p. 104.

The forest scene concludes with two key images. First we watch as Washizu, then Miki, react to the disappearance of the spirit, look around them, and then deliberately step forward into the white space vacated by the spirit. Here perhaps lies the meaning of the film, for they never really leave that space, or at least what it represents, again: they are *magicked*. And what this means is in one sense that they have become entirely creatures of the film, existing only in the space that was previously identified with the screen. They look back in surprise, behind them but at the camera, reacting to the fact that the frame through which they stepped is no longer there: they have crossed over into the Méliès world.[27] Then comes the second key image, as the camera moves away and reveals in the contiguous space of the forest a pile of bones, and military hardware.

So this was a death-place too, we now realize, and there too the heroes are forever stuck, doomed. The film now represents this by an almost tediously long sequence of the two men once again lost in the mist, galloping hither and yon until finally Kurosawa allows them, and us, to emerge and rest.

The spirit returns in a later scene when Washizu goes back to the forest after the death of Miki-Banquo, but we no longer have the same framing possibility, since there is only one warrior. This time the visions evoked by the witch-spirit force Washizu to turn around to look at them, implying that he is now surrounded by this magic and evil world. And the forest prophecy he hears has even more reso-nance than in Shakespeare, since it is this same Tangled Web Forest itself which will move toward the Spider Castle it has always till now protected with its deceptive and labyrinthine trails.

In Shakespeare's play a link is built up in several ways between the witches and Lady Macbeth. In Kurosawa, the visual images attached to the spirit since the first scene in the forest also establish a deliber-ate cinematic parallel with Washizu's wife: they have similar white Noh-theatre make-up, and both use a still and undemonstrative style of acting, making a very strong contrast with Toshiro Mifune. And indeed that contrast of the two styles enacts the two aspects of film tradition that we associate with Méliès and Lumière.

The Banquo's ghost scene is also managed with great skill. Two points are especially notable, first that when the ghost appears on screen it occupies the same position as that in which we first saw Washizu's wife, and it too is white. This links it back to the chain of imagery associated with the supernatural and the strange throughout

---

27. See Donaldson, p. 77. He reproduces two stills, before and after, to show the visual continuity between the stepping through the frame and noticing its absence.

the film. Second, we the cinema audience see the ghost only through Washizu's eyes, i.e. when the camera substitutes for his viewpoint. At the end, when we watch Washizu attack the ghost with his sword, the place is simply empty: Washizu can see it, but no-one else can, and nor can we. The contrast with the forest scene, when Washizu refrained from firing his arrow, is clear and important for the film's meaning. Illusion has now become delusion.

The largely successful use of film tradition for the supernatural in *Macbeth* films may also be used to point an important contrast between film and television. In April 1997 BBC television showed *Macbeth on the Estate*, a modern-dress version of the play set on the Ladywood estate in Birmingham, directed by documentary maker Penny Woolcock. This is a provocative and in many ways exemplary effort to get the best of both contemporary and Shakespearean worlds, but it is rather bizarre in its adaptation of the witches and what they represent. They become simply three very strange children, who sit in an inside space, a crowded living room adapted to childish fantasy and entered through hangings and low openings rather than doors. These "weird children", as Macbeth calls them, but apparently in the modern not the Shakespearean sense of *weird*, prophesy in television close-up, with fantasy ingredients like cloth picture dolls and a candle-lit *mise-en-scène*—passing strange, it is true, but manifestly not evil. Much evil there is in this teleplay, but its source is not mysterious at all: it resides quite clearly in the drug-driven underworld of gang rivalry in which the characters all live.[28] It is inherent in their social context, not in the supernatural, which has been—apart from these odd children—eliminated.[29]

The same reticence is clear in the way television deals with Banquo's ghost. Whereas Orson Welles exploited the cinema and its fundamental

---

28. A recent Hindi film, *Maqbool* (dir. Bharadwaj, 2003) similarly re-imagines the plot in the world of a crime syndicate in present-day Mumbai. As in Ionesco's *Macbett*, the motivation for the murder of the Duncan figure is the sexual attraction of his mistress for his henchman, Maqbool. The role of the witches is taken by two corrupt cops, one of whom has a talent for astrology. Their power is not supernatural but derives from their links with powerful and equally corrupt politicians. The film was well described by reviewers as Macbeth meets the Godfather. A more recent Australian film (dir. Wright, 2006) similarly sets the play (including, like Baz Luhrman's *Romeo + Juliet*, some of Shakespeare's language) in the Melbourne underworld. Here also the witches have little about them that is supernatural: they are seductive school girls. 29. A comic version of this plot-twist is the American black comedy *Scotland, Pa* (dir. Morrissette, 2001) in which Pat McBeth claims: 'We're not bad people, Mac... just underachievers who have to make up for lost time.' The witches here are reconfigured as giggling hippies (as the cast-list calls them) high on something quite strong and 'having a spell' that enables them to tell the future.

technique of montage or cross-cutting precisely to give us both possibilities, a deluded Macbeth and a horrifying presence, in TV that
chance is usually missed. The ghost is simply a delusion of the disturbed
Macbeth's drug-crazed psyche in Woolcock's sociological, documen-
tary-style version. In the fine 1979 Trevor Nunn-Philip Casson RSC-
Thames TV adaptation, as in the 1983 Shaun Sutton BBC/Time-Life
version, he is not visible to the audience. Perhaps it was felt the scene
would be too hard to accept in one's living room. Many made for TV
American horror or sci-fi shows, like *The X-Files* (cr. Carter, 1993-
2002) or *Buffy the Vampire Slayer* (cr. Whedon, 1997-2003), do bring
ghosts and other frights into that cosy space. So perhaps it was even the
fear of being thought too "American" that prompted the omissions, or
perhaps it was the fear of ridicule in the highbrow Shakespeare culture
with its persistent English reticence toward the supernatural. Even the
BBC witches are simply dirty and bedraggled, distasteful but not especially demonic women. In all these cases where the supernatural is sup-
pressed, the rationale is obviously that the psychological has replaced
the supernatural just as psychoanalysts have replaced priests. Only the
hoi polloi, it is thought, those benighted masses who turn out for those
contemporary Stephens—Spielbergs and Kings—continue to accept
screen magic of the Méliès kind. But TV Shakespeare thus aims at a
very restricted idea of what the respectable middle-class will buy.

This TV discomfort with the supernatural is palpable, and not only
in *Macbeth*. In the often admirable[30] sequence directed by Jane Howell
in 1982 for the BBC Time-Life series, the on-stage fiends of *1 Henry
VI* are simply omitted and Joan merely looks at the camera. Even the
ghosts who appear before the Battle of Bosworth in *Richard III* are
incorporated into dreams, reproducing that common retreat from the
supernatural into the psychological. A closeup takes us inside the head
of sleeping Richard, a voice-over repeats his mother's curse from 4.3,
then a nightmare sequence brings back the murdered victims who
mock Richard and revere Richmond.[31]

---

30. Graham Holderness praises this sequence for its refusal to accede to the series
director Jonathan Miller's programme for resolute television naturalism, "Radical Potentiality and Institutional Closure", in *Political Shakespeare*, ed. Jonathan
Dollimore and Alan Sinfield (Ithaca: Cornell University Press, 1985), pp. 192-3.
Holderness's argument resembles mine in that he distinguishes "illusionistic" and
its opposite as a basic contrast in film theory, but "opposite" for him means a Bre-
chtian awareness of the medium, not magic tricks. Thus his praise of Jane Howell is
based on her explicit and non-naturalistic use of the film studio as a stage. Whereas
Holderness studies the way the ideology of naturalism is subverted in some films,
reinforced in others, I celebrate here those films which reincorporate popular
magic alongside illusionistic naturalism.   **31.** See Alan Dessen, "The Supernatural
on Television", *Shakespeare on Film Newsletter*, Vol. 11, Dec 1986, pp. 1-8.

These examples show that television (or at least the realism that dominates TV drama) has been a less appropriate medium than film for presenting Shakespeare, who was himself, it seems, always fascinated with stage devices for presenting the supernatural. Early in his career, in *1 Henry VI*, Joan la Pucelle, as we just noted, talks to fiends who (in the folio direction) "walk and speak not", "hang their heads", "shake their heads", and eventually "depart"; the Duchess of Gloucester and Margery Jourdain summon spirits which appear on-stage and utter prophecies that come true in *2 Henry VI*. And in his last plays, Cerimon in *Pericles* resurrects Thaïsa with the help of spells, napkins and fire, while in *Henry VIII* there is (in Folio 4.2) "The Vision", in which a sleeping Queen Katherine is visited by six white-robed figures wearing golden vizards who bow, dance and hold a garland over her head. (Again the BBC TV version eliminates the supernatural, keying the scene instead to a religious mural seen by the queen as she starts to doze. Then in dream she imagines a younger self rising and dancing with those figures).

Indeed in the later plays, especially the romances which could use the new (1610-11) indoor artificially lighted Blackfriars Theatre as well as the Globe, Shakespeare exploited the contemporary popularity of magic for the miracles of *The Winter's Tale* and *The Tempest*, and used masque effects for the supernatural, as in the harpies' intervention to remove the banquet, or the descent of Jupiter on an eagle in *Cymbeline*. (Perhaps, as Nicholas Brooke proposes, the intrusive Hecate dance-scenes in *Macbeth* were added for Blackfriars performances.) All of this suggests that, along with the presence of both high and low culture within his plays, Shakespeare might have been happy to learn from the tradition of Méliès, from *trucage*, from horror movies, even from melodrama, just as Orson Welles or Kurosawa did. Prospero, who also alludes to Ovid's witch Medea, would then be his final version not only of the Renaissance magus in all his ambivalence, but also of the playwright as illusionist.[32] Peter Greenaway's "spell-stopped" film *Prospero's Books*, with its frames within frames, its "high charms", its rendering of the tempest-tossed ship as a child's toy galleon and the water world as a boy's fantasy of omnipotence as he pisses, is a baroque, dense, claustrophobically rich tribute to the connection of magician and playmaker, though it probably "reads" better on video than in the cinema, and might

---

32. See Barbara Mowatt, "Prospero, Agrippa, and Hocus-Pocus", *English Literary Renaissance* 11 (1981), 281-303, and Stephen Orgel's "Introduction" to his Oxford Shakespeare edition of *The Tempest* (Oxford University Press, 1987), pp. 20-23.

have made more use of popular magic and less of the austere and constantly writing magus.

Prospero-Shakespeare is comparable with the famous John Dee, Elizabeth's astrologer and magician. He was a highly ambivalent figure, both medieval and modern, using pure mathematics but often for superstitious or occult purposes. He had trouble with the authorities at various times. Yet Dee was first indicted, not for some egregious use of alchemical magic, nor even for using incomprehensible mathematical symbols, but for his role in a student play. At Cambridge, as a budding magician would, he invented a special effect, a giant flying beetle, for a student production of a classical play, Aristophanes *Peace*.[33] It is not clear whether the authorities regarded Dee's stage-trick as physically or spiritually dangerous, but arrest him they did. Add now to this composite image of the Elizabethan magus those "jugglers" of the street-corner and popular stage, and we can begin to imagine how the Shakespeare who invented both Prospero the masque-maker and Autolycus the trickster might have enjoyed making movies.

---

33. Barbara H. Traister, *Heavenly Necromancers: the Magician in English Renaissance Drama* (Columbia, MO: University of Missouri Press, 1984), p 18.

For Further Reading, Viewing, and Listening

SHAKESPEAREAN LANGUAGE

Booth, Stephen. *King Lear, Macbeth, Indefinition and Tragedy.* New Haven: Yale UP, 1983.

Shakespeare, William. *Macbeth.* Ed. A. R. Braunmuller. New York: CD-ROM. Voyager, 1994.

Shakespeare, William. *Macbeth.* Ed. Nicholas Brooke. Oxford: Clarendon Press, 1990.

Shakespeare, William. *Macbeth.* 1623. Electronic Text Center. 2002. University of Virginia Lib. http://etext.lib.virginia.edu/toc/modeng/public/ShaMacF.html.

Tobin, John. *"Macbeth and Christs Teares over Jerusalem."* *Aligarh Journal of English Studies* 7 (1982): 72–78.

STUART POLITICS, HISTORIOGRAPHY, RELIGIOUS DEBATE

Bushnell, Rebecca. *Tragedies of Tyrants: Political Thought and Theater in the English Renaissance.* Ithaca: Cornell UP, 1990.

Carroll, William C., ed. *William Shakespeare, Macbeth: Texts and Contexts.* Boston: Bedford/St. Martin's, 1999.

Galloway, Bruce. *The Union of England and Scotland 1603–1608.* Edinburgh: Donald, 1986.

King James VI and I: Political Writings. ed. Johann P. Sommerville. Cambridge: Cambridge UP, 1994.

Harris, Jonathan Gil. "The Smell of *Macbeth.*" *Shakespeare Quarterly,* 58:4 (Winter) 2007, 465–486.

Harrison, William. "The description of Scotland." In Raphael Holinshed, *The Second volume of Chronicles.* London, 1586. sig.B5v.

Macdonald, Michael. *"The Fearefull Estate of Francis Spira*: Narrative, Identity, and Emotion in Early Modern England." *Journal of British Studies* 31 (1992): 32–61.

Mapstone, Sally. "Shakespeare and Scottish Kingship: A Case History." *The Rose and the Thistle: Essays on the Culture of Late Medieval and Renaissance Scotland.* Ed. Sally Mapstone and Juliette Wood. East Lothian: Tuckwell, 1998. 158–189.

Mullaney, Steven. "Lying Like Truth: Riddle, Representation and Treason in Renaissance England." *ELH* 47 (1980): 32–47.

Norbrook, David. "*Macbeth* and the Politics of Historiography." *Politics of Discourse: The Literature and History of Seventeenth Century England.* Ed. Kevin Sharpe and Steven N. Zwicker. Berkeley: U of California Press, 1987. 78–116.

Poole, Kristen. "Physics Divined: The Science of Calvin, Hooker, and *Macbeth.*" *South Central Review* 26.1–2 (2009): 127–152.

WITCHCRAFT

King James I. *Daemonology, In Form of a Dialogue.* Edinburgh, 1597.

Macfarlane, Alan. *Witchcraft in Tudor and Stuart England: A Regional and Comparative Study.* New York: Harper, 1970.

Newman, Karen. "Discovering Witches: Sorciographics." *Fashioning Femininity and English Renaissance Drama.* Chicago: U of Chicago Press, 1991.

Stallybrass, Peter. "*Macbeth* and Witchcraft." *Focus on Macbeth.* Ed. John Russell Brown. London: Routledge, 1982.

ETHNICITY, GENDER AND THE RENAISSANCE BODY

Floyd-Wilson, Mary. *English Ethnicity and Race in Early Modern Drama.* Cambridge: Cambridge UP, 2003.

James, Susan. *Passion and Action: the Emotions in Seventeenth-Century Philosophy.* Oxford: Clarendon, 1997.

Maley, Willy and Andrew Murphy, ed. *Shakespeare and Scotland.* Manchester, Eng.: Manchester UP, 2004.

Siraisi, Nancy G. *Medieval and Early Renaissance Medicine: An Introduction to Knowledge and Practice.* Chicago: U of Chicago Press, 1990.

Zimmerman, Susan. "Duncan's Corpse." *A Feminist Companion to Shakespeare.* Ed. Dympna Callaghan. Malden, MA: Blackwell Publishers, 2000. 320–338.

PERFORMANCE HISTORY, RECEPTION HISTORY

Bristol, Michael. *Shakespeare's America, America's Shakespeare.* London: Routledge, 1990.

Gurr, Andrew. *Playgoing in Shakespeare's London,* 2nd Ed. Cambridge: Cambridge UP, 1996.

Holland, Peter, ed. *Macbeth and Its Afterlife. Shakespeare Survey* 57 (2004).

Jacobus, Mary. "'That Great Stage Where Senators Perform': *Macbeth* and the Politics of Romantic Theater." *Studies in Romanticism* 22.3 (Fall 1983): 353–387.

Kliman, Bernice. *Shakespeare in Performance: Macbeth*. Manchester, Eng.: Manchester UP, 1992.

Roach, Joseph. *The Player's Passion: Studies in the Science of Acting*. Newark, DE: U of Delaware Press, 1985. 23–57.

Rosenberg, Marvin. *The Masks of Macbeth*. Berkeley: U of California Press, 1978.

Rowe, Katherine. "Humoral Knowledge and Liberal Cognition in Davenant's *Macbeth*." *Reading the Early Modern Passions: Essays in the Cultural History of Emotion*. Ed. Gail Kern Paster, Katherine Rowe, and Mary Floyd-Wilson. U Penn Press, 2004.

Tiffany, Grace. "Borges and Shakespeare, Shakespeare and Borges." In *Latin-American Shakespeares*, ed. Bernice Kliman and Rick Santos. NJ: Fairleigh Dickinson UP, 2005. 145–65.

CRITICAL ACCOUNTS OF *MACBETH* ON SCREEN

Stephen M. Buhler. *Shakespeare in the Cinema: Ocular Proof*. New York: State University of New York Press, 2002.

Cartelli, Thomas and Katherine Rowe. *New Wave Shakespeare on Screen*. Cambridge, UK: Polity Press, 2007.

Donaldson, Peter S. *Shakespearean Films/Shakespearean Directors*. Media and Popular Culture 6. Boston: Unwin Hyman, 1990.

Lehmann, Courtney. "Out Damned Scot: Dislocating *Macbeth* in Transnational Film and Media Culture." *Shakespeare, the Movie, II: Popularizing the Plays on Film, TV, Video, and DVD*. Ed Richard Burt and Lynda Boose. New York: Routledge, 2003.

Rothwell, Kenneth S. *A History of Shakespeare on Screen: a Century of Film and Television*. Cambridge: Cambridge University Press, 1999.

Rowe, Katherine. "Crowd-sourcing Shakespeare: Screen Work and Screen Play in Second Life™." *Shakespeare Studies 38*, "After Shakespeare on Film," Winter 2010: 58–67.

Shakespeare in Europe (SHINE). May 2003. English Department, University of Basel, Switz. http://www.unibas.ch/shine/ linkstragmacbethwf.html. A useful finding list of translations of *Macbeth* in multiple languages.

Shohet, Lauren. "The Banquet of Scotland (PA)." *Shakespeare Survey 57: Macbeth and its Afterlife*. Ed. Peter Holland. Cambridge University Press, 2004. 186–195.

Starks, Lisa S. "Untimely Ripped: Mediating Witchcraft in Polanski and Shakespeare." *The Reel Shakespeare: Alternative Cinema and Theory*. Ed. Lisa S. Starks and Courtney Lehmann. Madison, NJ: Fairleigh Dickinson University Press, 2002.

SELECTED AUDIO, VIDEO, AND ONLINE ADAPTATIONS AND RESOURCES

Bardbox, http://bardbox.wordpress.com, cur. Luke McKernan. A collection of the best and most interesting examples of original Shakespeare videos online.

"Foul Whisperings, Strange Matters: Virtual *Macbeth*," http://virtualmacbeth.wikispaces.com/. Angela Thomas, Kerreen Ely-Harper, and Kate Richards. This sim in Second Life™ is dedicated to the exploration, adaptation and performance of Shakespeare's play.

Johnson, Robert, et al. "Come away, Hecate" and "The Witches' Dance". *Hark! Hark! the Lark*. London: Hyperion Records, 1998.

An International Database of Shakespeare on Film, Television, and Radio, created by the British Universities Film and Video Council. http://bufvc.ac.uk/shakespeare/.

Macbeth, dir. Orson Welles. Mercury Productions/Republic Pictures Corporation, 1948.

Macbeth, dir. Roman Polanski. Columbia Pictures/Caliban Films, 1971.

Macbeth, dir. Trevor Nunn-Philip Casson. RSC-Thames TV, 1979.

Macbeth, dir. Jack Gold. BBC TV Shakespeare. BBC. June 1982.

Maqbool (Hindi), dir. Vishal Bhardwaj, Kaleidoscope Entertainment Pvt. Ltd., 2003.

Opensourceshakespeare.org, http://www.opensourceshakespeare.org/. An online resource with excellent concordance and selection functions (allows printing by character lines/cues as well as by scene). Should only be used in conjunction with a modern edition (such as the Evans edition) because its text is a nineteenth-century edition that contains many errors.

Sangrador (Spanish). dir. Leonardo Henriquez. Centro Nacional Autónomo de Cinematografía/Post Meridian Cinema, 1999.

Scotland, Pa, dir. Billy Morrisette. Lot 49 Films, 2001.

Global Shakespeares, http://globalshakespeares.org/#. A growing video archive with robust search functions.

Throne of Blood/Kumonosu-jō, dir. Akira Kurosawa, Toho, 1957.